Durban & KwaZulu-Natal

Lizzie Williams

Credits

Footprint credits
Editor: Stephanie Rebello
Production and layout: Emma Bryers
Maps: Kevin Feeney

Publisher: Patrick Dawson
Managing Editor: Felicity Laughton
Advertising: Elizabeth Taylor
Sales and marketing: Kirsty Holmes

Photography credits
Front cover: Dirscherl Reinhard/
Superstock
Back cover: Roger de la Harpe/
Superstock

Printed in India by Thomson Press Ltd,
Faridabad, Haryana

Every effort has been made to ensure
that the facts in this guidebook are
accurate. However, travellers should
still obtain advice from consulates,
airlines, etc, about travel and visa
requirements before travelling. The
authors and publishers cannot accept
responsibility for any loss, injury or
inconvenience however caused.

The content of Footprint *Focus
Durban & KwaZulu-Natal* is based on
Footprint's *South Africa Handbook*,
which was researched and written
by Lizzie Williams.

Publishing information
Footprint *Focus Durban &
KwaZulu-Natal*
2nd edition
© Footprint Handbooks Ltd
January 2015

ISBN: 978 1 909268 76 0
CIP DATA: A catalogue record
for this book is available from
the British Library

Published by Footprint
6 Riverside Court
Lower Bristol Road
Bath BA2 3DZ, UK
T +44 (0)1225 469141
F +44 (0)1225 469461
footprinttravelguides.com

Distributed in the USA by
National Book Network, Inc.

Contents

5 Introduction
- 4   *Map: Durban and KwaZulu-Natal*

6 Planning your trip
- 6   Best time to visit Durban and KwaZulu-Natal
- 6   Getting to Durban and KwaZulu-Natal
- 9   Transport in Durban and KwaZulu-Natal
- 12   Where to stay in Durban and KwaZulu-Natal
- 14   Food and drink in Durban and KwaZulu-Natal
- 17   Essentials A-Z

23 Durban and the KwaZulu-Natal Coast
- 24   **Durban**
- 25   *Map: Greater Durban*
- 32   *Map: Durban*
- 45   Durban listings
- 61   **KwaZulu-Natal South Coast**
- 62   *Map: South Coast*
- 68   KwaZulu-Natal South Coast listings
- 75   **North Coast and Zululand**
- 76   *Map: Dolphin Coast*
- 79   *Map: Maputaland & Zululand game reserves*
- 85   *Map: Hluhluwe-Imfolozi Game Reserve*
- 91   *Map: St Lucia*
- 93   North Coast and Zululand listings
- 104   **Maputaland**
- 112   Maputaland listings

115 The Midlands, Battlefields and Drakensberg
- 116   **Pietermaritzburg and the Midlands**
- 118   *Map: Pietermaritzburg*
- 124   Pietermaritzburg and the Midlands listings
- 129   **Battlefields**
- 131   *Map: Ladysmith*
- 138   Battlefields listings
- 142   **uKhahlamba-Drakensberg Park**
- 148   *Map: Northern & central Drakensberg*
- 153   *Map: Monk's Cowl & Champagne Valley*
- 161   uKhahlamba-Drakensberg Park listings

173 Footnotes
- 174   Index

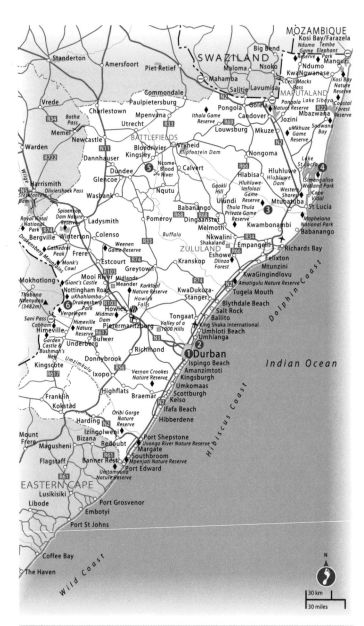

MOZAMBIQUE

Kosi Bay/Farazela

SWAZILAND

Standerton
Amersfoort
Piet Retief
Big bend
Ndumo Tembe
Game Elephant
Reserve Park
Ndumo
Manguzi

Maloma
Nsoko
KwaNgwanase
Cecil Macks
Pass

Commondale
Salitje
Lavumisa
MAPUTALAND
Kosi Bay
Nature
Reserve

Vrede
Paulpietersburg
Pongola
Golela
Pongola
Nature Reserve
Mbazwana
Coastal
Forest
Reserve

Charlestown
Mpenvana
Candover
Jozini
Sodwana
Bay

Botha
Pass
Utrecht
Louwsburg
Mkuze
uMkhuze
Game
Reserve

Memel
Newcastle
Wryheid
Klipfontein Dam
Nongoma
Lake
St Lucia

Warden
Dannhauser
Kingsley
Ntcme
Blood
River
Calvert
Hlabisa
Hluhluwe
Hluhluwe
Dam
Simangaliso
Wetland Park
Cape
Vidal

Harrismith
Dundee
Nqutu
Ggokli
Hill
Ulundi
Hluhluwe-
Imfolozi
Game
Reserve
Western
Shores
Mtubatuba
St Lucia

Oliviershoek Pass
Glencoe
Babanango
Thula Thula
Private Game
Reserve
Maphelana
National Park
Babanango

Royal Natal
Drakensberg
Spioenkop
Dam Nature
Reserve
Wasbank
Pomeroy
Dingaanstat
Melmoth
Kwambonambi

Bergville
Cathedral
Peak
Ladysmith
Colenso
Buffalo
Nkwalini
Shakaland
Eshowe
Empangeni
Richards Bay

Monk's
Cowl
Winterton
Frere
Weenen
Game Reserve
Kranskop
Dlinza
Forest
Felixton

Estcourt
Greytown
Mtunzini
KwaGingindlovu

Mokhotlong
Giant's Castle
Mooi River
Midlands
Karkloof
Nature Reserve
KwaDukuza-
Stanger
Amatigulu Nature Reserve
Tugela Mouth

Thabana
Ntlenyana
(3482m)
uKhahlamba
Drakensberg
Park
Nottingham Road
Meander
Howick Falls
Tongaat
Blythdale Beach
Salt Rock
Ballito

Sani Pass
Vergelegen
Midmar
Dam
Pietermaritzburg
Valley of
a 1000 Hills
King Shaka International
Umhloti Beach
Dolphin Coast

Cobham
Himeville
Himeville
Nature
Reserve
Howick
Bulwer
Umhlanga

Garden
Castle &
Bushman's
Nek
Underberg
Richmond
Durban

Kingscote
Donnybrook
Umzimkulu
Ixopo
Vernon Crookes
Nature Reserve
Ispingo Beach
Amanzimtoti
Kingsburgh
Indian Ocean

Franklin
Highflats
Braemar
Umkomaas
Scottburgh
Kelso

Kokstad
Harding
Oribi Gorge
Nature
Reserve
Ifafa Beach
Hibberdene

Mount
Frere
Izingolweni
Bizana
Port Shepstone
Uvongo River Nature Reserve

Magusheni
Redoubt
Margate
Southbroom
Hibiscus Coast

Flagstaff
Banner Rest
Mpenjati Nature Reserve
Port Edward

EASTERN CAPE
Umtamvuna
Nature Reserve

Lusikisiki
Libode
Port Grosvenor

Embotyi
Port St Johns

Coffee Bay
The Haven
Wild Coast

N
30 km
30 miles

KwaZulu-Natal manages to squash the country's most diverse features into a wedge of land between the towering Drakensberg Mountains and the long sweep of subtropical coastline. Here, visitors can go on safari, hike through dramatic wilderness, surf the country's best beaches and experience South Africa's strongest African culture. The mountains in the uKhahlamba-Drakensberg Park soar to over 3000 m, offering the country's finest hiking on an extensive network of remote trails. Zululand, rich in history and evocative landscapes, draws visitors both for its traditional Zulu lifestyles and the superb game reserves, some of the finest in South Africa. Hluhluwe-Imfolozi Game Reserve is the best known and has become famous for its rhino conservation programme, which has brought the rhino back from the brink of extinction. The iSimangaliso Wetland Park, lying to the north of Zululand, is an extraordinary area of undisturbed African wilderness, with subtropical lakes, wetlands and pristine coastlines, far off the usual tourist trail.

The landscape of the central region, dotted with small industrial towns and rolling farmland, makes up in history what it lacks in scenic drama. This area, better known as the Battlefields, still bears the scars of the Zulu Wars: the Zulu-Boer War, the Anglo-Zulu War and the Boer War. There are dozens of battlefield sites, but the most evocative are those at Isandlwana, Rorke's Drift and Blood River.

KwaZulu-Natal's beaches are some of the most beautiful in the country. While those around Durban and to the south are heavily developed, the coastline extending from the north towards Maputaland is relatively wild, with long empty sweeps of white sand backed by thick tropical dune forests – an excellent place for interesting wildlife encounters.

Planning your trip

Best time to visit Durban and KwaZulu-Natal

KwaZulu-Natal is situated on a subtropical latitude, and its shores are lapped by the warm waters of the Indian Ocean. It enjoys a pleasant, coastal climate with plenty of sunshine, quite a lot of humidity and a fair amount of light rainfall. Sea temperatures seldom fall below 17ºC – even in mid-winter – which makes it such a popular beach destination. Summer hits between September and April when temperatures are between 23-32ºC, with January being the hottest month, and because of the typically high humidity, conditions get sultry. This is also when the majority of rain falls, particularly in December, January and February, when there are often short tropical thunderstorms in the afternoons. Winters, with average daytime temperatures of 23ºC, are warm, dry and clear. Temperatures drop the further you go inland and in elevation, with the Drakensberg having daytime temperatures of up to 30ºC in summer, which may drop to below freezing on winter evenings and snow may fall on the highest peaks.

The dry winter months are the best time of year for game viewing, when vegetation cover is at a minimum and a lack of water forces animals to congregate around rivers and waterholes. Winter is also the best time for walking safaris and hiking, avoiding the high temperatures and frequent thunderstorms of the summer months. But summer has its advantages: lush greenery and flowers transform the reserves, animals are in good condition after feeding on the new shoots, and many young summer-born animals are around, which in turn attract the predators. However, the thick vegetation and the wide availability of water means that wildlife is far more widespread and difficult to spot.

All over the country December and January, followed by Easter, are by far the busiest periods for South African domestic tourism. The schools and universities shut and these are the times for special events and festivals. July and August are also popular with overseas visitors as they coincide with the European school holidays. Be sure to book your car hire and accommodation well in advance during these times.

Getting to Durban and KwaZulu-Natal

Air
The three main international airports in South Africa are: **OR Tambo International Airport** in Johannesburg, **Cape Town International Airport** in Cape Town and **King Shaka International Airport** in Durban (see page 24),

Don't miss...

1 Seaside holiday fun along Durban's Golden Mile and beaches, page 37.
2 World-class shopping at Gateway Mall in Umhlanga, page 53.
3 Seeing the Big Five in the Hluhluwe-Imfolozi Game Reserve, page 84.
4 Exploring the pristine coastline in the iSimangaliso Wetland Park, page 88.
5 A thought-provoking tour of the historical Battlefields, page 129.
6 Hiking in the uKhahlamba-Drakensberg Park, page 142.

Numbers relate to the map on page 4.

which opened in 2010 to replace the old Durban International Airport and is named after the Zulu king. **OR Tambo** is the regional hub with numerous daily flights to and from Europe, North America, Asia and Australia. Almost all international flights to South Africa first arrive in Johannesburg; the only international airline that flies directly to Durban's King Shaka International Airport is Emirates from Dubai (www.emirates.com).

Once in Johannesburg, there are connecting flights to Durban and the other domestic cities (see below); all of which are within a couple of hours' flying time of each other. Regardless of your eventual destination, immigration is done at Johannesburg, which usually means you have to pick up your luggage from international arrivals and check in again at domestic departures.

By booking early online, good deals can be found with all the airlines. You can either book directly or through the national booking agency **Computicket** ① *T011-340 8000, www.computicket.com*, or in South Africa at any of their kiosks in the shopping malls or any branch of **Checkers** and **Shoprite** supermarkets. **British Airways Comair** ① *T011-441 8600, www.britishairways. com*, has daily flights between Durban and Johannesburg, Cape Town and Port Elizabeth. **Kulula** ① *T0861-585 852 (in South Africa), T011-921 0111 (from overseas), www.kulula.com;* also owned by **British Airways**, is a no-frills airline with daily services between Durban and Johannesburg and Cape Town. **Mango** ① *T0861-162 646 (in South Africa), T011-359 1222 (from overseas), www.flymango.com*, another no-frills operator owned by **SAA**, has daily flights between Durban and Johannesburg and Cape Town. **South African Airways (SAA)** ① *T0861-359 722 (in South Africa), T011-978 1111 (from overseas), www. flysaa.com*, has daily flights between Durban and East London, Johannesburg, Cape Town, George and Maputo (Mozambique). They also have flights to/from Johannesburg and Pietermaritzburg and Richards Bay.

With a huge choice of routes and flights, you need to book well in advance for the best fares, especially over the Christmas and New Year period which is the peak summer holiday season in South Africa. Jet lag is not an issue if flying from Europe to South Africa as there is only a minimal time difference.

Rail

There are no international rail services between South Africa and its neighbouring countries, but South African long-distance passenger trains operate on a number of routes which all start and finish in Johannesburg. The network is run by **Shosholoza Meyl** ① *T0860-008 888 (in South Africa), T011-774 4555 (from overseas), www.shosholozameyl.co.za*. Shosholoza means 'to push forward' or 'to strive' and is the name of a popular traditional African song favoured particularly by hard-working men whose job it was to lay railway lines. Most of the major cities are linked by rail but train travel is very slow, and as all travel overnight, they arrive at some stations en route at inconvenient times. However the services are popular and seats should be reserved well in advance, and the trains have sleeping carriages, with coupés that sleep two or four people with a wash basin, fold-away table and bunk beds. The trains generally don't have a problem with security, but if you leave your compartment, make sure a train official locks it after you. Refreshments are available from trolleys or dining cars, but don't expect brilliant food and it's a good idea to take extra snacks. There is a service between Johannesburg and Durban (Monday, Friday, Wednesday and Sunday in both directions, 13 hours) via Newcastle, Ladysmith and Pietermaritzburg. Shosholoza Meyl also operates a more upmarket service, the **Premier Classe** ① *T011-774 5247, www.premier. co.za*, between Johannesburg and Durban and Johannesburg and Cape Town twice a week. This is a pleasant alternative to flying if you have the time, and the carriages are a lot nicer than the regular train, with two-bed coupés and extras like dressing gowns, toiletries and 'room service', and there's a good restaurant car serving breakfast, high tea and dinner; fares include all meals. Vehicles can be taken on the trains, which gives the option of taking the train in one direction and driving in the other.

Road

Bus **Greyhound** ① *T083-915 9000 (in South Africa), T011-276 8550 (from overseas), www.greyhound.co.za*, and **Intercape** ① *T0861-287 287 (in South Africa), T012-380 4400 (from overseas), www.intercape.co.za*, are the two long-distance bus companies that cover routes across South Africa's borders. The coaches are air conditioned and have a toilet; some sell refreshments and show DVDs. They will stop at least every four to five hours to refuel and perhaps change drivers and give passengers a chance to stretch their legs and buy snacks and drinks at a petrol station takeaway. For long journeys, the prices are reasonable (though always compare fares with the no-frills airlines). All bus tickets can be booked directly with the bus companies or through the national booking agency **Computicket**

① *T011-340 8000, www.computicket.com*, or in South Africa, at any of their kiosks in the shopping malls or any branch of **Checkers** and **Shoprite** supermarkets.

Greyhound runs services between Johannesburg/Pretoria and Maputo in Mozambique, and Harare and Bulawayo in Zimbabwe. Intercape runs services between Johannesburg and Windhoek in Namibia, and between Pretoria and Gaborone in Botswana, Pretoria and Bulawayo and Victoria Falls in Zimbabwe, which then continue to Livingstone, Lusaka and Ndola in Zambia, and Pretoria and Harare in Zimbabwe, which then continue to Blantyre and Lilongwe in Malawi. There are buses to and from Durban to connect with these services in Johannesburg/Pretoria.

Car If crossing any international borders in a private car, you must have a registration document, insurance and a driving licence printed in English with a photograph. With the exception of Zimbabwe, you should be able to take a hire car from South Africa into all the bordering countries, though check with the rental company first. You will need a letter of permission to take a car across a border if it is not registered in your name, and a ZA sticker (available from car rental companies or any AA shop in South Africa – usually found in the shopping malls). Botswana, Namibia, Lesotho, Swaziland, Mozambique and South Africa are all part of SADC's (Southern Africa Development Community) joint customs agreement, so if you are in your own car travelling on a carnet, you only have to produce this when crossing your first or last border to the SADC countries.

Transport in Durban and KwaZulu-Natal

Air
In Durban, domestic flights operated by the above airlines arrive and depart at **King Shaka International Airport** (see above and page 24), which is 35 km north of the city centre off the N2. There are regular flights to **Pietermaritzburg** (see page 117) and **Richards Bay** (see page 83).

Rail
On the long-distance rail service run by **Shosholoza Meyl** (above) between Johannesburg and Durban (Monday, Friday, Wednesday and Sunday in both directions, 13 hours), trains stop in Newcastle, Ladysmith and Pietermaritzburg en route. However, the arrival and departure times in these places are at inconvenient times late at night/early hours of the morning.

Road
Bus and coach Baz Bus ① *reservations Cape Town T021-422 5202, www. bazbus.com*, is a hop-on, hop-off bus that offers a convenient and sociable

alternative to the main long-distance bus services. It is specifically designed for backpackers visiting South Africa and remains one of the most popular ways of seeing the country on a budget. One of the best aspects of the service is that the bus collects and drops off passengers at their chosen backpacker hostel. There are a few exceptions where the bus will drop off on a main road, and the hostels will then meet you for an extra charge, though you must arrange this in advance. The Baz Bus route is Cape Town–Durban along the coast, and Durban–Johannesburg via the N3 with a diversion to the northern Drakensberg, with an extra shuttle from Johannesburg to Pretoria if there is the demand. Visit the website for the full timetable.

Tickets are priced per segment, for example from Durban to Johannesburg. You are allowed to hop off and on the bus as many times as you like in the given segment, but must not backtrack. This is where the savings are made, since the long-distance bus companies charge high prices for short journeys. However, note that for long distances without stops, the other buses may be better value.

Intercity coaches: Greyhound ① *T083-915 9000 (in South Africa), T011-276 8550 (from overseas), www.greyhound.co.za*; **Intercape** ① *T0861-287 287 (in South Africa), T012-380 4400 (from overseas), www.intercape.co.za*; and **Translux** ① *T0861-589 282 (in South Africa), T011-774 3333 (from overseas), www.translux. co.za*, are the three major long-distance bus companies that run between towns and popular destinations, and to some cities in South Africa's neighbouring countries (see page 8). You can either book directly or through the national booking agency **Computicket** ① *T011-340 8000, www.computicket.com*, or in South Africa, at any of their kiosks in the shopping malls or any branch of **Checkers** and **Shoprite** supermarkets. The coaches are air conditioned and have a toilet, and will stop at least every three to four hours to give the passengers a chance to stretch their legs and buy refreshments at petrol stations. Note that long-distance buses are more than twice as fast as the trains.

Car hire Hiring a car for part, or all, of your journey is undoubtedly the best way to see South Africa; you get to travel at your own leisurely pace and explore more out-of-the-way regions without being tied to a tour or a timetable. Driving isn't challenging; the roads are generally in excellent condition and, away from the major urban centres, there is little traffic. Petrol, not a major expense, is available 24 hours a day at the fuel stations in the cities and along the national highways; an attendant fills up, washes the windscreen and, if necessary, checks oil, water and tyre pressure, for which a tip of a few rand is the norm. Parking is easy and the sights and shopping malls have car parks. For street-side parking in the cities and towns, you pay a uniformed attendant between 0800 and 1700. Parking costs on average around R5-7 per hour. In less formal places and at night, you pay a 'car guard' about the same to watch over your car – they are usually identified by a badge or work vest. Driving is on the left side of the road and speed limits are

60 kph in built up areas, 80 kph on minor roads and 120 kph on highways. Speed traps are common. Remember that if you are caught by a speed camera, the fine will go to the car hire company who have every right to deduct the amount from your credit card, even if it is some time after you have left South Africa.

The minimum age to rent a car is usually 23. A driver's licence (with a translation if it's not in English) and a credit card are essential. Tourist offices usually recommend large international organizations such as **Avis** or **Budget**, but there are a number of reliable local companies, usually with a good fleet of cars and follow-up service, and it is worth asking at hotels for recommendations. Most of the larger companies have kiosks at the airport and partner with the airlines, so it's also possible to book a car online with your flight.

Costs for car hire vary considerably and depend on days of the week, season, type of vehicle and terms (insurance, excess, mileage, etc). A compact car starts from as little as R250-350 per day; a fully equipped 4WD or camper van with tents and equipment from R800-1300 per day. If this is shared among a group of 4 it's the most affordable way to get around. The cost of fuel is about two-thirds of what Europeans are used to, but distances travelled can be considerable so longer holidays will run up a hefty fuel bill.

In the event of an accident, call your car hire company's emergency number. For emergency breakdown and traffic update information contact the **Automobile Association of South Africa** ① *T083-84322, www.aa.co.za*.

Make sure you have the correct documents from the rental company if you wish to take the car into one of the neighbouring countries. See page 9.

Hitchhiking This is not common in South Africa and is not recommended as it can be very dangerous. Women should never hitch, under any circumstances, even in a group. If you have to hitch, say if your vehicle has broken down, be very wary of who you are accepting a lift from, and a car with a family or couple is usually the best option.

Minibus taxi The majority of South Africa's population travel by minibus taxis and, in many areas, including inner cities, they are the only way of getting around. However, the accident rate of such vehicles is notoriously high, with speeding, overcrowding and lack of maintenance being the main causes. There is also the problem of possible robbery, especially at the taxi ranks, so many visitors and locals are wary of using them. Nevertheless, minibus taxis remain the cheapest and most extensive form of transport in the country. Many routes have experienced little or no crime, but you should exercise extreme caution and always ask people in the know before using them.

Taxi Regular taxis are not hailed in the street, and except in the major cities there are few taxi ranks in South African towns so it's normal to phone for one;

any hotel or restaurant can do this for you. Taxis are metered and charge around R11-14 per kilometre. Groups should request a larger vehicle if available as these can carry up to seven people. Some can also accommodate wheelchairs.

Where to stay in Durban and KwaZulu-Natal

There is a wide variety of accommodation in this region from top-of-the-range five-star hotels, luxury game lodges and tented camps that charge R3000-8000 or more per couple per day, to mid-range safari lodges and hotels with air-conditioned double rooms for R1500-3000, to guesthouse or B&Bs that charge R500-1500 and dormitory beds or camping for under R200 a day. Generally, there are reasonable discounts for children and most places offer family accommodation. During the popular domestic tourism seasons and the long school holidays such as Christmas, New Year and Easter, reservations should be made well in advance, especially for the parks and along the coast. All accommodation in South Africa is graded a star value by the **Tourism Grading Council of South Africa** ① *www.tourismgrading.co.za*, and the website has comprehensive lists in all categories. There are numerous other resources for independently booking accommodation: the regional tourism websites listed in each area, **AA Travel Guides** ① *www.aatravel.co.za*, **SA-Venues** ① *www.sa-venues.com*, and **Sleeping Out** ① *www.sleeping-out.co.za*, are recommended.

Hotels There are some delightful family-run and country hotels, boutique hotels with stylish interiors in the cities and towns and chains such as Tsogo **Sun**, **Protea** and **City Lodge**. Many of the more upmarket hotels offer additional facilities like spas, golf courses and some fine restaurants, which are almost always open to non-guests. Every small town also has at least one hotel of two- or three-star standard: usually aimed at local business travellers, they may be in characterless buildings with restaurants serving bland food, but they nevertheless represent good value.

Guesthouses Guesthouses can offer some of the most characterful accommodation in South Africa, with interesting places springing up in both cities and small towns. Standards obviously vary enormously; much of what you'll get has to do with the character of the owners and the location of the homes. Some are simple practical overnight rooms, while at the more luxurious end, rooms may be in historic homes filled with antiques, and offering impeccable service. Breakfast is almost always included and, in some, evening meals can be prepared if you phone ahead. For listings look at the websites of the **Guest House Association of Southern Africa** ① *www.ghasa. co.za*, or the **Portfolio Collection** ① *www.portfoliocollection.com*.

Price codes

Where to stay

$$$$ over US$350 $$$ US$150-350

$$ US$75-150 $ under US$75

Prices refer to the cost of a double room, not including service charge or meals unless otherwise stated. See page 20 for exchange rates.

Restaurants

$$$ over US$30 $$ US$15-30 $ under US$15

Prices refer to the cost of a two-course meal for one person including a soft drink, beer or glass of wine.

Backpacker hostels Apart from camping, backpacker hostels are the cheapest form of accommodation, and a bed in a dormitory will cost as little as R120 a night. Some also have budget double rooms with or without bathrooms, while others have space to pitch a tent in the garden.

You can usually expect a self-catering kitchen, hot showers, a TV/DVD room and internet access. Many hostels also have bars and offer meals or nightly *braais*, plus a garden and a swimming pool. Most hostels are a good source of travel information and many act as booking agents for bus companies, budget safari tours and car hire. The Baz Bus (see page 9) caters for backpackers and links most hostels along the coast between Cape Town and Durban, and some on its route between Durban and Johannesburg via the Drakensberg. Coast to Coast ① *www.coastingafrica.com*, publishes a free annual backpackers' accommodation guide and is available in all the hostels.

Camping and caravan parks Camping is the cheapest and most flexible way of seeing South Africa. Every town has a municipal campsite, many of which also have simple self-catering chalets. As camping is very popular with South Africans, sites tend to have very good facilities, although they may be fully booked months in advance, especially during the school holidays in the most popular game reserves and national parks. Even the most basic site will have a clean washblock with hot water, plus electric points and lighting. All sites have *braai* facilities, with charcoal, wood and firelighters available in campsite shops. Some sites also have kitchen blocks. At the most popular tourist spots, campsites are more like holiday resorts with shops, swimming pools and a restaurant – these can get very busy and are best avoided in peak season.

Camping equipment is widely available in South Africa if you don't want to bring your own. Lightweight tents, sleeping bags, ground mats, gas lights, stoves and cooking equipment, etc, can be bought at good prices in all the major cities and some car hire companies rent out equipment. Cape Union Mart is a quality outdoor adventure shop for gear, as well as outdoor clothing, and branches can be found in the larger shopping malls across the country, www.capeunionmart.co.za.

Self-catering Self-catering chalets, cottages or apartments are particularly popular with South African holidaymakers, and the choice is enormous along the KwaZulu-Natal coast and in the game reserves. They can be excellent value and the cost could be as little as R100-200 per person per day and are ideal for families or a group of friends on a budget. The quality and facilities of course vary, but in Durban and the other seaside towns, you can expect holiday apartments to have a couple of bedrooms and a fully equipped kitchen, and perhaps additional facilities like restaurants, shops, swimming pool and children's playground, and there will always be nearby access to the beach. The self-catering accommodation in KwaZulu-Natal's game reserves ranges from simple huts, which share communal bathrooms and kitchens with campers, to spacious multiple bedroom units with at least two bathrooms and quite often a view of a river or floodplain for game viewing.

Luxury game lodges There are numerous private game reserves dotted around KwaZulu-Natal. Most are in prime wildlife areas and the attraction is the combination of exclusive game viewing in a spectacular natural setting, with top-class accommodation, fine dining and high levels of service.

The cost of staying in a luxury game lodge varies from R3000-8000 or more per couple per day. But this includes all meals, most drinks and game-viewing activities such as game-drives or walks. In order to get the most from the experience, guests tend to stay for at least two nights. The lodges are often isolated and not easily accessible by road so many reserves offer shuttle transfers from the nearest city, and some have their own airstrips where charter aircraft can land. These can be arranged through the game lodge when you book accommodation.

Food and drink in Durban and KwaZulu-Natal

Food

South African food tends to be fairly regional, although a ubiquitous love of meat unites the country. As well as quality steak and Karoo lamb, South Africa offers plenty of opportunities to try an assortment of game such as popular ostrich or springbok. One of the first local terms you are likely to learn will be *braai*, which quite simply means barbecue. The *braai* is incredibly popular, part of the South African way of life, and every campsite, back garden and picnic spot has one. Given the excellent range of meat available, learning how to cook good food on a *braai* is an art that needs to be mastered quickly, especially if you are self-catering. A local meat product, which travellers invariably come across, is biltong – a heavily salted and spiced sun-dried meat, usually made from beef but sometimes made from game. Non-red meat eaters and vegetarians need not despair though as most fruit and vegetables are grown in South Africa (and indeed exported) and there is an excellent choice of local produce. Fish and seafood too is plentiful and the likes of Cape salmon and West Coast mussels come from South Africa's Atlantic coast, while prawns, sea bass and snapper come from Mozambique.

Supermarkets have a similar selection of groceries to that found in Europe and in most cases considerably cheaper, especially meat and fresh fruit and vegetables. There are several large supermarket chains, and the larger ones also feature extensive counters for pre-prepared food, hot meals, pizzas and sandwiches (in some, even sushi). Across the region there are also plenty of farmers' markets (and often on the roadside, padstalls – Afrikaans for 'farm-stalls'), for tasty home-made goodies, organic vegetables, wine and olives.

Drink
South Africa is a major player in the international market and produces a wide range of excellent wines. The Winelands in the Western Cape have the best-known labels but there are a number of other wine regions dotted around the country. South Africa also produces a range of good beer. Major names include Black Label, Castle and Amstel. Windhoek, from Namibia, is also widely available and more popular than some of the South African beers. Home-brewed beer, made from sorghum or maize, is widely drunk by the African population. It has a thick head, is very potent and not very palatable to the uninitiated. No liquor may be sold on Sundays (and public holidays) except in licensed bars and restaurants. The standard shop selling alcohol is known as a bottle store, usually open Monday-Friday 0800-1800, Saturday 0830-1400 (some may stay open until 1600). Supermarkets do not sell beer or spirits, stop selling wine at 2000, and don't sell alcohol on Sundays. A bottle of wine and beer bought from a bottle store starts from an affordable R30 and R10 respectively.

Soft drinks Tap water in South Africa is safe to drink. Bottled mineral water and a good range of fruit juices are available at most outlets – the Ceres and Liquifruit brands are the best. Another popular drink is Rooibos (or red bush) tea – a caffeine-free tea with a smoky flavour, usually served with sugar or honey, that is grown in the Cederberg Mountains in the Western Cape.

Eating out
There is an excellent variety of restaurants that represent every kind of international cuisine as well as a good choice of quality South African dishes. In particular, because of the Indian influence in KwaZulu-Natal, the best curries are found in and around Durban and the authenticity of the dishes are better

South Africanisms

English, the official language, is understood and spoken by the majority of South Africans, but it is peppered with a host of other commonly used words; some borrowed from Afrikaans and the numerous African languages, while others are completely fabricated slang that is uniquely South African.

Bakkie Pick-up truck.

Babbelas Hangover.

Boerewors Afrikaans for 'farmer's sausage' made from beef or game meat and grilled in a spiral.

Born frees South Africans who were born into a democratic South Africa (after 1994).

Braai Barbeque.

Bushveld Grassland dotted with thick scrubby trees and bush. Veld means 'field' in Afrikaans.

Dorp Afrikaans for 'village'; usually refers to a small rural town with just a few farmers wandering around.

Eish An isiXhosa word used to express surprise, wonder, frustration or outrage; used across all the languages.

Howzit How is it going? How are you?

Ja Yes. From Afrikaans and pronounced *yaa*.

Ja-Nee Yes-no (*yaa-near*), but actually means so-so or maybe.

Jol To have fun; can refer to anything from a picnic to an all-night party.

Lapa Thatched shelter for entertaining, especially when *braaiing*.

Lekker Nice, good, great, cool or tasty.

Kopjie A hill or outcrop of rocks; a common feature on wide open plains.

Madiba The universal affectionate name for Nelson Mandela (it was his clan name).

Now-now and just-now Widely used to indicate concepts of time.

Potjiekos Stews cooked over coals in three-legged cast-iron pots of the same name; means 'little-pot food' in Afrikaans.

Robot South African term for traffic lights.

Shebeen Traditional township pub/bar; once illegal under Apartheid.

Stoep A veranda in front of a house.

Traffic circle Roundabout.

Yebo Yes, for sure; derived from isiZulu.

than you would expect in Europe. Eating out can be very good value, and a two-course evening meal with wine in a reasonable restaurant will cost under R300 for two people, and you can be pretty assured of good food and large portions. For the budget traveller there are plenty of fast-food outlets, and almost every supermarket has a superb deli counter serving hot and cold meals.

A great starting point for choosing a restaurant is the **Eat Out** ① *www.eatout.co.za*, which features South Africa's best restaurants, or you can buy their magazine, available at CNA and Exclusive Books. **Dining Out** ① *www.dining-out.co.za*, is another excellent resource and provides hundreds of reviews and contact details for restaurants throughout the country.

Essentials A-Z

Accident and emergency

Police, T10111; **Medical**, T10177; **Fire**, T10111. All emergencies from a cell phone, T112.

Children

The region is a popular family holiday destination with plenty to do, and there are significant discounts on accommodation, transport and entry fees. You will find plentiful supplies to feed and look after your little ones, and many restaurants have kids' menus. Hygiene throughout the country is good; stomach upsets are rare and the tap water everywhere is safe to drink.

Most accommodation options welcome families; many hotels have family or adjoining rooms, there are plenty of self-catering chalets or apartments, and children love camping, either with your own camping equipment or an upmarket tented camp.

In the parks and reserves, seeing animals on safari is very exciting for children, especially when they catch their first glimpse of an elephant or lion. However, small children may get bored driving around a hot game park all day if there is no animal activity. Keep them interested by providing them with their own animal and bird check-lists and perhaps their own binoculars and cameras. While in the bush, be sure to protect your children from the sun's intense rays, and be aware of the potential dangers of wild animals, snakes and insects.

Disabled travellers

Facilities for disabled travellers are generally of a high standard and the airports are fully wheelchair accessible and can provide wheelchairs for less mobile travellers. Modern hotels have specially adapted rooms, but it is worth enquiring in advance at older hotels or more remote places. Almost all shopping malls, museums and tourist attractions have ramps or lifts and disabled parking right by the entrance.The more modern transport, for example Durban's **People Mover** bus (page 27), is accessible for wheelchairs. With notice, the larger car hire companies, such as **Avis**, **Budget** and **Hertz**, can organize cars with hand controls.

Customs and duty free

The official customs allowance for visitors over 18 years includes 200 cigarettes, 50 cigars, 250 g of tobacco, 2 litres of wine, 1 litre of spirits, 50 ml of perfume and 250 ml of eau de toilette. Tourists can reclaim the 14% VAT on purchases bought in South Africa whose total value exceeds R250. You can do this when departing at the VAT reclaim desks at airports in Johannesburg,

Cape Town and Durban or at border posts. For more information visit www.taxrefunds.co.za.

Electricity

Voltage 220/230 volts AC at 50 Hz. Most plugs and appliances are 3-point round-pin (1 10-mm and 2 8-mm prongs). Hotels usually have 2-pin sockets for razors and chargers.

Embassies and consulates

For embassies and consulates of South Africa, see http://embassy.goabroad.com/

Health

See your GP or travel clinic at least 6 weeks before departure for general advice on travel risks and vaccinations. Make sure you have sufficient medical travel insurance, get a dental check, know your own blood group and if you suffer a long-term condition, such as diabetes, epilepsy or a serious allergy, obtain a Medic Alert bracelet/necklace (www.medicalert.co.uk). If you wear glasses, take a copy of your prescription.

Vaccinations
Confirm your primary courses and boosters are up to date. Courses or boosters usually advised: diphtheria, tetanus, poliomyelitis, hepatitis A. Vaccines sometimes advised: tuberculosis, hepatitis B, rabies, cholera, typhoid. The final decision on all vaccinations, however, should be based on a consultation with your doctor or travel clinic. A yellow fever certificate is required if over 1 year old and entering from an infected area. If you don't have one, you'll be required to get one at the airport before being permitted entry. Specialist advice should be taken on the best anti-malarials to use.

Health risks
Diarrhoea Diarrhoea can refer either to loose stools or an increased frequency of bowel movement, both of which can be a nuisance. Symptoms should be relatively short lived but if they persist beyond 2 weeks specialist medical attention should be sought. Adults can use an antidiarrhoeal medication to control the symptoms but only for up to 24 hrs. In addition keep well hydrated by drinking plenty of fluids and eat bland foods. Oral rehydration sachets are a useful way to keep well hydrated. These should always be used when treating children and the elderly.

The standard advice to prevent problems is to be careful with water and ice for drinking. If you have any doubts then boil the water or filter and treat it. Food can also transmit disease. Be wary of salads (what were they washed in, who handled them), re-heated foods or food that has been left out in the sun having been cooked earlier in the day. On the positive side, very few people experience stomach problems in South Africa.

HIV/AIDS Southern Africa has the highest rates of HIV and AIDS in the world. Visitors should be aware of the dangers of infection and take the necessary precautions with sex, needles, medical treatment and in the case of a blood transfusion.

Malaria South Africa only has a very low seasonal risk of malaria in the extreme east of the country along the Mozambique border. This includes parts of the Kruger National Park and the extreme east of KwaZulu-Natal including Ndumu and Tembe game reserves. The risk period is between December and April. If you are travelling there during this time, consult your doctor or travel clinic about taking anti-malarials and ensure you finish the recommended course.

The best prevention is to try to avoid getting bitten. The most vulnerable times are between dusk and dawn; cover exposed skin with light clothing and insect repellents, and in accommodation use mosquito nets or ensure netted screens are kept closed.

Sun Protect yourself adequately against the sun. Apply a high-factor sunscreen (greater than SPF15) and also make sure it screens against UVB. Prevent heat exhaustion and heatstroke by drinking enough fluids throughout the day.

If you get sick
There are plenty of private hospitals in South Africa, which have 24-hr emergency departments and pharmacies, run by **Medi-Clinic** (www.mediclinic.co.za) or **Netcare** (www.netcare.co.za). It is essential to have travel insurance as hospital bills need to be paid at the time of admittance, so keep all paperwork to make a claim. If you need to have a vaccination or buy malaria prophylactics in South Africa, visit one of the **Netcare Travel Clinics** in the major cities, www.travelclinic.co.za.

Holidays

South African school holidays are mid-Dec to mid-Jan; mid-Apr to early May; early Aug to early Sep. Exact dates can be found at www.schoolterms.co.za. Accommodation rates are often higher during school holidays in the parks and along the coast, but generally stay the same year-round in the cities.

When a public holiday falls on a Sun, the following Mon becomes a holiday. Most businesses will close but shopping malls and large supermarkets in city centres remain open (public holidays are some of their busiest days – especially if a holiday weekend coincides with month-end pay day). All tourist attractions are open on public holidays.

1 Jan New Year's Day
21 Mar Human Rights' Day
Mar/Apr Good Friday; Family Day
(Mon following Easter Sun)
27 Apr Freedom Day
1 May Workers' Day
16 Jun Youth Day
9 Aug National Women's Day
24 Sep Heritage Day
16 Dec Day of Reconciliation
25 Dec Christmas Day
26 Dec Day of Goodwill

Money

→ *US$1 = R10.97; £1 = R17.58; €1 = R13.87 (Oct 2014).*
For up-to-the-minute exchange rates, visit **www.xe.com**.

Currency
The South African currency is the **rand** (R), which is divided into 100 **cents** (c). Notes are in 200, 100, 50, 20 and 10 rand, and coins are in 5, 2, 1 R and 50, 20, 10 and 5 cents. You can carry your funds in traveller's cheques (TCs), currency cards, credit and debit cards, or rand, US dollars, euros or pounds sterling cash. Note that rand can easily be exchanged in all South Africa's neighbouring countries and in Lesotho, Swaziland, Namibia, Mozambique and Zimbabwe, it is used interchangeably alongside the local currency.

Changing money
South Africa's main banks are **ABSA**, **First National**, **Nedbank** and **Standard Bank**. All have foreign exchange services. You can also change money at **Bidvest**, www.bidvestbank.co.za, and **Master Currency**, www.mastercurrency.co.za, which has branches at the main airports and large shopping malls. Larger hotels offer exchange facilities, but these often charge exorbitant fees.

Currency cards
If you don't want to carry lots of cash, prepaid currency cards allow you to preload money from your bank account, fixed at the day's exchange rate. They look like a credit or debit card and are issued by specialist money changing companies, such as **Travelex** and **Caxton FX**, as well as the **Post Office**. You can top up and check your balance by phone, online and sometimes by text.

Credit and debit cards
Lost or stolen cards American Express, T0800-110929; **Diners Club**, T0800-112017; **MasterCard**, T0800-990418; **Visa**, T0800-990475.

You can get all the way around South Africa with a credit or debit card. Not only are they a convenient method of covering major expenses but they offer some of the most competitive exchange rates when withdrawing cash from ATMs. You can only hire a car with a credit (not debit) card. The chip and pin system is common, though not yet universal. ATMs are everywhere: **Plus**, **Cirrus Visa**, **MasterCard**, **American Express** and **Diners Club** are all accepted. The amount you can withdraw varies between systems and cards, but you should be able to take out at least R2000 a day. Note that theft during or immediately after a withdrawal can be a problem, so never accept a stranger's help at an ATM, be aware of your surroundings and avoid using street-side ATMs. Instead, go into a bank or shopping mall, where guards are often on duty.

Opening hours

Banks Mon-Fri 0830-1530, Sat 0830-1130; bureaux de change in the airports and shopping malls are open longer hours 7 days a week.

Post offices Mon-Fri 0830-1600, Sat 0800-1200. **Shops** Mon-Fri 0830-1700, Sat 0830-1300, Sun 0900-1300. Larger branches of the supermarkets stay open until late in the evening. Large shopping malls in the cities may stay open until 2100.

Safety

The most common crimes facing tourists are pickpocketing, purse-snatching and thefts from vehicles, and, on occasion, carjacking. Guns are prevalent and you should be aware that your assailant may well be armed and any form of resistance could be fatal. South Africa has had more than its fair share of well-publicized crime problems. But despite the statistics, much of the serious violent crime is gang-based and occurs in areas that tourists are unlikely to visit. The crime rate in the districts where most of the hotels, restaurants and shops are located has dropped significantly in recent years, due mainly to an increase in security measures; you should experience few problems in these areas. Nevertheless, listen to advice from locals about which areas to avoid, and the general common sense rules apply to prevent petty theft: don't exhibit anything valuable and keep wallets and purses out of sight, and avoid deserted areas and always take a taxi after dark. If you're driving, plan your route beforehand, avoid driving after dark, always keep car doors locked and windows wound up, and it's a good idea to bring (or hire) a mobile phone; useful in any case if you break down.

Telephone

→ *Country code: +27; international direct dialling code 00; directory enquires T1023; international enquires T1025.*

You must dial the full 3-digit regional code for every number in South Africa, even when you are calling from within that region.

The telephone service is very efficient. Card and coin phones are widespread and work well. Cards are available in supermarkets, some pharmacies and Telkom vending machines. Even in remote national parks there are usually card phones from which one can dial direct to anywhere in the world. Note that hotels usually double the rates and even a short international call can become very expensive.

Mobile phones
Overseas visitors should be able to use their mobiles on international roaming. Alternatively, you can buy a local SIM card and start-up pack from any of the phone shops and at the 3 international airports, which also offer phone and SIM hire.

Time

South Africa has only 1 time zone: GMT +2 hrs (+1 during UK Summer Time Mar-Oct), 8 hrs ahead of USA Eastern Standard Time, 1 hr ahead of Europe; 8 hrs behind Australian Eastern Standard Time. There is no daylight saving.

Tipping

Waiters, hotel porters, stewards, chambermaids and tour guides should be tipped 10-15%, according to the service. When leaving tips make sure it goes to the intended person. It is common practice to tip petrol pump attendants, depending on their service – around R5 for a fill up, oil and water check and comprehensive windscreen clean. It is also customary to tip car guards R2-5 if parking on the street. They are usually identified by a work vest or badge. On safari you are expected to tip guides. If in any doubt, ask the company that you booked with for advice on how much to tip.

Tourist information

South African Tourism (SATOUR), T011-895 3000, www.southafrica.net, has a very useful website with information on special interest travel, maps, latest travel news, airlines, accommodation and national parks. The website is published in 15 languages and each version provides specific information for people coming from each individual country. SATOUR also has offices around the world, which are useful for pre-travel information. Regional and local tourism authorities are some of the best sources of information once in the country; even the smallest town will have a tourist office with details of local sights and accommodation. Local tourist offices are listed under individual towns.

Visas and immigration

Most nationalities including EU nationals and citizens from the USA, Canada, Australia and New Zealand don't need visas to enter South Africa. On arrival, visitors from these countries are granted temporary **visitors' permits**, lasting up to 90 days. You must have a valid return ticket or voucher for onward travel and at least one completely empty page in your passport to get a permit; without these you maybe denied entry.

It is possible to apply for an extension to the permit at one of the offices of the **Department of Home Affairs**; Durban T031-308 7930; www.home-affairs.gov.za. Citizens of countries other than those listed above should consult the South African embassy or consulate in their country for information on visa requirements.

Weights and measures

The metric system is used in South Africa.

Contents

24 Durban
    24 Arriving in Durban
    28 Background
    30 Places in Durban
    41 Around Durban
    45 Listings

61 KwaZulu-Natal
**   South Coast**
    61 South of Durban
    64 Hibiscus Coast
    68 Listings

75 North Coast
**   and Zululand**
    75 Dolphin Coast
    78 Zululand
    81 Ithala Game Reserve
    83 Empangeni and
       around
    84 Hluhluwe-Imfolozi
       Game Reserve
    88 iSimangaliso
       Wetland Park
    93 Listings

104 Maputaland
    104 Arriving in
        Maputaland
    106 uMkhuze Game
        Reserve
    107 Sodwana Bay
    108 Coastal Forest Reserve
        and Lake Sibaya
    109 Ndumo Game Reserve
    110 Tembe Elephant Park
    111 Kosi Bay Nature
        Reserve
    112 Listings

Footprint features

26 Durban by bus
34 Bunny chow
57 Tours with Durban Tourism
63 The Greatest Shoal on Earth
105 Maputaland turtles

Durban & the KwaZulu-Natal Coast

Durban

The sprawling conurbation of Durban is KwaZulu-Natal's principal city and South Africa's largest port. Although its appeal is not immediately apparent – few original buildings survive and it can feel overcrowded – it is renowned for its steamy tropical climate and magnificent bathing and surfing beaches, which stretch from Durban harbour in the south to the upmarket suburb of Umhlanga in the north. The beachfront paved promenade, the Golden Mile, is a major feature of the city centre and runs between its two most popular attractions: uShaka Marine World and Suncoast Casino complex.

Away from the CBD are the attractive suburbs that climb the hills above Durban, where tropical foliage spills from the ornate balconies of Victorian and Edwardian houses and the parks are awash with colour in spring and summer. The city also has one of the country's most interesting cultural mixes, and exhibits a mix of Indian, Zulu and post-colonial influences. Durban is home to South Africa's largest Indian population, reflected in the tasty curries and colourful markets, while half an hour out of town in the Valley of 1000 Hills is the chance to experience Zulu rural life.

Arriving in Durban → *Phone code: 031.*

Getting there
King Shaka International Airport ① *La Mercy on the Dolphin Coast, 35 km north of the city centre off the N2, T032-436 6000, flight information T0867-277888, or check the Airports Company of South Africa (ACSA) website, www.acsa.co.za,* has regular domestic flights to and from South Africa's other principal cities. However, with the exception of Emirates, there are few international flights and most people change in Johannesburg (see Planning your trip, page 6). There are numerous facilities in the terminal building including restaurants, shops, banks with ATMs and foreign exchange services, mobile phone shops and Wi-Fi. Tourist information can be found at the desks of both **Tourism KwaZulu-Natal** ① *T032-436 0013, www.zulu.org.za, daily*

0700-2100, and **Durban Tourism** ⓘ *T031-322 6046, www.durbanexperience. co.za, daily 0700-2100*.

Taxis and car hire offices can be found outside the terminal building, and many hotels offer airport transfer services. The **King Shaka Airport Shuttle Bus** ⓘ *T031-465 5573, www.airportbustransport.co.za*, departs and arrives at the dedicated stop outside the terminal, 0500-2200, R50 one way to Umhlanga and R70 to Durban city centre, tickets are bought on the bus. From the airport, buses depart every 45 minutes and go to all the large hotels in Umhlanga and in Durban's city centre and beachfront, as well as the Gateway Mall in Umhlanga and Durban's central bus station in the CBD. In the other direction the buses must be pre-booked (so they know which hotels to stop at) and again they run at 45-minute intervals. **King Shaka Airport Shuttle Services** ⓘ *T031-822 7783 www.kingshakashuttles.co.za*, has a desk in the arrivals hall (among other shuttle companies) and provides shuttle buses to Umhlanga, R200, and Durban CBD, R300, for one to four passengers. They can also go to Durban's outlying suburbs. The **Margate**

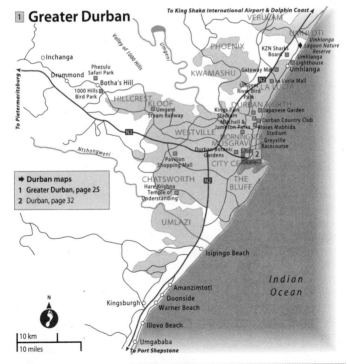

Greater Durban

➡ **Durban maps**
1 Greater Durban, page 25
2 Durban, page 32

Durban by bus

Bus public transport in Durban has improved significantly in the last few years, and is now generally safe, simple to use and efficient. The city centre bus station is opposite the Workshop Mall on the corner of Monty Naicker Road and Samora Machel Street. For enquiries call the 24-hour, toll-free **Durban Transport Information Call Centre** (T0861-000 834), which offers assistance for all buses run by Durban Transport, Mynah and People Mover.

On all these buses you can pay in cash or you can get a **Muvo Card**. This is a smartcard that is loaded with money, and cards are 'tapped' in and out on the bus so the fare is calculated, and is interchangeable on the routes of all three bus companies. They can be bought and loaded at the main bus stations or interchanges or from some local convenience shops such as **7-Eleven** (look for the 'Muvo accepted here' signs). It costs R25 to get a card and you need to load a minimum of 10 trips. Information on where you can get a card, plus fares and timetables for all buses can be found at www.muvo.co.za.

There is a fleet of over 460 green and white municipality buses called **Aqualine** (also known as **Durban Transport**; T031-309 3250). They run 0600-1900, but are not especially useful for visitors as they generally ferry commuters in and out of the city to outlying suburbs in the general metropolitan area. Fares start from R6 for a short trip. However Durban Transport also run **Mynah** (T031-309 3250), a frequent service of about 20 'short' buses (roughly 0630-1730) between the city centre and the northeast

Mini Coach, also stops at the airport on its service to the south coast (see pages 59 and 74).

Durban **railway station** is on Masabalala Yengwa Road (M12) to the north of the CBD. Behind is the **motorcoach terminal** for major long-distance buses run by **Translux**, **Intercape** and **Greyhound**. ➤ *For more detailed information, see Transport, page 58.*

Getting around

Most of Durban's oldest buildings, museums, galleries and the commercial centre are concentrated in a relatively small area in the CBD. However, in parts, the CBD is a pretty rough-and-ready district, and although security had improved in recent years, it's still sensible to take common sense precautions in terms of safety. While most of the sights in the CBD can now be explored on foot, remember that it is still a bustling, congested place and street crime may occur. You'd be advised to catch a bus (see box, above) or take a taxi between the sites. The other alternative is to take one of Durban Tourism's walking tours suburbs just outside the Durban CBD such as Berea, Musgrave, Morningside and Mitchell Park. Short fares start from R5; it's very useful if you want to get to town from accommodation in these suburbs, and one of the routes goes from the CBD to the Botanical Gardens via Berea Road.

By far the most useful service for visitors are the green **People Mover** (T031-309 2731) buses, which run 0500-2200 and pass by about every 15 minutes. The wide windows are ideal for sightseeing along their scenic routes and the buses are wheelchair accessible. The three routes are the Beach Line between Suncoast Casino and Entertainment World in the north and uShaka Marine World in the south; The City Line, which stops close to the City Hall, the Playhouse Theatre, Tourist Junction, the Inkosi Albert Luthuli International Convention complex, and the Victoria Street Market among other sights in the CBD; and the Circle Line, a wider loop that also takes in the Victoria Embankment in the south and sights such as the Kwa Muhle Museum and Kingsmead cricket stadium as well as the Durban railway station and long-distance bus terminal in the north. The interchange between the Beach Line and the City Line is on the beachfront at the end of Dr Pixley Ka Seme Street, while the interchange between the Beach Line and the Circle Line is further north on the beachfront at the end of KE Masinga Road; although the routes cross over in other places. Fares start from R5.50 for a short trip; R16 for a day pass; and R50 for 10 trips.

or the Ricksha Bus tour (for details of these see box, page 57). The extensive beachfront can be easily explored on foot and security is good. To explore the outlying suburbs, there are a number of day tours to join, but for the greatest flexibility, it's always a good idea to rent a car.

Tourist information

The main office of **Tourism KwaZulu-Natal** ① *160 Monty Naicker Rd, CBD, T031-366 7500, www.zulu.org.za, Mon-Fri 0800-1700, Sat 0900-1400,* is at Tourist Junction in the old station building and is very helpful and a useful place to pick up maps and brochures for the whole province. They also have kiosks at **King Shaka International Airport** ① *T032-436 0013, daily 0700-2100,* and at **uShaka Marine World** ① *T031-337 8099, daily 0900-2100.* **Durban Tourism** is the city's tourist information service, which is also very helpful and produces a range of brochures, including accommodation, restaurant and events guides. It also runs extremely good city tours (see box, page 57). The **head office** ① *90 Florida Rd, T031-322 4164, www.durbanexperience.co.za, Mon-Fri*

0800-1600, is in Berea and they have other **tourist information offices** ① *corner of OR Tambo Parade and KE Masinga Rd, North Beach T031-322 2404-5, daily 0800-1700,* at the beachfront; in the **uShaka Marine World** ① *T031-337 8099, daily 0900-2100*; **Gateway** ① *T031-561 4257, Mon-Thu 0900-1900, Fri-Sat 0900-2100, Sun 0900-1800,* and at **King Shaka International Airport** ① *T031-322 6046, daily 0700-2100.* There are also satellite offices at the Valley of 1000 Hills (page 43), and Amanzimtoti (page 61).

Orientation

Durban lies within the metropolitan eThekwini Municipality (from *itheku* meaning 'bay' or 'lagoon'), which covers 2300 sq km from Umkomaas in the south, to Tongaat in the north, moving inland to Ndwedwe, and ends at Cato Ridge in the west. The many approaches to Durban pass through coastal tourist resorts, industrial areas, townships and eventually reach the Central Business District (CBD). This crop of high rises is bordered to the west by the Indian district, to the south by the harbour, and to the east by the beaches. The significant feature of the beachfront is the Golden Mile, or promenade, which runs for 5 km from South Beach (where **uShaka Marine World** is) to North Beach (**Suncoast Casino** and **Entertainment World**). Beyond, the city extends north alongside the ocean to include the holiday towns such as Umhlanga and Umdloti, surrounded by the inland rolling hills of sugar cane. South of the CBD and beyond the entrance to the harbour are the Bluff beaches and further south, the coastal town of Amanzimtoti which marks the start of the string of resorts along the South Coast. A 30-minute drive inland from the CBD takes you to the suburbs of Westville, Kloof, Hillcrest, and the Valley of 1000 Hills. These western suburbs are notably elevated with both Hillcrest and Kloof being around 850 m above sea level.

Background

The area around the bay was once covered with mangroves and inhabited by pelicans, flamingos and hippos. The earliest inhabitants were members of the Lala tribe who fished in the estuary, and hunted and grew crops in the fertile tropical forests along the coast. The first Europeans to land here were Portuguese explorers en route to the east. On 25 December 1497, Vasco da Gama sighted land and called it Natal, though this was probably off the coast of present-day Eastern Cape. The Portuguese cartographer Manuel Perestrello mapped the coast of Natal in 1576, but it was nearly 200 years after the earliest European sighting that the first trading ships arrived. In 1684 the *Francis* began a new era when she sailed to Natal to buy ivory.

After the relative success of the first trading expedition, the Dutch East India Company planned to open a trading post here (after buying land off

Chief Inyangesi for 1000 guilders worth of beads, copper rings and iron). But after a few technical hitches involving the estuary's sandbars, trade was never really developed and in 1730 the Dutch established an alternative trading station at Delagoa Bay.

The first British traders arrived in 1823 on the *Salisbury*, spurred on by news of Shaka, the powerful chief of the Zulus and his Empire. Lieutenant Francis and George Farewell arrived in the Bay of Natal and were blown over the sandbars in a storm. They returned in May 1824, with Henry Francis Fynn and a group of other adventurers, and set up their first camp in what is now known as Farewell Square. Fynn was the first European trader to make contact with Shaka. Fynn and the other adventurers claimed (falsely) to be envoys of King George and were well received. Fynn became a favourite of the royal household after he helped Shaka recover from a stab wound sustained during a battle. In thanks Shaka granted Fynn a huge tract of land, over 9000 sq km.

Fynn and his young colleague Nathaniel Issacs ran this area as their own personal fiefdom, taking many Zulu wives and fathering dozens of children. Fynn declared himself King of Natal and wielded power in the same brutal manner as his infamous neighbour, Shaka. Even though Fynn and his men broke many Zulu laws, including the prohibition on all but the king from trading in ivory, they were treated with great respect by Shaka (though the chiefs they bought the ivory from were invariably executed).

The area remained undeveloped, however, with just a few dozen European settlers, and the British refused to annex the region. It was not until the establishment of the Voortrekker republic of Natalia in 1838 that the British felt their interests to be under threat. The capital of Natalia was in Pietermaritzburg, but settlements had also been established at Weenen and Durban, giving the Voortrekkers access to the sea. The possibility of a viable independent Voortrekker republic wasn't acceptable to the Cape Colony and an expeditionary force was sent from the Cape in 1842. Although they were besieged by the Voortrekkers on their arrival, by June of that year the parliament in Pietermaritzburg had accepted British rule. The Cape Colony annexed Natal in 1844, and the security given by becoming part of the Cape Colony encouraged many new settlers in search of land to come to Durban.

The development of the sugarcane industry in the 1860s encouraged the growth of Durban as a port and gave the city one of its most peculiar characteristics. Initially the sugarcane industry suffered from a lack of cheap labour, so the planters imported a large number of indentured labourers from India, who lived in conditions not dissimilar to slavery. After working off their five-year indenture contracts some returned home, but a number remained in Natal. Many continued farming and eventually came to dominate the local fruit and vegetable market. Others established small businesses and gradually built up important trade connections with India. These ex-indentured labourers were joined by a number of more affluent traders, mainly from Gujarat, who arrived direct from India to set up business.

With the development of the Golden Mile in the 1970s, Durban was promoted as a seaside resort for white holidaymakers, particularly for families from Gauteng. During Apartheid, the extensive beach was split according to colour – black people were permitted to walk the length of the whole beach but, on the whites-only Addington Beach, they were not allowed to sit down or go into the sea.

As Apartheid broke down in the late 1980s, a huge influx of workers from Zululand transformed the fabric of the city centre and it took on a distinctly vibrant African feel. Additionally there came another influx: that of black holidaymakers, particularly from the wealthier sectors of urban black Johannesburg, which would have been unheard of during Apartheid. The Golden Mile was redeveloped in 2009 in time for the 2010 FIFA World Cup™, when it was resurfaced and widened between uShaka Marine World and the new Moses Mabhida Stadium. Today, more than three and half million people live in the metropolitan area of Durban, and after Johannesburg, it is the second-largest city in South Africa.

Places in Durban → For listings, see pages 45-60.

City centre
The small area surrounding City Hall between Dr A B Xuma Street and Anton Lembede Street in central Durban is one of the city's more interesting spots. The colonial buildings and gardens offer a striking contrast between Durban's past and the present. High-rise office blocks tower over the remains of Durban's colonial history, where pastel-coloured art deco buildings are dwarfed by mirrored skyscrapers.

Luthuli Farewell Square is the hub of this area and is named after the first British settler who built his home here out of wattle and daub in 1824, as well as liberation struggle leader Albert Luthuli. Today the square has a busy street market, but at night it resembles, rather incongruously, a Victorian cemetery, as this is where most of Durban's commemorative statues have been placed. There is a cenotaph to those who died in both world wars, a memorial to the dead of the Boer War and statues of Queen Victoria, in commemoration of her diamond jubilee, and Natal's first two prime ministers.

The **City Hall**, on Anton Lembede Street, faces directly onto the Luthuli Farewell Square. This is one of Durban's most impressive buildings and reflects the town's municipal might at the turn of the 20th century. The neo-Baroque building was completed in 1910 and in its day was one of the British Empire's finest city halls in the southern hemisphere. What are particularly appealing about the building are the palms lining the street outside. You will also find the Natural Science Museum and Durban Art Gallery here.

The **Natural Science Museum** ① *T031-311 2265, Mon-Sat 0830-1600, Sun 1100-1600, free, gift shop and coffee shop*, has an assortment of scientific displays, including a huge gallery of stuffed African mammals. More interestingly, the museum also houses an extremely rare Dodo skeleton and South Africa's only Egyptian mummy. The **KwaZuzulwazi Science Centre** has an excellent series of displays dedicated to the Zulu culture.

The **Durban Art Gallery** ① *T031-311 2265, Mon-Sat 0830-1600, Sun 1100-1600, free*, on the upper floor of City Hall, was first established in 1892, and is home to some fine British, French and Dutch paintings, objets d'art such as French and Chinese ceramics, early glass vases by Lalique and bronzes by Rodin. However more interesting are the exhibits of contemporary art that represent the peoples of KwaZulu-Natal.

The Playhouse is directly opposite the Anton Lembede Street entrance to the City Hall. It was built in 1935 and was originally used as a bioscope, which seated 1900 people. The lounge bar became popular with visiting sailors during the 1970s and was notorious for its heavy drinking sessions and occasional fights. The cinema was eventually forced to close after a fire and has now been restored and converted into an arts complex with five theatres (see Entertainment, page 52).

St Paul's Church was originally built in 1853, and was rebuilt in 1906 after a fire. The church is purely British in architectural style and inside there are commemorative plaques to Durban's early settlers. The chapel of St Nicholas on the left side of the aisle was part of the Mission to Seamen between 1899 and 1989. Reverend Wade, who was rector of the church between 1952 and 1961, was the father of tennis one-hit-wonder Virginia Wade, who won the ladies singles title at Wimbledon in 1977.

The **post office**, built in 1885, was originally Durban's first city hall. There is a plaque on the southern corner of the building, which commemorates Winston Churchill's speech after his escape during the Boer War. The grand structure that is now home to **Tourist Junction** is Durban's old railway station. The building, modelled on a traditional British Victorian railway station, was completed in 1892. The roof is capable of supporting more than 5 m of snow, the result of a mistake by the architects in London who had mistakenly switched the roof plans with those for a station in Toronto, Canada. The flat roof that was destined for Durban collapsed during the first winter in Toronto. A bust just inside the front door commemorates Mahatma Gandhi's first step in his struggle against all forms of discrimination and oppression when he boarded a train at the station on 7 June 1893; he was forcibly removed from the whites-only carriage when the train got to Pietermaritzburg.

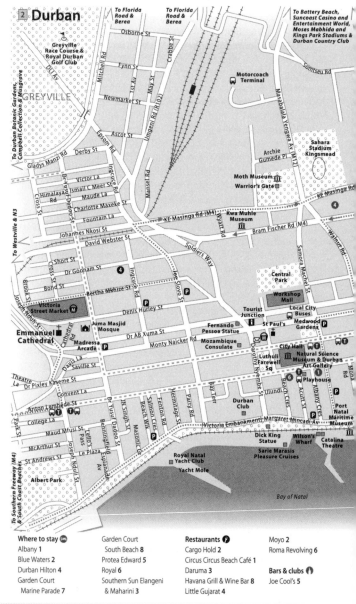

Where to stay 🛏
Albany **1**
Blue Waters **2**
Durban Hilton **4**
Garden Court
  Marine Parade **7**

Garden Court
  South Beach **8**
Protea Edward **5**
Royal **6**
Southern Sun Elangeni
  & Maharini **3**

Restaurants 🍴
Cargo Hold **2**
Circus Circus Beach Café **1**
Daruma **3**
Havana Grill & Wine Bar **8**
Little Gujarat **4**

Moyo **2**
Roma Revolving **6**

Bars & clubs 🍸
Joe Cool's **5**

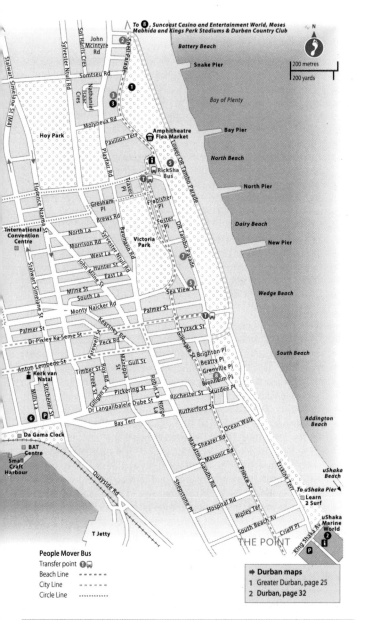

To 8, Suncoast Casino and Entertainment World, Moses Mabhida and Kings Park Stadiums & Durban Country Club

N

Battery Beach

Snake Pier

200 metres
200 yards

Bay of Plenty

Bay Pier

North Beach

North Pier

Dairy Beach

New Pier

Wedge Beach

South Beach

Addington Beach

uShaka Beach

To uShaka Pier

uShaka Marine World

THE POINT

John Mcintyre Rd

Shell Parade

Sol Harris Cres

Sylvester Ntuli Rd

Somtseu Rd

Nathaniel Isaac Cres

Molyneux Rd

Amphitheatre Flea Market

Pavilion Terr

Hoy Park

Playfair Rd

Lower OR Tambo Parade

RickSha Bus

Gresham Pl

Frobisher Pl

Brews Rd

Foster Pl

Travers Pl

Baumann Rd

International Convention Centre

North La

Sylvester Ntuli Rd

Florence Nzama St

Morrison Rd

West La

Victoria Park

DR Tambo Parade

John Mline St

Hunter La

East La

Milne St

South La

Sea View St

Stalwart Simelane St

Monty Naicker Rd

Palmer St

Palmer St

Kearsney Rd

Tyzack St

Dr Pixley Ka-Seme St

Brewer St

Peck Rd

Gillespie St

Brighton Pl

Beatty Pl

Anton Lembede St

Timber St

Roy Rd

Gull St

Grenville Pl

Kerk van Natal

Creek St

Pickering St

Blenheim Pl

Kitchener St

Gilligan St

Mazeppa St

Robin St

Horge St

Rochester St

Sturdee Pl

Dr Langalibalele Dube St

Rutherford St

Mills St

Bay Terr

Ocean Walk

Da Gama Clock

Shearer Rd

Masonic Rd

BAT Centre

Plince St

Erskine Terr

Small Craft Harbour

Quayside Rd

Sheppstone Pl

Mahatma Gandhi Rd

Hospital Rd

Ripley Terr

South Beach Av

Crieff Pl

Learn 2 Surf

King Shaka Av

T Jetty

People Mover Bus

Transfer point 🚏🚌

Beach Line   - - - - -
City Line   - - - - -
Circle Line   . . . .

➡ Durban maps
1 Greater Durban, page 25
2 Durban, page 32

Bunny chow

One of the more popular and delicious takeaway meals in Durban is bunny chow: a quarter, half or whole loaf of bread with the middle scooped out and filled with curry. The scooped-out bread is then used instead of a spoon to soak up the sauce. There are lots of theories about where it got its name but it's generally thought the dish was originally created for Indian caddies, known as bunnies, at the Royal Durban Golf Course in the 1940s. They were unable to get off work for long enough to nip into Grey Street for a curry at lunchtime, so the story goes that they got their friends to go and buy the curry for them and that it was brought back to the golf course in hollowed-out loaves of bread because there were no disposable food containers at the time. There's quite an art to eating a bunny: after eating the scooped-out piece of bread, you tear pieces off of the side of the loaf and dip them into the curry. The trick is to avoid tearing off pieces of loaf which are below the current gravy line otherwise you end up with a steaming-hot mass in your lap. You should also check whether your bunny chow was made from the end of a loaf or whether it is a 'funny bunny' made from the middle and without a crust at the bottom.

The Workshop, also on Dr A B Xuma Street, lies directly behind the old railway station and is an enormous shopping mall that has been built inside the old train sheds. With the transition of major shops to the Pavilion and Gateway malls in the suburbs, the Workshop has suffered a decline in recent years and is starting to look shabby and doesn't have very many interesting shops. You can get authentic Indian snacks at the food court though.

Around 500 m north of the Workshop, on Bram Fischer Road near Warrior's Gate, is the **Kwa Muhle Museum** ① *T031-311 2223, Mon-Sat, 0830-1600, free*, housed in the old Native Affairs Department building (1923). This was the authoritative body responsible for enforcing punitive Apartheid legislation and was once the most hated buildings in the city as it was where blacks were issued with their passes. It's a fascinating and moving exhibition of what it was like to be an African under the old regime and is also known locally as the **Apartheid Museum**. There is a collection of waxwork figures in hostels along with a series of photographs of incidents and riots of the past 25 years. Another display features the Indian merchants of (formerly) Grey Street; here you can learn more about the first trade union, the Grey Street mosque, Bertha Mkhize Street beer hall, the Bantu Social Centre and bunny chow (see box, above). One of the exhibits is on the 'Durban System', a method for Durban's city council to raise revenue to finance the administration of African affairs during Apartheid without using a penny of white taxpayers' money: they gave themselves the monopoly on brewing sorghum beer, which they sold for a fine profit in African-only public beer houses.

The **Warrior's Gate Moth Museum** ① *Masabalala Yengwa (NMR) Av, T031-307 3337, Tue-Sun 1100-1500, free,* can be found opposite Kingsmead cricket stadium and has a large collection of military memorabilia from the First and Second World Wars and battlefield relics from the Anglo-Boer and Zulu wars. The museum was started by First World War veterans and is now the international headquarters of the MOTH (**Memorable Order of Tin Hats**) organization. The gate itself was built in 1936 and was designed on the lines of a Norman gatehouse.

Indian district

Two waves of Indian emigration, one of indentured labour under British rule beginning in 1860 and the second by traders arriving from the 1920s onwards, helped make Durban home to what is considered the highest concentration of Indians outside India. The area around Bertha Mkhize Street, Denis Hurley Street and Dr Yusuf Dadoo Street (formerly Grey Street) is one of the oldest areas of Durban still standing. It is a good 20-minute walk west from the centre down Dr A B Xuma Street or Monty Naicker Road, or take a bus or taxi to Bertha Mkhize Street. Indian traders built the pastel-coloured shopping arcades in the 1920s and 1930s. Originally they were designed so families could have their homes over their shops. In 1973, however, legislation was introduced which prohibited Indians from living in the area, though not from trading. Family labour living above the shops was seen as integral to their success and the legislation was deliberately introduced in an effort to reduce their competition with white-owned businesses. With the new legislation, much of the residential population was forced to move out to Chatsworth or Phoenix; the wealthier traders moved to Westville.

Thankfully the new residential rules did not succeed in destroying the Indian-owned businesses and many have continued to prosper. A number of original shops are still here, selling spices, saris and other goods from India, but it is now very much a commercial, rather than residential, area.

The main entrance to **Victoria Street Market** ① *T031-306 4021, www. indianmarket.co.za, Mon-Sat 0600-1800, Sun 1000-1600*, is on the corner of Denis Hurley Street and Bertha Mkhize Street. The original market was established in 1910 but was destroyed in 1973 by fire. Today's concrete building (with its purple Indian minarets) was built in the 1980s and is rather dingy, but there are over 170 crammed stalls inside. The ground floor has a fish and seafood market, plus fresh meat, fruit and vegetables, and the main attraction here are the stalls selling spices and dried beans imported from India, with men in their traditional *kurtas* and women in their *saris* selling their wares. The top floor offers more conventional shopping for souvenirs, crafts, jewellery and fabrics, and there are a variety of food stalls serving up delicious snacks such as bunny chow, samosas and Durban curries. The nearby Warwick Junction Market focuses primarily on traditional African herbs and medicinal compounds. The markets get extremely busy, so beware of pickpockets and don't take anything valuable with you.

The entrance to the **Madressa Arcade** ① *Tue-Sat 1000-1700*, is on Dr Yusuf Dadoo Street (formerly Grey Street) and links to Cathedral Road. The bazaar-like arcade was built in 1927 and is little more than a narrow and winding alley lined with 50 or so little shops. Here you can buy everything from plastic trinkets to household utensils and Indian music. Behind the arcade, the **Juma Masjid Mosque** ① *corner of Denis Hurley St and Dr Yusuf Dadoo St, T031-306 0026, open to all Mon-Fri 0900-1600 but not during prayer times, free but donation appreciated*, was also built in 1927 and claims to be the largest mosque in the southern hemisphere, despite the fact that Muslims are a minority in Durban, which is largely Hindu. Its gilt-domed minarets tower over the bustling commercial area, but inside is a peaceful and elegant marble hall. Women and men must cover their legs and remove their shoes at the door before entering. At the other (western) end of Madressa Arcade is the Gothic-style redbrick **Roman Catholic Emmanuel Cathedral** (1904) ① *contact for mass times, T031-306 3595, www.emmanuelcathedral.org.za*, on the corner of Cathedral Road and Denis Hurley Street, and is clearly visible when driving on the N3 flyover into Durban. Denis Hurley (after which the street was named) was Archbishop of Durban from 1946 until 1992.

Margaret Mncadi Avenue (Victoria Embankment)

The Victoria Embankment was originally built in 1897 and was a grand and desirable residential area facing a beautiful stretch of beach. Very little of this remains today, and at first glance the Embankment seems like any other busy road lined with skyscrapers. There are still a few sights worth seeking out though, and it's a short 500 m stroll past the Royal Hotel from Luthuli Farewell Square.

At the junction of Dorothy Nyembe Street and Victoria Embankment is the **Dick King Statue,** which commemorates Dick King's epic 10-day ride to Grahamstown in 1842 while Durban was under siege. The **Durban Club** is on the opposite side of the embankment at 93-96 Margaret Mncadi Avenue and was built in 1904. This is one of the few original buildings left on the Victoria Embankment, a grand edifice which gives an inkling of what the Victoria Embankment once looked like.

To the west, the **Royal Natal Yacht Club** ① *Yacht Mole, T031-301 5425, www.rnyc.org.za, daily 0700-2030, free if you're eating there*, was founded in 1858 as the Durban Regatta Club, and is the oldest yacht club in Africa and much of the history of early Durban can be linked to this club. Regattas are still popular occasions, and today the club open to the public and the Britannia Room on the first floor of the clubhouse is the perfect place to sip a gin and tonic or eat a Durban curry as you watch the yachts in the harbour. The lawns around the lower deck have a swimming pool and a jungle gym for children.

Heading east from the Dick King Statue, **Wilson's Wharf** is a modern development overlooking the harbour and is home to a couple of cafés and fast food restaurants, and the Catalina Theatre (page 51). Just beyond is the **Port Natal Maritime Museum** ① *entrance is on the docks opposite the junction of Samora Machel St and Margaret Mncadi Av, T031-311 2230, Mon-Sat 0830-1600, Sun 1100-1600, entry by donation.* Among the boats on display, visitors can walk through a minesweeper, the *SAS Durban*, two tugs, the *Ulundi* and the *JR More*, and the Khayalethu a deep-sea fishing boat made out of the hull of a flying boat. In the small exhibition hall on dry land are photographs and drawings documenting the development of the Port of Durban.

About 200 m after the Maritime Museum is the Small Craft Harbour and the excellent non-profit making **BAT (Bartle Arts Trust) Centre** ① *T031-332 0451, www.batcentre.co.za.* This is a popular arts centre with a concert hall and a bar and restaurant, as well as several little shops selling excellent contemporary Zulu crafts. At the eastern end of the embankment is the ornate Da Gama Clock. A good example of late-Victorian design, this large cast-iron clock was erected to commemorate the 400th anniversary of Vasco da Gama's discovery of the sea route to India in 1487.

Beachfront

The most popular beachfront area extends along the length of Marine Parade (now OR Tambo Parade). Traditionally known as the **Golden Mile**, it's a favourite with South African holidaymakers. It is lined with high-rise hotels, gardens with children's paddling pools, and an attractively paved broad promenade that runs for 5 km from South Beach (where **uShaka Marine World** is) to North Beach (**Suncoast Casino** and **Entertainment World**); the People Mover bus (see page 27) runs from one to the other. The beaches, all of which are impressive stretches of long, golden sand broken up by piers, are divided into areas designated for surfing, boogie boarding and swimming. All are protected with shark nets and lifeguards are on patrol daily 0800-1700.

Durban Tourism ① *corner of OR Tambo Parade and KE Masinga Rd, North Beach, T031-322 2404-5, daily 0800-1700,* has a kiosk on the beachfront, which is near the People Mover bus interchange between the Beach Line and the Circle Line. Also here on Sunday (0900-1600) is the Amphitheatre Flea Market, which sells a variety of goods from arts and crafts to clothing and snacks. Along the promenade there are also several stands where extravagantly dressed rickshaw drivers wait for tourists. The options are either a quick and painless photograph with the driver, or a photograph and ride up and down OR Tambo Parade, usually costing around R20.

The leading Golden Mile attraction is **uShaka Marine World** ① *1 King Shaka Av, T031-328 8000, www.ushakamarineworld.co.za*. To get here drive down Mahatma Gandhi Road from the city centre and it's on the beach at The Point (there's plenty of parking). The People Mover bus also stops here (see page 27). There are a few components to this large beachfront complex. **Village Walk** ① *shops daily 0900-1900, restaurants vary*, is an attractive open-air shopping mall that (not surprisingly) features curio, surf and holiday clothing shops, as well as numerous cafés and fast-food joints, and it has access to the promenade and beach. Both **Tourism KwaZulu-Natal** and **Durban Tourism** have kiosks here (see page 57). **Wet 'n' Wild** and **Sea World** ① *daily 0900-1700, Wet 'n' Wild closed Mon-Tue Apr-Oct, both R149, children (3-12) R115, combined ticket R199/149, under 3s free*, is an enormous waterpark. **Wet 'n' Wild** has a huge choice of impressive swimming pools, waterslides and rides including a 450-m river float on inflatable tubes around the complex. **Sea World** is an impressive aquarium that is reputed to be the largest in the southern hemisphere, where the highlight is the phantom ship, where visitors walk through glass tunnels surrounded by ragged-tooth sharks and game fish. It also has a dolphinarium, seal and penguin pools, a dive tank and a snorkel reef. Finally **Dangerous Creatures** ① *daily 0900-1630, R40 per person, under 3s free*, is a snake and reptile park where you can also see the likes of tarantulas and scorpions.

At the northern end of the Golden Mile and OR Tambo Parade, **Battery Beach** is perhaps the most attractive of Durban's beaches, with good swimming and fewer crowds. It's also the location of the **Suncoast Casino and Entertainment World** ① *Suncoast Blvd, OR Tambo Parade, T031-328 3000, www.suncoastcasino. co.za*, which is a huge glitzy complex built in Miami Beach Art Deco style architecture and has a casino, cinemas, a selection of bars, takeaway joints, themed restaurants, two hotels and a car park for 2000 vehicles. Directly in front of the complex is the promenade and beach.

A 10-minute walk of about 800 m from Suncoast, the unmissable attraction behind Battery Beach is the impressive **Moses Mabhiba Stadium** ① *Isaiah Ntshangase Rd, off Masabalala Yengwa Av (M12), 1 road back from the beachfront, T031-582 8242, www.mmstadium.com*, which was built for the 2010 FIFA World Cup™ and named after anti-Apartheid activist Moses Mabhida, who was both general secretary of the South African Communist Party and vice-president of the South African Congress of Trade Unions. With its 'arc of triumph' constructed over the top, this has, unlike some of the other stadiums built in South Africa for the tournament, become somewhat of an attraction in its own right. The 350-m-long and 105-m-high arc, which holds up the roof of the 62,000-seater stadium, is not only a striking feature to admire (and beautifully lit at night), but provides some entertaining activities. You can do a 30-minute **tour of the inside of the stadium** ① *departing hourly on the hour*

Mon-Fri 1100-1600, Sat-Sun 0900-1600, R30, children (6-12) R15, under 6s free, and ride to the top of the arc on the **SkyCar** ① *daily 0900-1700, last trip 1630, R55, children (6-12) R30, under 6s free*, a funicular railway car that carries up to 20 passengers. The excellent views from 106-m at the top of the stadium take in the sweeping Golden Mile and ocean, the high-rises of the CBD and inland towards the hilly suburbs. On the opposite side of the arc from the Skycar is the **Adventure Walk** ① *Sat-Sun 1000, 1300 and 1600, R90 per person, no children under 10*, where visitors can go on a guided climb while attached to a safety harness up and down the 550 steps to the top of the arch. These can be followed by the **Big Rush Swing** ① *1000-1600 daily except Tue and Thu, R695, no children under 10*, a bungee-like 220-m swing beneath the arc. There is an attractive landscaped piazza and park at the base of the stadium with a café.

Berea

The Berea is a ridge above and to the northwest of the CBD and is also the collective name for Durban's oldest and most attractive suburbs including Essenwood, Musgrave, Morningside and Windermere. There are some good ocean and city views, and fine whitewashed mansions and Victorian bungalows with their tin roofs and verandas line the quiet streets. This is one of the best places to head for restaurants and nightlife, especially on and around fashionable Florida Road, about 3 km north of the CBD straddling Windermere and Morningside. Stretching from Sandile Thusi Road in the south to Innes Road in the north, this 2-km tree-lined street is a hive of art galleries, restaurants, sidewalk cafés and coffee shops, and bohemian boutiques, many of which are in restored Victorian, Edwardian and art deco listed buildings. The Mynah bus (see box, page 26) does some useful loops around Berea.

In Musgrave opposite the Greyville Racecourse are the **Durban Botanic Gardens** ① *70 John Zikhali Rd, T031-309 1271, www.durbanbotanicgardens. org.za, www.musicatthelake.co.za, daily 0730-1715, until 1730 in summer, free.* The gardens were founded in 1849, making them the oldest botanical gardens in Africa, and they cover almost 15 ha. There are some impressive avenues of palms crossing the park, an ornamental lake where you can feed the ducks, and an impressive orchid house. They are at their best in summer (November-February), after the spring rains. The tea garden (daily 0930-1615) is a pleasant place to relax and serves traditional high tea with scones, jam and cream. Music by the Lake is a popular programme of concerts on Sunday afternoons, especially over winter (May-August), which can feature anyone from Johnny Clegg and Ladysmith Black Mambazo to the KwaZulu-Natal Philharmonic Orchestra. The drill is to take a picnic and bottle of wine and enjoy the performances from a rug on the lawns.

There are two other smaller parks in Berea worth visiting. **Mitchell Park** ① *corner of Innes and Ferndale roads, Morningside, T031-303 2275, daily*

0730-0800, zoo 0800-1700, free but a small entry fee to the aviaries and animal enclosures, are public gardens named after Sir Charles Mitchell, an early governor of Natal, with an open-air café, the Blue Zoo Restaurant and Tea Garden (see page 50), aviaries and a few small animals like monkeys and reptiles in cages. The adjoining **Jameson Park** ① *350 Montpelier Rd, Morningside, T031-312 2318, free*, has extensive rose gardens (proving that roses can grow in a subtropical climate), which are at their best during flowering season between September and November. The park is named in honour of Robert Jameson, a mayor of Durban from 1895 to 1897, who during his 30-year tenure with the Town Council, was instrumental in planting trees throughout Durban. There's a good view of Durban from the top of the park and look out for a prominent house on the ridge; this is the Elephant House which is the highest point in Berea built in the early 1850s and is now a guesthouse. It earned its name due to repeated attacks by elephants on their way up a path (now Florida Road) to drink at the Greyville marsh (today part of the Royal Durban Golf Course). The house is now a National Monument.

The **Campbell Collection** ① *220 Gladys Mazibuko Rd, Essenwood, T031-260 1722, www.campbell.ukzn.ac.za, house and gardens open to the public by appointment only Mon-Fri 0830-1630, R20 per person*, is a museum and African library in a Cape Dutch style house called Muckleneuk, which was built in 1914 for sugar farmer and politician Sir Marshall Campbell (1848-1917), and still has most of its original decorations. There are some fine examples of Cape furniture and early South African oil paintings, displays of African sculpture, weapons, musical instruments and a rare collection of paintings by Barbara Tyrrell. Most of the paintings are of Africans dressed in traditional clothes from the 19th century; the paintings form part of a unique record of what people wore before contact with European settlers.

North of the CBD
About 7 km north of the CBD, on the way to Umhlanga, the Umgeni River estuary and its associated mangroves provide a rich and important feeding ground for numerous water birds. When the water is low during summer, thousands of waders forage in the mud and large flocks of terns roost on the sandbanks. If the water level is higher, birders may be lucky enough to see flocks of white and pink-backed pelicans, while herons and woolly-necked storks roost on the flooded grassy islands in the river. A visit to the estuary is highly recommended after a severe cold front in winter, which brings up the southern seabirds such as the Cape gannet and Cape cormorant. Along Riverside Road on the northern bank are lay-bys to pull over and bird-watch and there are a couple of birding attractions in this area. Riverside Road (M21) is reached by taking the first off-ramp from the M4 North after crossing the Umgeni River and turning left at the first T-junction.

Umgeni River Bird Park ① *490 Riverside Rd, T031-579 4601, T031-260 1722, www.umgeniriverbirdpark.com, daily 0900-1700, free-flight show Tue-Sun 1100 and 1400, R50, children (4-12) R30, under 4s free, Cockatoo Café,* is home to over 700 exotic and indigenous birds from more than 180 species, from flamingos to macaws and there are plenty of pathways through the aviaries and open ponds. There is an impressive free-flight show where large birds such as owls, raptors and vultures fly over the heads of the audience to perches at the top of the open-air auditorium and a presenter tells you a bit about the various species. A little further up the M4 are the **Japanese Gardens** ① *Prospect Hall Rd, T031-563 1333, daily 0730-1600, free,* where there are some pleasant paths through the gardens with their many water features, bridges and gazebos. Species include paradise and black flycatchers, various weavers, Egyptian geese and in summer various species of swallow and martin can be skimming over the lawns and water.

Around Durban → *For listings, see pages 45-60.*

Umhlanga

Umhlanga is 17 km north of the CBD, and while it was once no more than a sleepy holiday resort, these days with its sprawl of high-rises, office and shopping parks, and modern housing developments, it is now the wealthiest and most upmarket suburb of the eThekwini Metropolitan Municipality. **Umhlanga Tourism** ① *1 Chartwell Dr, T031-561 4257, www.umhlanga-rocks. com, Mon-Fri 0800-1630, Sat 0900-1200,* is just west of the **Oyster Box Hotel** and can book accommodation and has maps and brochures to pick up.

Background The town's name means 'Place of Reeds' in Zulu, after the reeds that are washed down the river to the north and onto the pristine beaches. The area was once covered with dune forest; today, only small pockets of original vegetation have been preserved in surrounding nature reserves. In the 19th century, the land was part of a large sugar estate, Natal Estates Ltd, owned by Sir Marshall Campbell. The estate was managed from Mount Edgecombe in the interior; a track was built from here to the coast and local farmers began to lease small plots on the beach and build holiday cottages. The first cottage was built in 1869 and was known as the Oyster Box; today the site is the location of the five-star **Oyster Box Hotel** (see Where to stay, page 47).

While once it was referred to as Umhlanga Rocks, in the 1970s it merged with neighbouring La Lucia and gained urban status, and is now referred to as just Umhlanga. It remains a popular seaside resort, with boxy beachfront hotels and beaches filled with umbrellas and sun worshippers, but above the town on Umhlanga Ridge, which used to be largely covered in sugarcane, is a much sought-after retail, office and residential area, which has incredible ocean views. In a similar fashion to Sandton in Johannesburg, many of the larger businesses have relocated from central Durban to Umhlanga. After the beach, the massive **Gateway**, KwaZulu-Natal's premier shopping mall, which is allegedly the largest in the southern hemisphere (see page 53), is Durban's most popular attraction.

Places in Umhlanga In high season, wealthy South Africans flock to Umhlanga, a beautiful stretch of wave-lashed sand with a belt of high-rise hotels and condominiums. Access to the water is almost exclusively through the resort and hotel complexes, although there is a 3-km stretch of promenade that spans the front of these, which has been attractively landscaped with indigenous plants along the dune belt next to the beach. The **Umhlanga Lagoon** lies just to the north of town at the end of the promenade, where a trail continues through a beautiful expanse of wetland and forest to an unspoilt, open beach yet to be concreted by the developers.

A popular local landmark is the **Umhlanga Lighthouse**. The distinct red and white circular concrete tower stands 21 m above the beach and acts as a fixed point to help ships waiting to dock in Durban harbour confirm their exact position in the outer anchorage. The lighthouse tower has stood here since November 1954, occupying the centre point on the beach, right in front of the Oyster Box Hotel. The lighthouse has never had a keeper; instead it was operated by the owner of the Oyster Box Hotel from controls in the hotel office, though now it's fully automated.

Umhlanga Lagoon Nature Reserve ① *the gate is just past Breakers Hotel at the end of Lagoon Dr, daily 0600-1800, free,* is at the end of the promenade, about 2 km from the lighthouse, and covers around 25 ha of coastal forest and dunes around the lagoon. There are 4 km of leisurely walks, some on boardwalks, and the area is rich in birdlife and you may see bushbuck, duiker and vervet monkeys.

The KZN Sharks Board

① *1 Herrwood Dr, T031-566 0400, www.shark.co.za, display hall and curio shop Mon-Fri 0800-1600, tour and film Tue-Thu 0900 and 1400, 1st Sun of the month 1300, R45, children (4-12) R25.*

Set inland from the resort, this place studies the life cycles of the sharks that inhabit the sea off the coast of KwaZulu-Natal and investigates how best to protect bathers with various forms of netting. Umhlanga became the first beach to erect shark nets in 1962, following a series of attacks along the whole coast in December 1957. Today the Sharks Board is responsible for looking after more than 400 nets, which protect nearly 50 beaches. Tours at the Sharks Board begin with a 25-minute audio-visual show on the biology of sharks and their role as top predators in the marine food chain. This is followed by a (optional) stomach-churning shark dissection. The display hall has a variety of replicas of sharks, fish and rays, including that of an 892-kg shark.

It is also possible to accompany researchers on the **Sharks Board boat** ① *T082-403 9206 (booking essential), R300 per person, no children under 6, min 6 people, max 12 people, 2 hrs*, as they conduct daily servicing of the shark nets off Durban's Golden Mile. The boat goes from Wilson's Wharf (see page 37) in Durban at 0630. You won't necessarily see sharks in the nets, but you have a good chance of spotting dolphins and sea birds and there are good views back across to Durban. The ride out beyond the harbour walls can be bumpy.

Hare Krishna Temple of Understanding
① *Bhaktiveedante Swami Rd, Chatsworth, take the Higginson Highway (M10) from the N2 south of the CBD, or follow the M10 from Berea, T031-403 3328, tours 1000-1300, 1400-2000, daily, free, restaurant.*
This striking temple is situated in Chatsworth, a large suburb created in the 1950s to house the predominantly Indian population under the Group Areas legislation. It's in the South Durban basin, roughly 22 km southwest of the CBD. Also known as the Sri Sri Radhanath Temple of Understanding, it was built in the shape of a giant lotus leaf and opened as an ashram in 1985. It is the largest Hare Krishna temple in Africa. It has a castle-like moat, gilt domes and extensive ornamental gardens, and inside the interior is just as lavish with gold-tinted windows, marble tiles, crystal chandeliers and ceiling frescoes. The temple is also renowned for its good vegetarian restaurant; allow about an hour for a tour and a meal here.

Valley of 1000 Hills
Between Durban and Pietermaritzburg the landscape quickly climbs some 700 m over a series of rolling hills characteristic of the suburbs around the two cities. To the north of the N3, the Valley of 1000 Hills is a peaceful area, supposedly named at the end of the 19th century by the writer Mark Twain after the dozens of hills which fold down towards the Umgeni River. From Botha's Rest, there are many viewpoints on the R103 from where you can see the valley unfold. The fertile hills are dotted with villages, farms and encroaching townships closer to Durban. The valley has historically been a Zulu stronghold and, in the early 19th century, it became a refuge for dispossessed Zulus who had lost their farmland through battle further north. It is an easy 35-km drive from Durban. Follow the N3 north out of the city and leave at the Westville/ Pavilion Mall exit to join the R103 (the old Pietermaritzburg road) and drive through the suburbs of Kloof and Hillcrest. Here you will pick up signs for the Valley of 1000 Hills Meander, which runs along the lip of the valley through the villages of Botha's Hill, Drummond, Monteseel and Inchanga. Tourism has

gone into overdrive along this route, with a variety of craft shops, restaurants, B&Bs, guesthouses, farm stalls and several Zulu cultural villages. The **Comrades Marathon**, a gruelling 90 km between Pietermaritzburg and Durban, follows this route in June (see page 52). For information contact **Durban Tourism** ① *47 Old Main Rd, Botha's Hill, T031-777 1874, www.durbanexperience.co.za, Mon-Fri 0800-1600, Sat 0900-1400.*

About 500 m before the tourist office, if coming from the city, children will enjoy the **1000 Hills Bird Park** ① *1 Clement Stott Rd, off Old Main Rd, Botha's Hill, T031-765 6090, www.birdpark.co.za, Tue-Sun 0900-1530, R65, children (under 10) R35, zip line ride R35 per person,* which has parrots, hornbills, falcons and cranes and many other species in aviaries, as well picnic and *braai* sites, a café and a 150-m-long zip line ride.

About 2 km beyond the tourist office, the most popular of the Zulu cultural villages is **PheZulu Safari Park** ① *5 Old Main Rd, Botha's Hill, T031-777 1000, www.phezulusafaripark.co.za, daily 0830-1630, Zulu shows daily 1000, 1130, 1400, 1530, R100, children (3-12) R65, under 3s free, Crocodile & Snake Park R45/35, combo ticket R140/100, additional 1-hr game-drives R220/110.* There are commanding views of the valley from here, a reptile farm, a small game park with zebra and antelope, curio shops, and the **Croctilians** restaurant which specializes in croc steaks. The main attraction here is the Zulu show, where visitors are taken into traditional beehive-shaped huts and Zulu beliefs, rituals and artefacts are explained. There follows an impressive dancing display.

Umgeni Steam Railway's **1000 Hills Choo-Choo** ① *Kloof Station, Village Rd, T082-353 6003, www.umgenisteamrailway.co.za, 2 daily departures on the last Sun of each month, 0830 and 1230, R180, children (2-12) R130 return,* is a vintage 1912 steam train that runs along a line built 1877-1880. On departure days there are two round trips, between Kloof and Inchanga stations, and it's a leisurely way to enjoy the scenery. At Inchanga Station is a tea room and small railway memorabilia museum to visit before the return journey.

⦿ Durban listings

For hotel and restaurant price codes and other relevant information, see pages 12-16.

⦿ Where to stay

Where you stay in Durban depends on where your interests lie. The hotels in Central Durban mostly appeal to visitors attending events at the **Inkosi Albert Luthuli International Convention Centre (ICC)**; the beachfront has a wide selection of typical holiday accommodation a stone's throw from the sand; while smaller guesthouses but with a wider choice of restaurants close by are found in the Berea suburbs. The more luxurious accommodation is found to the north of the city, in Umhlanga.

City centre *p30, map p32*
$$$ Durban Hilton, 12-14 Walnut St, next to the ICC, T031-336 8100, www3.hilton.com. All the trappings you'd expect from a modern 5-star 'name' city hotel. Popular with conference delegates but just as good for tourists, with 327 rooms with all-mod cons, restaurant, 2 bars, gym, spa and pool.
$$$ Royal Hotel, 267 Anton Lembede St, T031-333 6000, www.theroyal.co.za. The hotel originally built on this site in 1842 was made of wattle and daub; it now has 204 smart a/c rooms, with Wi-Fi, DSTV, pleasant decor, some with great harbour views, attractive outdoor pool, gym, sauna, bars and 2 excellent restaurants (see Restaurants, page 48).

$$ Albany, 225 Anton Lembede St, T031-304 4381, www.albanyhotel.co.za. Classic art deco hotel in a big pink block, 72 a/c rooms, with DSTV and Wi-Fi, some have views over gardens, restaurant, 2 bars, comfortable and affordable 3-star option and central location opposite City Hall and Playhouse, but remember the CBD is a rather run-down area.

Beachfront *p37, map p32*
$$$ Protea Hotel Edward, 149 OR Tambo Parade, T031-337 3681, www.proteahotels.com. The most luxurious of the beachfront hotels with a restored art deco façade, 101 elegant a/c rooms, with DSTV and minibar, most have sea views, lavish lobby and lounge, 2 restaurants, bar, small rooftop pool and deck, excellent service.
$$$ Southern Sun Elangeni & Maharani, 63 Snell Parade, North Beach, T031-362 1300; **$$ Garden Court South Beach**, 70 OR Tambo Parade, South Beach, T031-337 2231; and **$$ Garden Court Marine Parade**, 167 OR Tambo Parade, South Beach, T031-337 3341, www.tsogosunhotels.com. Managed by quality chain **Tsogo Sun**, imposing modern towers with between 295-480 rooms each, all 200 m from the beach and with spectacular views of the Golden Mile from the higher floors, spacious and comfortable with a/c, DSTV and Wi-Fi, a full range of facilities including pools, spas and several restaurants (some listed under Restaurants, below). Impersonal for some, but

high standards and good all-round holiday options. **Tsogo** also runs the **$$$ Suncoast Towers**, T31-314 7878, with 37 rooms, and the **$$ SunSquare Suncoast**, T031-314 7878, with 128 rooms, which are both at the **Suncoast Casino and Entertainment World** (see page 38).

$$ Blue Waters, 175 Snell Parade, North Beach T31-327 7000, www. bluewatershotel.co.za. Attractive retro block with 252 rooms, 80 of which have 2 bedrooms, with DSTV, Wi-Fi and excellent views of the ocean and the Moses Mabhida Stadium, restaurant, pool, the **Blue Dolphin** cocktail bar (see page 51), well priced given its location next to the beach.

Berea *p39*

$$$$ Audacia Manor, 11 Sir Arthur Rd, Morningside, T031-303 9520, www. africanpridehotels.com. Beautifully restored home built in 1928, 10 opulent rooms with fine mahogany furniture and sweeping drapes, a/c, Wi-Fi, DSTV and DVD players, some with balconies and spa baths, the rooms in the Coach House have double-vaulted ceilings and oregon floors. Gourmet restaurant, 22-m pool, and bar and veranda with magnificent views of Durban's CBD and harbour.

$$$ Quarters, 101 Florida Rd, Morningside, T031-303 5246, www.quarters.co.za. 4 historic homes have been converted to create this boutique hotel, with a refreshingly modern feel, 23 rooms, with luxury fabrics and black and white photos on the walls, DSTV and Wi-Fi. Excellent restaurant, shaded courtyard, modern bar. Good location close to restaurants.

$$ Bali on the Ridge, 268 South Ridge Rd, Glenwood, T031-261 9574, www.baliridge.co.za. Close to the University of KwZulu Natal, spectacular views of city and harbour, 10 stylish a/c B&B rooms with elegant Bali furniture, attractive polished wooden floors, high ceilings and DSTV, bar, pool, a short drive to restaurants.

$$ The Benjamin, 141 Florida Rd, Morningside, T031-303 4233, www. benjamin.co.za. Classy boutique hotel in a great location close to restaurants on Florida Rd. 43 tastefully decorated rooms with a/c, Wi-Fi and DSTV, centred around a nicely restored historic building, pleasant lounge with antiques, sunny breakfast room overlooking the pool.

$$ The Concierge, 37-43 St Marys Av, Greyville, north of the racecourse, T031-309 4434, www.the-concierge. co.za. Well-priced and quirky option just a short walk from the southern end of Florida Rd, with 12 rooms with fashionable decor around a leafy courtyard behind original 1920s street façades, the **Freedom Café** offers breakfasts, snacks and Wi-Fi.

$$-$ Tekweni Backpackers, 169 Ninth Av, Morningside, T031-303 1433, www.tekwenibackpackers. co.za. One of the liveliest, most popular hostels in Durban, with dorms and double rooms set across 2 rambling houses, space for a couple of tents, kitchen, bar, small pool, internet access, travel desk, all meals available. Often in a party mood, easy stroll to restaurants on Florida Rd.

North of the CBD *p40*

$$$-$$ Riverside Hotel & Spa, Northway St, Durban North, next to the Umgeni River bridge on Masabalala Yengwa Av (M12), T031-563 0600, www.riversidehotel.co.za. Large modern hotel overlooking the Umgeni River, a good spot for birdwatching in the estuary (see page 41), 169 spacious a/c rooms with DSTV, friendly service and a great café/restaurant (see Restaurants, page 50) and popular bar, pool and spa.

$$ Beside Still Waters Guest House, 30 Braemar Av, La Lucia, Durban North, T031-572 7797, www.beside stillwatersguesthouse.com. Set in an acre of tropical gardens with fishponds and gazebos, 14 modern a/c self-catering units with modern bright decor, DSTV and Wi-Fi, pool, very friendly management, breakfast and dinner available.

$$-$ On the Beach, 17 Promenade, Durban North, T031-562 1591, www.durbanbackpackers.com. Peaceful location on the beach, north of the city centre and with easy access to Gateway. Smart budget set-up with mix of B&B en suite doubles with TV and self-catering dorms, most rooms have floor-to-ceiling glass windows with ocean views, bar, pool, internet and DSTV.

Umhlanga *p41*

There is no budget accommodation in Umhlanga, although good deals can be had out of season. **Lighthouse Property Group**, T031-561 5838, www.lighthouse.co.za, can arrange holiday apartments on the coast between Umhlanga and Ballito (see page 76); contact well in advance if you are planning on renting a family-sized apartment during any local school holidays.

$$$$ Oyster Box Hotel, Lighthouse Rd, T031-561 2233, www.oysterbox. co.za. The area's 1st hotel dating back to the 1940s, when it was popular with British travellers visiting the colonies, is in a spectacular setting behind the dunes, the beach and the lighthouse. It now features 86 super-luxury suites, some with private plunge pools, a spa, 2 restaurants, an oyster bar, 2 heated pools, a cinema and a gym. Stop here for the sumptuous afternoon tea in the beautiful drawing room or on the terrace at the foot of the lighthouse.

$$$$-$$$ Teremok Marine, 49 Marine Dr, T031-561 5848, www. teremok.co.za. A boutique lodge set in a tropical garden, contemporary and stylish decor and design, 8 luxury a/c suites with stand-alone baths, rain showers, Wi-Fi, spacious lounge, pool, spa, lovely breakfast room with picture windows opening on to a giant milkwood tree. No children under 16.

$$$ Beverly Hills Hotel, Lighthouse Rd, T031-561 2211, www.tsogo sunhotels.com. Smart luxury hotel overlooking the beach that first opened in 1964, 90 a/c rooms with ocean views, choice of top-end restaurants including the **Sugar Club** and **Elements** cocktail bar, swimming pool, gym, tennis and squash courts. **Tsogo Sun** also runs **Cabana Beach Resort** (**$$$-$$**), 10 Lagoon Dr, T031 561 2371, which has Mediterranean village style architecture and 217 self-catering cabanas sleeping up to 6; and the (**$$**) **Garden Court Umhlanga**, corner of Aurora Dr and Centenary Blvd, T031-514 5500, which has 204 modern rooms and is close to Gateway in Umhlanga Ridge. From all 3 is a thrice-daily courtesy shuttle bus to the **Suncoast Casino & Entertainment World** (see page 38).

$$ Chartwell Guest House, 88 Chartwell Dr, T083-280 2102, www.88chartwell.co.za. Affordable for its location, this is close to the beach, shops and restaurants and has 5 neat a/c B&B rooms, pretty garden with *braai* and swimming pool. The whole house can also be taken on a self-catering basis.

$$ The Square Boutique Hotel & Spa, 250 Umhlanga Rocks Dr, T031-566 1814, www.thesquareboutique hotel.co.za. A smart offering close to Gateway, with 50 comfortable modern rooms with Wi-Fi, DSTV and contemporary decor, pool, spa, and the stylish **Cosmopolitan** restaurant and bar.

❼ Restaurants

Local specialities include spicy Indian food, fresh seafood, and organic vegetables and produce from the fertile KwaZulu-Natal Midlands. Most hotels have restaurants and many more are within the confines of a shopping mall but, thanks to good architecture, in the most part you will not be aware that you are eating in a mall. For a lively streetside scene, head to Berea; especially Florida and Windermere roads in Morningside and Davenport Rd in Glenwood.

City centre *p30, map p32*
$$$ Royal Grill, **Royal Hotel**, see Where to stay, page 45. Mon-Sat 1200-1430, 1830-2300. The **Royal Hotel**'s 70-year-old flagship restaurant, serving the likes of Norwegian salmon and roast duck in an opulent setting with chandeliers, grand piano, soaring ceilings and potted palms. An elegant, colonial dining experience. Save room for something from the dessert trolley.

$$ Roma Revolving, John Ross House, Margaret Mncadi Av (Victoria Embankment), T031-368 2275, www. roma.co.za. Mon-Sat 1200-1430, 1800-2230. Old-fashioned and kitsch concept, this long-running Italian restaurant is set on the 32nd floor, with a revolving floor offering excellent city views. Italian dishes, seafood and pasta, heavily laden dessert trolley, good-value 3-course set meals.

$$ Ulundi, **Royal Hotel**, see Where to stay, page 45. Mon-Fri 1200-1430. Excellent lunchtime Indian restaurant with a feel of colonial Natal, turbaned waiters, rattan furniture, ceiling fans, tandoori grills and traditional Durban curries served in little copper bowls on platters to share. Good choice for vegetarians.

$ Little Gujarat, 43 Dr Goonam St, T031-305 3148. Mon-Fri 0830-1600, Sat 0830-1330. Basic spot in the Indian district famous for its ridiculously cheap, very tasty and authentic vegetarian and vegan Indian food. Choices include *samosas*, vegetable curries, *masala dosas*, *rotis*, *pakoras* and pickles, and bunny chows (see box, page 34), which can be washed down with sweet, milky *chai* (tea).

Beachfront *p37, map p32*

$$$ Cargo Hold, uShaka Marine World, see page 38, T031-328 8065. Daily 1200-1500, 1800-2200, no children under 8 for dinner. Great location spread over 3 floors in the phantom ship, with a glass wall looking into the shark tank – ragged tooth sharks sidling by as you eat. Impressive menu, including good seafood, steaks, warm salads and Mediterranean starters. Reservations essential.

$$$ Daruma, ground floor, **Southern Sun Elangeni & Maharani**, see page 45, T031-362 1322, www. daruma.co.za. Mon-Sat 1200-1400, 1800-2230, Sun 1800-2130. Pricey but superb Japanese cuisine from sushi and sashimi to teppanyaki and teriyaki – the Durban seafood tempura is especially good. It's one of several restaurants in this large hotel.

$$$ Havana Grill & Wine Bar, Suncoast Casino & Entertainment World, see page 38, T031-337 1305, www.havanagrill.co.za. Daily 1200-1500, 1800-2200, bar open late. Great veranda with views of the beachfront and Cuban-inspired decor and menu, well known for its aged steaks seafood and tapas. There are several other quality restaurants at Suncoast plus a food court for snacks.

$$$-$$ Moyo, uShaka Marine World, T031-332 0606, www.moyo. co.za. Open 1100-2230. Good ocean views from either tables on the beachfront or at the end of uShaka Pier, a pan-African menu with dishes from Morocco tagines to Mozambique curries and traditional South African *potjieko*, live music, Xhosa face

painting, fantastic atmosphere and professional service.

Cafés

Circus Circus Beach Café, Snell Parade, Bay of Plenty, T031-337 7700, www. circuscircus.co.za. Mon-Thu 0600-1700, Fri-Sun 0600-1900. Good seaside vibe with tables strung along the promenade and on the beach, popular with surfers for early breakfasts and with families for brunch on Sun, plus a long menu of salads, pastas, burgers, toasted sandwiches and wraps.

Berea *p39*

Durban's most popular nighttime hubs are around Florida Rd in Morningside and Musgrave Rd in Berea, both with numerous bars and restaurants.

$$$ 9th Avenue Bistro, Avonmore Centre, 9th Av, Morningside, T031-312 9134, www.9thavenuebistro.co.za. Tue-Fri 1200-1430, Mon-Sat 1800-2200. Classic bistro atmosphere with a smart, traditional setting and award-winning wine list, inventive menu including good oxtail, roast duck, seared tuna and lobster bisque, beautifully presented dishes, plenty of loyal local regulars.

$$ Café 1999, corner of Silverton and Vasue roads, Musgrave, T031-202 3406, www.cafe1999.co.za. Mon-Fri 1230-1430, Mon-Sat 1830-2230. Interesting menu of tapas and finger food to share, poached duck leg, honey-glazed lamb cutlets, or chickpea and feta burgers. Sheltered outdoor eating area and relaxed, stylish interior, attracts a young, well-dressed crowd.

$$ Indian Connection, 485 Lilian Ngoyi Rd, Morningside, T031-312 1440, www.indian-connection.co.za. Daily 1100-1500, 1730-1030. Traditional suburban home, which has been converted into a modern, stylish Indian restaurant, refreshingly free of the usual curry house decor, the interior is white with wooden floors. Mix of north and south Indian dishes, choice of tandooris, tikkas and biriyanis, plus local coconut prawn curries.

Cafés
Blue Zoo Restaurant and Tea Garden, in Mitchell Park (page 39), 6 Nimmo Rd, Morningside, T031-312 9134. Daily 0800-1630. Pleasant spot in the picturesque park with outside tables, build-your-own breakfasts, sandwiches, salads and light meals, plus seafood and curries.

North of the CBD p40
$$-$ Mojo's, Riverside Hotel & Spa, see page 47. Daily 0600-2300. Informal setting on a terrace around the pool with good leisurely breakfasts and light meals like tortilla wraps, and a more sophisticated menu of seafood and grills in the evening. **Hops**, the pub and cocktail bar next door, is popular for after work drinks on a Fri when there's live music and a happy hour 1700-1800.

Umhlanga p41
For gourmet eating and fine wines in a luxurious setting with ocean views, head to the restaurants in the 5-star hotels: the **Oyster Box**, or the **Beverly Hills**. Umhlanga's restaurant and nightlife 'strip' is on Chartwell Dr.

There are also numerous restaurants at Gateway.
$$$-$$ Little Havana, Granada Centre, Chartwell Dr, T031-561 7589, www.littlehavana.co.za. Formal place with crisp white-linen tablecloths and gliding waiting staff, well-known for its excellent steaks, seafood and winelist, unusual combinations like seared tuna and fillet beef, make room for the rich desserts.
$$ Lord Prawn, Umhlanga Plaza, Lagoon Dr, T031-561 1133, www.lordprawnumhlanga.co.za. Daily 1200-1430, 1730-2200. Recommended for its good-value seafood dishes, including surf 'n' turf combos, fish and chips, 1 kg of prawns, and very good Durban prawn curries. Cheerful maritime decor with an informal atmosphere.
$ Steak & Ale, Chartwell Centre, 16 Chartwell Dr, T031-561 7234. Tue-Sun 1200-2200. Home-style pub grub like steak and sauces or their signature pork belly and mash, broad outside deck, good choice of local and international beers, the bar stays open late and gets busy at the weekend.

Cafés
Ferrucci Classical Bakery & Café, Chartwell Centre, 16 Chartwell Dr, T031-5614140, www.ferrucci.co.za. Mon-Fri 0700-1700, Sat 0700-1500, Sun 0700-1300. A good stop to make up a picnic for the beach for the flaky croissants, cakes, pastries and artisan breads made from stone-ground flour. Also coffees, milkshakes, breakfasts, gourmet sandwiches and salads:

🍸 Bars and clubs

Durban *p24, maps p25 and p32*
The best resource for Durban's nightlife is *Durban Live*, www.durbanlive.com.
Billy the Bums, 504 Lilian Ngoyi Rd, Morningside, opposite the **Indian Connection** restaurant (see above), T031-303 1988, www.billythebums. co.za. Open 1200-2430. Well-established and lively bar in old townhouse with lattice balconies and covered patio, regular party theme nights, long cocktail list, food includes shared platters and 'burgers 'n beer' specials. (BUMS stand for Basic Upmarket Socialite.)
Blue Dolphin, at the **Blue Waters Hotel** (page 46), 175 Snell Parade, North Beach. Daily 1000-2400. Pleasant hotel bar with great ocean views and tables scattered on a terrace around the swimming pool, good venue for a cocktail or mocktail at sunset, also pizzas and coffee and cake.
Café Vacca Matta, **Suncoast Casino and Entertainment World**, Snell Parade, T031-368 6535, www. vaccamatta.co.za. Tue-Sat 1900-late. Sleek bar and club with enormous interiors, ultra-chic decor, lounge areas and bar-dancers. Strictly over 25s and smart dress code.
Joe Cool's, OR Tambo Parade, North Beach, T031-368 2858, www.joecools. co.za. Daily 0800-0400. Durban's most famous beach bar popular with surfers for breakfast, sun-worshipers for lunch of seafood, grills and pizza, and die-hard drinkers until the early hours. Always a party atmosphere, cocktail happy hour 1500-1800 and DJs on the upper deck from sunset.

Vogue Nightclub, T031-303 8836, 672 Umgeni Rd, Windermere, www. voguedurban.com. Fri-Sun 0900-0500. Cavernous modern dance club, lots of DJs, varied music and theme nights, a 10-min taxi ride from bars and restaurants in Florida Road.

🎭 Entertainment

Durban *p24, maps p25 and p32*
Cinema
All the latest Hollywood (and in Durban, Bollywood), and home-grown releases can be seen at multi-screen cinemas in the shopping malls and casinos. The 2 major cinema groups are **Nu Metro**, www.numetro.co.za, and **Ster-Kinekor**, www.sterkinekor. com. New films are released on Fri. Newspapers have full listings. Gateway in Umhlanga also has a separate **Cinema Nouveau**, which screens international and art-house films (information and bookings also at **Ster-Kinekor**).

Theatre
All tickets for live performances can be purchased from **Computicket**, T011-340 8000, www.computicket. com, or at their kiosks at the larger shopping malls, as well as in **Checkers** and **Shoprite** supermarkets.
Barnyard Theatre, Gateway, Umhlanga, T031-566 3045, www. barnyardtheatre.co.za. Popular supper theatre for comedy and fun tribute band theme evenings.
Catalina Theatre, Wilson's Wharf, Margaret Mncadi Av, T031-305 6889, www.catalina theatre.co.za. 175-seater

venue for comedy, theatre and music with new productions every 2-3 weeks. **The Playhouse**, 231 Anton Lembede St, T031-369 9596, www.playhouse company.com. Performances in 3 auditoriums: the **Opera**, **Loft**, and **Drama** theatres. Eclectic range from Shakespeare to modern dance and contemporary political satire.

⊕ Festivals

Easter Festival of Chariots, North Beach, www.festivalofchariots.net. A multi-faith spiritual festival with origins from the Ratha Yatra festival in India's ancient city of Jagannatha Puri. Held over Easter weekend on the lawns and beach around Snell Parade, includes an alternative arts and crafts market, a parade of giant chariots, and a collective prayer for peace when thousands of sky lanterns are released over the ocean.
May or Jun Comrades Marathon, www.comrades.com. Established in 1921 to commemorate South African soldiers killed during the First World War, this is the oldest and one of the most gruelling ultra-marathons in the world. The direction of the race alternates each year between the 'up' run (87 km) starting from Durban and the 'down' run (89 km) starting from Pietermaritzburg. Attracts more than 20,000 runners from all over the world. Also see page 44.
Top Gear Festival Durban, at the Moses Mabhida Stadium, www. topgearfestivaldurban.co.za. South Africans just love the BBC's Top Gear, and Durban is the country's venue for this massively popular 2-day event.

Jeremy Clarkson, Richard Hammond and James May (Jezza, the Hamster and Captain Slow) do their stuff in front of more than 70,000 visitors; book tickets and accommodation well in advance.
Jul Durban July, Greyville Racecourse, www.vodacomdurbanjuly.co.za. Usually held on the 1st Sun of Jul, this day of horseracing has been going since 1897 and now attracts more than 50,000. It's just as well-known as a glamorous social get together and fashion spectacle. Again book tickets and accommodation well in advance.
Taste of Durban, at **Suncoast Casino and Entertainment World** (see page 38), www.tasteofdurban.co.za. Hugely popular event where some of the city's top gourmet restaurants showcase their food; buy a book of coupons and a wine glass for tastings.
Mid-Oct to mid-Nov Durban Dilwali Festival, details from the South African Hindu Maha Sabha organization, www.sahms.org.za. A 3-day festival celebrating the annual Dilwali (the festival of lights), the biggest event in the Hindu religious calendar; the date is determined by the new moon. Entertainment includes live music, yoga demonstrations, classical Indian dancing, and a parade of colourful floats through the CBD finishing off with fireworks.

O Shopping

Durban *p24, maps p25 and p32*
Arts, crafts and curios
African Art Centre, 94 Florida Rd, Morningside, opposite **Quarters Hotel** (see page 46), T031-312 3804, www.

afriart.org.za. Mon-Fri 0830-1700, Sat 0900-1500. One of the best places in Durban to buy quality Zulu beadwork, baskets and ceramics and a non-profit making outlet for rural craftspeople.

Antiques and Bygones, 437 Lilian Ngoyi Rd, Morningside, T031-303 8880, www.antiquesandbygones. co.za. Mon-Fri 0900-1700, Sat 0900-1300. Established in 1949 and the oldest antiques shop in KwaZulu-Natal selling a range of valuable items from South Africa's Georgian, Victorian and Edwardian periods, plus paintings and sculptures by well-known local artists.

BAT Centre, Margaret Mncadi Av, T031-332 0451, www.batcentre.co.za. Mon-Fri 0900-1630, Sat-Sun 1000-1600. A collection of curio and craft studios selling contemporary Zulu art and jewellery and you can watch the artists at work.

KZNSA Gallery, 166 Bulwer Rd, Glenwood, T031-277 1705, www. kznsagallery.co.za. Tue-Fri 0900-1700, Sat 0900-1600, Sun 1000-1500. Home of the **KwaZulu-Natal Society of Arts**, the gallery features changing exhibitions by local and international artists. The gallery shop contains an excellent selection of imaginative arts and crafts, and the **Arts Café** serves breakfasts, lunches and teas and has a children's playground.

The Stables Lifestyles Market, Jaco Jackson Dr, opposite the Kings Park Stadium, off Masabalala Yengwa Av (M12), T031-312 3058. www.stableslife stylemarket.co.za. Wed and Fri 1800-2200, Sun 1000-1700. As the name suggests set in a converted stables with the 100 or so horse stalls making interesting arts, crafts, antiques and decor shops. Also known as the 'moonlight market' as it's open in the evening, it also has food stalls, live music and bars.

Books and maps

Exclusive Books, www.exclus1ves. co.za. National bookshop chain, the best branches are at Gateway and the Pavilion (see shopping malls below), which also have cafés. Particularly good for maps, guide books and coffee-table books on Africa and carry a full range of international magazines and newspapers.

Camping and hiking equipment

Cape Union Mart, www.capeunion mart.co.za. Excellent shop selling outdoor equipment, clothing, backpacks, tents, mosquito nets, and a great range of walking shoes. There are branches at Gateway, the Pavilion, La Lucia Mall in La Lucia, and the Galleria Mall, in Amanzimtoti.

Gold

Scoin Shop, www.scoinshop.com. Krugerrands, South Africa's famous gold coins, can be bought here as an investment or souvenir. The company also produces collector's coins such as the Mandela Medallion. There are branches at Gateway, the Pavilion, and La Lucia Mall in La Lucia.

Shopping malls

Shop opening hours are listed; the restaurants and cinemas stay open later, until 2200 or 2300.

Gateway, Umhlanga Ridge, Umhlanga, close to the N2/M41 interchange,

T031-514 0500, www.gatewayworld. co.za. Mon-Thu 0900-1900, Fri-Sat 0900-2100, Sun 0900-1800. Also known as the Gateway Theatre of Shopping (its original name when it was built in 2001, which became too much of a mouthful rather quickly), this vast complex is supposedly the largest mall in the southern hemisphere – easily believable once you step inside. Covering more than 220,000 sq m of retail space, it features a huge variety of shops and restaurants, an 18-screen **Ster-Kinekor** cinema, and the **Barnyard Theatre** (see page 51). **Electric Avenue** is a family entertainment centre (daily 0900-2300) which offers 10-pin bowling, go-karts and arcade games among other activities, while the **Wave House** (Sat 1200-1700, Sun 0900-1700) is an artificial surf wave with the world's only man-made double-point break (for those who understand surf jargon). Also here is a championship skateboard park, an indoor climbing wall (reputedly the world's highest), a children's science centre and a mini-funfair; you can easily spend a day here without going into a shop and it reputedly gets 2 million visitors a month.
La Lucia Mall, William Campbell Dr, La Lucia, T031-562 8420, www.lalucia mall.co.za. Mon-Fri 0900-1800, Sat 0830-1700, Sun 0900-1730. Serving the northern suburbs, this mall has 130 shops including large branches of supermarkets, and is another option to Gateway to stop for provisions if heading north on the N2; it's 4.4 km to the N2/M41 interchange.
Musgrave Centre, 115 Musgrave Rd, Berea, T031-201 5129, www.musgrave

centre.co.za. Mon-Sat 0900-1800, Sun 0900-1700. Over 110 shops with a mix of trendy boutiques and national chain stores, plus supermarkets, a food court and a 7-screen **Ster-Kinekor** cinema.
The Pavilion, accessed from the N3, Westville, T031-265 0558, www.thepav. co.za. Daily 0900-1900. After Gateway, this is Durban's 2nd-largest mall with 230 shops, 40 restaurants, a food court and a 12-screen **Nu Metro** cinema.

⏱ What to do

Durban *p24, maps p25 and p32*
Boat trips
Durban Charter Boat Association, T031-301 1115, www.dcba.co.za. This represents a number of charter boats that depart from either the Yacht Mole near the Durban Yacht Club, or the Small Craft Harbour near the BAT Centre along Margaret Mncadi Av (Victoria Embankment), for deep-sea and shark fishing. Most take 4-8 people, and prices (from R500 per person for 3-4 hrs) include all equipment, bait and tackle. Non-fisherman can also go to enjoy the views of Durban, and whale watching in season. Check the website for contact details of each operator, plus information about trips offered.
Ocean Ventures, on the promenade, uShaka Marine World (see page 38), T086-100 1138, www.oceanventures. co.za. Daily 0900-1600. Offers numerous boat trips including an inflatable boat launched off the beach for dolphin watching, 1 hr, R300, children (5-15) R150; whale watching in season (Jun-Dec), 2 hrs, R450, children (5-15) R300; and exciting

speed-boat trips, 30 mins, R150 per person. Also surfing and ocean kayaking lessons and hires out boards and kayaks from R100 per hr.

Sarie Marasis Pleasure Cruises, T031-305 4022, Margaret Mncadi Av (Victoria Embankment), at the Gardiner Jetty, www.sariemaraiscruises.co.za. A good way to get a grip on the size and workings of Durban Harbour is to go on a short harbour cruise on an engine-powered ferry boat, which departs every 30 mins 0900-1600 from the jetty, R60, children (under 12) R35. The little boats are able to get right beneath the hulls of the massive container ships moored at the docks.

Cricket

Sahara Stadium Kingsmead, Masabalala Yengwa Av (M12), just north of the ICC, T031-335 4200, www.dolphinscricket.co.za, tickets from **Computicket**, T011-340 8000, www.computicket.com, or at their kiosks in the larger shopping malls, as well as in **Checkers** and **Shoprite** supermarkets. The 1st Test match was played here in 1923 between South Africa and England, and it is now home to the KwaZulu-Natal Dolphins, and all Durban's big matches are played here, usually Oct-Apr.

Cycling

Bike & Saddle, T031-813 5633, www.bikeandsaddle.com. Offers a 3-hr guided bike tour along the Golden Mile and to sights around City Hall; departures at 0900 or 1300 from the **Southern Sun Elangeni & Maharani**, 63 Snell Parade, North Beach (see

page 45); reservations essential, R880 per person including coffee and a pastry. Also rents out bikes for your whole holiday with pick-up/drop-offs in Durban, Johannesburg and Cape Town (like car rental).

Diving

Operators dive from Durban or can arrange trips to other sites such as Sodwana Bay or the Aliwal Shoal, see page 63. Visibility is at its best during the winter months.

Calypso Dive & Adventure Centre, at Village Walk, **uShaka Marine World** (page 38), T031-332 0905, www.calypsoushaka.co.za. Daily 0900-1800. A 5-star PADI dive school offering a number of courses and numerous daily dives to the nearby sites including the *T-Barge* and the *Fontao* wrecks off Umhlanga; both boats that were sunk to create artificial reefs and provide habitats for tropical fish. Can also organize dives in the Tropical Tank and the Ray Tank in uShaka's aquarium from R170 (no under 12s).

Golf

Durban Country Club, Isaiah Ntshangase Rd, T031-313 1777, www.dcclub.co.za. Close to the Moses Mabhida Stadium, attractive 18-hole course with lush vegetation next to the ocean. The club was established in 1922 and the clubhouse is a fine example of Cape Dutch architecture. **Royal Durban Golf Club**, Mitchell Crescent, Greyville, T031-309 1350, www.royaldurban.co.za. A club has existed here since 1892, and got its royal prefix after Edward VIII visited in 1925. Today it's a 9-hole course which is uniquely set in the middle of the Greyville Racecourse (see below). There are also several top-class courses along the coast to the north and south of Durban.

Horse racing

Race meetings are held at one of Durban's racecourses operated by the Golden Circle Turf Club: **Greyville**, 150 Avondale Rd, Greyville, T031-314 1651; and **Clairwood Park**, 89 Barrier Lane, Merewent, T031-469 1020, www.goldcircle.co.za. Each has regular stands and an indoor buffet restaurant overlooking the course. Check the website for racing calendars. The prestigious **Durban July** (see page 52) is held at Greyville.

Rugby and football

Kings Park Stadium, Isaiah Ntshangase Rd, off Masabalala Yengwa Av (M12), 1 road back from the beachfront, across the road from Moses Mabhida Stadium, information on fixtures, T031-308 8400, www.sharksrugby.co.za, tickets from **Computicket** T011-340 8000, www. computicket.com, or at their kiosks in the larger shopping malls, as well as in **Checkers** and **Shoprite** supermarkets. This 52,000-seat stadium fondly known as the 'shark tank' is the home ground to the KwaZulu-Natal Rugby Union team, The Sharks, who consistently rank as one of South Africa's best. A match here is a spirited and fun occasion, and Sharkie, the team's mascot, runs around the stadium in a full shark suit. The club rugby fields outside double up as a parking and *braai* area. While the national football team, Bafana Bafana, usually play its Durban fixtures across the road at Moses Mabhida Stadium (built for the 2010 FIFA World Cup™), **Kings Park** still hosts a number of domestic football matches, as well as the occasional music concert. Rugby is played Feb-Oct, football through the year.

Surfing

There are several designated surfing and boogie-boarding beaches along the Golden Mile tucked between the series of piers; the most popular are Bay of Plenty, New Pier, North Beach, Wedge and Dairy.
Learn 2 Surf, Addington Beach, T0831-40567, www.learn2surf.co.za. Daily 0800-1600. Offers lessons from R200 per hr and students can pick up the basics in their first lesson. Will teach children as young as 6.
Ocean Ventures, on the promenade at **uShaka Marine World** (see page 38), T084-823 9470, www. surfandadventures.co.za. Daily 0900-1600. Rents out boards and rash vests for R100 per hr, and a number of surf shops on the beachfront also have boards for hire.

Tour operators

Expect to pay in the region of R500-600 for a half-day city tour, and R700-900 for a full-day tour to the outlying regions such as Valley of 1000 Hills. The operators use minibuses, have registered guides and pick up from hotels. This is far from an exhaustive list; hotels can make recommendations, the tourist offices (see page 27) can

Tours with Durban Tourism

Durban Tourism (www.durban experience.co.za) runs two fun and informative three-hour walking tours, and a three-hour bus tour that are a good, safe way of getting to know the city. Both walking tours depart from the Tourist Junction, 160 Monty Naicker Street (the old station building) (T031-322 4205 or book at any of the Durban Tourism offices, Monday-Friday at 0900 and 1330, and Saturday at 0900, R100, children (5-18) R50, under fives free), and they must be booked at least a day in advance. Oriental Walk-About gives an account of Mahatma Gandhi in South Africa and the history and culture of Durban's Indians and Zulus. It goes through the Indian arcades to the Juma Musjid Mosque, the Emmanuel Cathedral and into Victoria Street Market. Historical Walk-About goes through the CBD and includes a look at the historical monuments and buildings around Luthuli Farewell Square and visits the City Hall, Natural Science Museum and Durban Art Gallery.

There are two daily three-hour Ricksha Bus tours (T031-322 4209, or book at any of the Durban Tourism offices, 0900-1200 and 1300-1600, R100, children (5-18) R50, under fives free), on an open-top double-decker bus and depart from the North Beach office of Durban Tourism on the corner of OR Tambo Parade and KE Masinga Road. The route goes in a loop from the beachfront past uShaka Marine World, Victoria Street Market, the Juma Musjid Mosque, Francis Farewell Square, Mitchell Park, Florida Road, the Moses Mabhida Stadium and back to the beachfront.

recommend numerous tour operators, or go on one of **Durban Tourism**'s tours (see box, above).

1st Zulu Safaris, office at uShaka Marine World, T031-337 3103 www.1stzulusafaris.co.za. Comprehensive half day tours including the city and Valley of 1000 Hills, plus longer tours to Pietermaritzburg and the Midlands Meander, Sani Pass, Hluhluwe-Imfolozi and Shakaland; long days (11-14 hrs) but ideal if you're short of time.

Hylton Ross, T031-275 3836, www. hyltonross.com. Again long day tours, but good for an exploration of KwaZulu-Natal on a short timeframe, including Isandlwana and Rorke's Drift in the battlefields, Giant's Castle and San (Bushmen) paintings in the Drakensberg, and Hluhluwe-Imfolozi and other game parks.

Jikeleza Tours, T031-702 1189, www. jikelezatours.co.za. Township tour starting at the Kwa-Muhle Museum to explain the nature of Apartheid, before visiting the Umlazi or Nanda township. Also evening trips with local guides for drinks at the township shebeens, plus wider city tours.

Strelitzia Tours, T031-579 5681, www. strelitziatours.com. A comprehensive range of tours in the province 1-3 days with regular departures. City tours and day trips to townships and Valley of 1000 hills.

Tekweni Ecotours, T082-303 9112, www.tekweniecotours.co.za. Excellent cultural tours including a half-day city tour which includes a visit to the Hare Krishna Temple of Understanding and the Indian township of Chatsworth, and to the Victoria Street Market and a traditional healer. Also Valley of 1000 Hills, and overnight tours to Hluhluwe-Imfolozi and Sani Pass in the Drakensberg.

⊖ Transport

Durban *p24, maps p25 and p32*
From Durban it is 1642 km to **Cape Town** (via the Garden Route); 1639 km (via Bloemfontein), 589 km to **Johannesburg**, 642 km to **East London**, 1154 km to **Knysna**, 552 km to **Maseru** (Lesotho), 540 km to **Mbabane** (Swaziland), 584 km to **Maputo** (Mozambique, via Swaziland), 707 km to **Nelspruit**, and 897 km to **Port Elizabeth**.

Air

For information on **King Shaka International Airport**, see Getting there, page 24, and for details of the international airlines serving South Africa, see Planning your trip, page 6. **King Shaka International Airport** has numerous daily flights to/from **Johannesburg** and **Cape Town**, though for smaller cities and regional destinations, in the most part, you'll have to change in Johannesburg. By booking early online, good deals can

be found with all the airlines, and you can either book directly or through **Computicket**, T011-915 8000, www.computicket.com, or in South Africa, at any of their kiosks in the shopping malls or any branch of **Checkers** and **Shoprite** supermarkets.

South African Airways (**SAA**) run in conjunction with its subsidiaries **SA Airlink**, and **SA Express**, T011-978 5313, www.flysaa.com, has daily flights between Durban and **East London**, **Johannesburg**, **Cape Town**, **George** and **Maputo** (Mozambique). **British Airways Comair**, T011-441 8600, www.britishairways.com, has daily flights between Durban and **Johannesburg**, **Cape Town** and **Port Elizabeth**. **Kulula**, T0861-585 852 (in South Africa), T011-921 0111 (from overseas), www.kulula.com, also owned by **British Airways**, is a no-frills airline with daily services between Durban and **Johannesburg**, and **Cape Town**. **Mango**, T0861-162 646 (in South Africa), T011-359 1222 (from overseas), www.flymango.com, another no-frills operator owned by **SAA**, has daily flights between Durban and **Johannesburg** and **Cape Town**.

Bus

Local For details of Johannesburg's public buses, see box, page 26. Additionally to the formal bus companies, minibus taxis also serve all areas of the city on fixed routes but with no timetables or formal stops and are flagged down on the street. They are generally fine to use for a short journey along a main road, but are best avoided on longer journeys as they are generally driven rather recklessly and there is often no way of knowing where they're heading. Most trips cost around R6, and they stop running at about 2000.

Long-distance Greyhound, www. greyhound.co.za, **Intercape**, www. intercape.co.za, and **Translux**, www. translux.co.za, cover routes from Durban to **Cape Town** via **Mthatha**, **East London**, **Port Elizabeth**, **Knysna** and **Swellendam**, or via **Harrismith**, **Bloemfontein** and **Beaufort West**; **Pretoria** and **Johannesburg** on the N3 or via **Richards Bay** and the N2.

Full timetables can be found on the websites, and tickets can be booked through **Computicket**, T011-915 8000, www.computicket.com, or in South Africa, at any of their kiosks in the shopping malls or any branch of **Checkers** and **Shoprite** supermarkets For more information, see Getting around, page 26.

These and other smaller bus companies depart and arrive at the **Motorcoach Terminal** just north of the CBD, which is also where the railway station is (see below). It's easiest to enter from Masabalala Yengwa Av (M12), entrance not from Umgeni Rd (R102). Many of the buses and trains depart and arrive late at night or early in the morning, so make sure you have pre-arranged a pickup with your hotel or take a metered taxi. **Margate Mini Coach**, T039-312 1406, www.margatecoach. co.za, advance booking essential, runs in both directions between **King Shaka International Airport**, and the **Wild Coast Sun** in the Eastern Cape, via (from north to south), **Durban Station**, **Amanzimtoti**, **Scottburgh**, **Hibberdene**, **Port Shepstone**, **Margate** and **Port Edward**. There are at least 3 services per day, R230 for the full one-way trip, which takes 3¼ hrs. Fares and timetables can be found on the website.

Underberg Express, T033-701 2750, www.underbergexpress. co.za, runs between **Underberg**, **Howick**, **Pietermaritzburg**, **Hillcrest**, **Kloof**, the **Pavilion Mall**, **Durban**, **Umhlanga** and **King Shaka International Airport**. It departs Underberg Tue-Sun at 0800 and arrives in central Durban at 1100 and at King Shaka International Airport at 1130, from where it leaves again at about 1300 and arrives back again in Underberg at around 1730. There is a service on Mon that departs Underberg at 0500, so adjust times of arrival accordingly. The full one-way fare between Underberg and the airport is R600. Fares and timetables can be found on the website.

Baz Bus, reservations Cape Town T021-422 5202, www.bazbus.com, is the best option for backpackers, and has a daily service between Durban and **Port Elizabeth**, and **Johannesburg** and **Pretoria**. See Planning your trip, page 9, for full details of the service.

Car hire
All offices are at King Shaka International Airport. Check the websites for city centre locations. **Avis**, T032-436 7800, www.avis.co.za; **Budget**,

T032-436 5500, www.budget.co.za; **Dollar Thrifty**, T032-436 3040, www.thrifty.co.za; **First Car Rental**, T032-436 0100, www.firstcarrental.co.za; **Hertz**, T032-436 0300, www.hertz.com.

Train

The Durban railway station is located between Umgeni Rd (R102) and Masabalala Yengwa Av (M12) just to the north of the CBD. It is also where the Motorcoach Terminal is (see above). It is the terminus of Shosholoza Meyl long-distance services and the hub of a network of Metrorail commuter rail services.

Local Metrorail, enquiries T031-813 0000, www.metrorail.co.za, operates suburban commuter trains across the Durban metropolitan region as far as **KwaDukuza-Stanger** to the north, **Kelso** to the south, and **Cato Ridge** inland. However, few routes are useful for tourists and while these trains are fine to use in rush hour (0700-0800 and 1600-1800), are best avoided at quieter times due to the possibility of petty crime. But in saying that, CCTV cameras have been installed at larger stations to monitor activities on the platforms and there are visible security guards on trains, making the service safer than it was in the past. They generally operate 0400-2100 and run about every 20 mins in peak periods. Short single fares start from R8, and routes and timetables are published on the website.

Long-distance Passenger trains are run by **Shosholoza Meyl**, central reservations, T0860-00888 (in South Africa), T011-774 4555 (from overseas), www.shosholozameyl.co.za. There is a service between **Johannesburg** and Durban (Mon, Fri, Wed and Sun in both directions, 13 hrs) via **Newcastle**, **Ladysmith** and **Pietermaritzburg**. Shosholoza Meyl also operates a more upmarket service, the **Premier Classe**, T011-774 5247, www.premierclasse.co.za, between **Johannesburg** and Durban twice a week. It has a dedicated lounge for boarding passengers at Durban station. For more information on all rail services, see Transport, page 9.

❶ Directory

Durban p24, maps p25 and p32
Consulates Mozambique High Commission, 306-310 Matthews Meyiwa Rd, Windermere, T031-303 7130, www.embamoc.co.za. Mon-Fri 0800 1500. Issues visas for Mozambique in the same day or up to 72 hrs, depending on the fee paid. **Medical services** Netcare, St Augustine's Hospital, 107 JB Marks Rd, Bulwar, Berea, T031-268 5000, the largest private hospital in KwaZulu-Natal; for 24-hr medical services and ambulances T082-911, to locate any **Netcare** hospital T011-301 0000, www.netcare.co.za. **Netcare Travel Clinic**, Umhlanga Medical Centre, 321 Umhlanga Rocks Dr, Umhlanga, T031-582 5302, www.travelclinic.co.za, Mon-Fri 0730-1800, Sat 0830-1300, useful stop to update vaccinations and pick up anti-malarials if heading to Mozambique or parts of Kruger National Park.

KwaZulu-Natal South Coast

The south coast of KwaZulu-Natal stretches from Durban to the start of the Eastern Cape's Wild Coast. Beyond the city suburbs, the first stretch is a long line of built-up concrete holiday resorts popular with domestic tourists, which won't appeal much to overseas visitors. However the further south you go, the coastline opens up to reveal beautiful beaches and attractive sub-tropical vegetation in the numerous nature reserves. Secluded coves and lagoons, beach walks and abundant birdlife – more than 400 bird species have been recorded along the south coast – are the highlights, while the towns such as Scottburgh, Hibberdene, Margate and Ramsgate have all the facilities you may want on a typical sun, sea and sand type of holiday. There is plenty for the more active including several golf courses, scuba diving at Aliwal Shoal and Protea Banks, and adventure activities in Oribi Gorge.

South of Durban → *For listings, see pages 68-74.*

Amanzimtoti to Scottburgh
Driving down the N2 immediately south of Durban, the road first goes through an extensive industrial belt and then to Amanzimtoti, or 'toti', only 22 km south of Durban, which is effectively a suburb and an unattractive high-rise holiday resort with little appeal. **Inyoni Rocks** and **Pipeline Beach** are the two main beaches for swimmers and sunbathers. The **Galleria Mall** (see page 72), the largest shopping mall on the south coast, is worth a stop to pick up provisions and has easy access from the N2. You can get information on the South Coast at the helpful office of **Durban Tourism** ① *95 Beach Rd, T031-903 7498, www.durbanexperience.co.za, Mon-Fri 0800-1630, Sat 0900-1400.*

Amanzimtoti Bird Sanctuary ① *Umdoni Rd, T031-903 1203, daily 0900-1800, tea garden 0800-1600, free,* covers 4 ha around a large pond. There are picnic sites, a 1-km walking trail through a patch of indigenous forest and three hides from which to see many of the 150 species of water birds present here including greenback heron, white-faced duck, and large flocks of spur-winged geese.

Between Amanzimtoti and Umgababa are a series of coastal resorts known collectively as **Kingsburgh**. This 8-km stretch is known for its good beaches and is popular with surfers and jet-skiers. Travelling down the coast from Amanzimtoti, the first beach you reach is **Doonside**; across the Little Manzimtoti

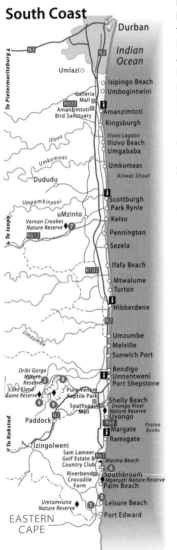

South Coast

River is **Warner Beach**. **Winkelspruit** is one of the more developed parts of the area. Across the Lovu River is **Illovo** beach, which is backed by a lagoon at the mouth of the river. **Karridene** is at the mouth of another river, the Msimbazi. **Umkomaas** is the last resort in this area, which is 48 km south of Durban and is where the Umkomaas River spills into the sea at the largest estuary on the south coast.

Scottburgh

Zulu King Shaka and his entourage were among some of the early visitors to this area, and stopping to rest and drink from a spring, he was distracted by the myriad of birds at the mouth of the river beside which the town was later to be built. He wondered how each bird would know to which nest it should return, and named the river Mpambanyoni which translates to 'confuser of birds'. Today's Scottburgh, 58 km south of Durban, was named after Natal Governor John Scott, and was the first town to be laid out south of Durban in 1860. It's another popular resort and the beach by the estuary of the Mpambanyoni has

Where to stay 🛏
Estuary Country Hotel **1**
The Gorge Private Game
  Lodge & Spa **2**
Ku-Boboyi River Lodge **3**
Lake Eland Game Reserve **4**

Mondazur **6**
Nyengelezi Hutted Camp **7**
Oribi Gorge Camp **8**
Oribi Gorge **9**

The Greatest Shoal on Earth

Each year around June or July in the warm winter months millions of sardines travel northwards along the east coast of South Africa close to the beaches, known locally as 'the Sardine Run'. Their sheer numbers create a feeding frenzy along the coastline attracting dolphins, sharks, game fish and birds, and the ocean teams with life. The shoals are often more than 7 km long, 1.5 km wide and 30 m deep and are clearly visible from planes or from the surface of the ocean. The sight of wheeling squadrons of gannets folding their wings to plummet into the water around schools of hundreds of dolphins in hot pursuit of the shimmering mass of panic-stricken fish is an extraordinary spectacle. Little is known about this phenomenon, but their main spawning grounds are on the Agulhas banks off the southern Cape coast, where the adults gather for a prolonged breeding season through spring and early summer. Sardines are cold-water fish and are usually associated with areas of cold ocean upwelling, where deeper, cooler, nutrient-rich water currents surge to the surface when they strike shallow coastal areas. It is believed that the water temperature has to drop below 21°C in order for the migration up the coast of KwaZulu-Natal to take place. The melee of predators accompanying the sardines can be problematic, as the sardines come so close to shore, the shark nets that protect bathers and surfers can take a heavy toll on sharks and dolphins. The KZN Sharks Board (see page 42) monitors the situation carefully and in parts lifts the shark nets before the arrival of the Sardine Run. It's often dubbed 'the Greatest Shoal on Earth', and a number of high profile television documentaries, including the BBC's Blue Planet series, have featured the run.

terraced lawns, tidal and paddling pools, a miniature railway and is protected by shark nets. The Green Point Lighthouse, a national monument, was erected in 1905. There's an office for **South Coast Tourism** ① *Scott St, T039-976 1364, www.gosouthcoast.co.za, Mon-Fri 0800-1700, Sat 0800-1300, Sun in season*.

The **Aliwal Shoal** lies just north of Scottburgh, and after Sodwana Bay is one of South Africa's most popular diving areas (see page 73). The shoal is a rocky reef which is the remains of an ancient sand dune approximately 5 km off the coast. It's inhabited by many kinds of hard and soft corals and a variety of tropical and subtropical fish. It is named after the near-sinking of the vessel Aliwal in 1849. The shoal is especially known for its abundance of grey nurse sharks (known locally as ragged tooth sharks or 'raggies') between August and November when the sharks congregate there to mate.

Vernon Crookes Nature Reserve
ⓘ *On the R612, 12 km inland from the N2, turn off 3 km past the town of uMzinto and it's 6 km to the entrance gate, T039-974 2222, www.kznwildlife.com, Apr-Sep 0700-1700, Oct-Mar 0600-1800, R20, children (under 12) R10.*

Surrounded by eucalyptus and sugarcane plantations and named after a 19th century sugar magnet, this 2189 ha reserve is 22 km east of Scottburgh. The unusual patch of grassland and thornveld near the coast supports blue wildebeest, impala, mountain and common reedbuck, blesbuck and zebra, and of over 300 birds, it is especially renowned for its variety of grassland large species including grey crowned cranes, ground hornbills, trumpeter hornbills and secretary bird. There is a 19-km network of dirt roads, 15 km of hiking trails, picnic sites and viewpoints and accommodation is in the **Nyengelezi Hutted Camp** (see Where to stay, page 69).

Hibiscus Coast → *For listings, see pages 68-74.*

The Hibiscus Coast is the most southern part of KwaZulu-Natal's south coast and stretches from Hibberdene to Port Edward on the border with the Eastern Cape. There is less industrial development along this section of the coast, but the overall impression as you drive south is of a long line of caravan parks and holiday homes, albeit set in a lush subtropical strip of forest. The ocean is the highlight here.

Hibberdene
Hibberdene, 97 km south of Durban, was named after C. Maxwell-Hibberd, the former postmaster-general of Natal, and has five popular beaches, four of which are netted and thus safe for swimming. On the beachfront there's **South Coast Tourism** ⓘ *Barracuda Blvd, T039-699 3203, www.gosouthcoast.co.za, Mon-Fri 0800-1630, Sat 0800-1300, Sun 0900-1300*. Continuing south from Hibberdene, the road goes through a stretch of coastal bush and the oceanside hamlets of Umzumbe, Melville, Sunwich Port, Bendigo and Umtentwini, before crossing the mouth of the Umzimkulu River into Port Shepstone.

Port Shepstone
Located at the mouth of the Umzimkulu River, 124 km south of Durban, Port Shepstone was founded in 1867 when marble was discovered nearby. Today it is the largest town on the south coast and is more of an industrial centre than a tourist resort. On the southern bank of the river, look out for the striking black-and-white chequered 8-m-tall **Port Shepstone Lighthouse** that was manufactured in Britain, shipped to Natal and erected in 1905. In the lighthouse there's an office for **South Coast Tourism** ⓘ *T039-682 2455,*

www.gosouthcoast.co.za, Mon-Fri 0900-1700, Sat-Sun in season, and from here excellent views of the river-mouth and the wide Port Shepstone beach.

West of Port Shepstone

From Port Shepstone the N2 passes through an extensive agricultural area of sugarcane fields, eucalyptus plantations and cattle pastures. **Oribi Gorge Nature Reserve** ① *T039-679 1644, www.kznwildlife.com, gates 0630-1930, office 0800-1230, 0400-1630, R20, children (under 12) R10*, is 21 km west of Port Shepstone off the N2. It covers 1917 ha and was established in 1950 to protect an area of thick woodland and towering cliffs where the Umzimkulu and Umzimkulweni rivers meet. The views from the top of the sandstone cliffs, some of which are up to 280 m high, look out over the forest, which clings to the sides of the ravines below. The cliffs provide nesting sites for birds of prey, and the forest, home to the African python, is so thick that although leopard live here they are never seen. One of their prey, the samango monkey, can sometimes be seen in small groups, although ironically, oribi are not common and are very rarely seen. Birdlife here is prolific, with over 250 species present, including the Knysna lourie, narina trogon, trumpeter hornbill and five kingfisher species.

    Samango Falls, **Hoopoe Falls** and **Lehr's Falls** are the most spectacular waterfalls in the gorge and are best seen after heavy rain when vast quantities of water come crashing down into the ravines below. There are a series of tracks leading to viewpoints over the gorge, and several clearly marked hikes, from 1 km to 9 km. A tarred road winds down 4 km from the camp to a picnic spot next to the bridge crossing the Umzimkulweni River. The Umzimkulweni River is not safe to swim in as it is infected with bilharzia but there is a pleasant swimming pool in the camp. There are also a number of activities to do in the gorge operated by **Wild 5 Adventures** (see page 73).

    Lake Eland Game Reserve ① *follow the N2 for 11 km west of Port Shepstone, then turn right to Oribi Flats East and follow the D251 for 26 km to the entrance, the last 4 km is on dirt, T039-687 0395, www.lakeeland.co.za, day visitors 0700-1700, R40, children (2-8) R30, under 3s free, zip line tour 0800-1430, R500 (no under 5s), curio shop and restaurant 0800-1600*, is a 5000-ha private reserve that covers similar landscape to the Oribi Gorge Nature Reserve, and also has spectacular views of the gorge a little further upstream. There is a network of self-drive gravel tracks leading to a number of viewpoints. The highlights here are the 80-m suspension bridge that spans the gorge, and a 4.5-km-long Zip Line tour which soars across the gorge 300 m high in places. Wildlife in the reserve includes giraffe, zebra, wildebeest, eland, mountain reedbuck and bushbuck, while grassland bird species like the ground hornbill, martial eagle and secretary bird are fairly common. Most of the accommodation in the reserve is on the picturesque Eland Dam at the bottom of the gorge (see Where to stay, page 70).

Shelly Beach and around

Shelly Beach is 8 km south of Port Shepstone on the R61, or follow Marine Drive (R620) along the coast. It is quite a large suburb with one of the region's biggest shopping malls (the **Southcoast Mall**; page 72), and the beach here is a popular launch site for fishing and diving charter companies. Like the Aliwal Shoal further north, the Protea Banks, 7 km offshore from Shelly Beach, is known for its abundance of ragged tooth sharks between August and November. Activities at the **Pure Venom Reptile Park** ① *5 km inland from Shelley Beach off off the Izotsha road, T039-685 0704, www.purevenom.com, 0900-1700, R80, children (3-12) R60, under 3s free*, include having your photo taken with pythons, mambas, cobras or vipers. There's a restaurant and petting animal farmyard for kids.

Uvongo, 5 km south of Shelley Beach, is built on cliffs looking out to sea and is one of the more pleasant resorts on the south coast. The beach, protected by shark nets, is safe for swimming and surfing. On Marine Drive (R620) you'll cross a bridge over the iVungu River at Uvongo. The 28-ha **Uvongo River Nature Reserve** ① *sunrise-sunset, free*, stretches upstream from this bridge and the entrance is on the south bank. It was established to protect an array of riverine birds and rare species found here include the grey sunbird, purple-banded sunbird and grey waxbill. The 23-m-high waterfall tumbling over cliffs into the beachside lagoon is the reserve's main feature, and there are some steps to a viewpoint overlooking the falls.

Margate and Ramsgate

Originally a palm-fringed stretch of sand, the town of Margate was laid out in 1908, and was named after another seaside resort on the northern coast of Kent, in England. It is now a highly developed family resort dominated by high-rise apartments crammed in towards the beachfront. The beach is excellent and is consistently awarded with Blue Flag status. It has all the facilities and entertainment a typical holiday resort could offer, but apart from the beach, it's not especially attractive and as primarily a destination with holidaymakers from Gauteng, can get very crowded during the school holidays. There's an office for **South Coast Tourism** ① *Panorama Parade, T039-312 2322, www.gosouthcoast.co.za, Mon-Fri 0830-1630, weekends in season*, in the middle of town on the beachfront.

Ramsgate is 2 km south of Margate and is now practically a suburb, but the beach here is a little quieter and has a tidal pool for swimming and some pedalos and canoes available for hire, and there's a wooden whale deck on Marine Parade for hopeful surveys of the ocean.

Southbroom

Southbroom is a popular resort with sub-tropical trees coming down to the beach. It consists mainly of private holiday homes belonging to wealthy people from Gauteng and can feel deserted out of season. There is safe swimming in a tidal pool just down the coast at Marina Beach, a beautiful 4-km stretch of sand and rolling dunes.

Riverbend Crocodile Farm ① *Old National Rd, T039-316 6204, www. crocodilecrazy.co.za, daily 0900-1630, feeding time Sun 1500, R36, children (3-6) R22*, breeds around 200 Nile crocodiles per year. As well as tours of the farm, visitors may be able to watch crocodile hatching from January until mid-March. There is also a snake house, with snake handling demos every day at 1430, and at 1100 on Tuesday and Thursday (pre-booking only) one hour tours are conducted to the banana plantations and packing sheds on the farm. There is also has a tea garden, restaurant, farm stall and art gallery.

Mpenjati Nature Reserve ① *T039-313 0531, www.kznwildlife.com, Oct-Mar 0600-1800, Apr-Sep 0700-1700, R20, children (under 12) R10*, is 9 km south of Southbroom and 12 km north of Port Edward and well signposted off the R61. It is popular with hikers, windsurfers and canoeists and covers 60-ha of coastal forest and wetlands along the edge of the lagoon. The 1.8-km-long Yengele trail on the north bank takes hikers through one of the largest dune forests on the KwaZulu-Natal south coast, and is good for spotting wetland and woodland birds, including a resident pair of breeding fish eagles. The 1.2-km-long Ipithi Trail on the south bank holds the promise of sighting the shy blue, red and grey duiker, as well as the resident troop of vervet monkeys. There are observation platforms on each trail and picnic and *braai* spots along the Mpenjati River and around the lagoon.

Port Edward

This small sleepy resort, roughly 21 km from Southbroom and 163 km south of Durban, has a large palm-fringed beach backing onto tropical forest. The village was laid out in 1925 and named in honour of the Prince of Wales, who later became King Edward VIII. Its prominent landmark is the 24-m-tall Port Edward Lighthouse built in 1968.

Umtamvuna Nature Reserve

① *8 km north of Port Edward towards Izingolweni, T039-313 2383, www.kzn wildlife.com, Oct-Mar 0600-1800, Apr-Sep 0700-1700, R20, children (under 12) R10*. Covering 3257 ha and a 28-km-long section of the Umtamvuna River and surrounding cliffs and plateaus, this is the southernmost and one of the lesser-visited reserves in KwaZulu-Natal. But it has some of the finest hiking in the region and there are a number of trails varying from one to three hours to an all-day hike. The sheer walls of lichen-covered rock, dropping down into thick rainforest at the bottom of the gorge, are the centre of this dramatic landscape. The reserve is known for its displays of wild flowers in the spring and its colony of Cape vultures, and it's usually fairly easy to spot bushbuck, blue and common duiker, and the ubiquitous chacma baboons.

Towards the Wild Coast
Just south of Port Edward, the R61 crosses the Umtamvuna Bridge over the river into the Wild Coast in the Eastern Cape. Built in 1966, this is the largest steel suspension bridge in South Africa and has a span of 206 m and the highest point of the arch is 35 m. Maintenance is a real challenge on this bridge, as the steel is exposed to the salty sea air. The Wild Coast stretches roughly 280 km from the Umtamvuna River to East London and is so named because of its rugged, virtually deserted coastline. Instead of full-blown resorts, there are small seaside villages backed by protected stretches of verdant coastal forest and windswept dunes, with a number of caves, beaches, cliffs and shipwrecks to explore. This used to be the Transkei, the former homeland for the Xhosa people during Apartheid. The area is far less developed than much of South Africa's coast, and most of the people live in rural settlements and work on the land. The contrast between KwaZulu-Natal and the former homeland could hardly be more marked – crossing the bridge over the old border is like crossing into another, much poorer country. Road conditions deteriorate immediately and this is not a good route for access to the Wild Coast. The alternative route is along the N2 from Port Shepstone via Kokstad and Mthatha to Port St Johns on a tarred road.

◉ KwaZulu-Natal South Coast listings

For hotel and restaurant price codes and other relevant information, see pages 12-16.

◉ Where to stay

The south coast has been a popular holiday destination for decades and, as such, features some older and somewhat soulless self-catering blocks of apartments or faded hotels. If you are looking for upmarket quality accommodation, then the north coast has a better choice.

Amanzimtoti to Scottburgh
p61, map p62
$$$ Selborne Hotel & Spa, Old Main Rd, Pennington, off the N2 14 km south of Scottburgh, T039-688 1800, www.selborne.com. Set on an attractive golf estate surrounded by tropical palms, 4-star hotel with 49 rooms and colonial decor, DSTV, a/c, garden or golf course views, a short walk to the beach, restaurant, pool, spa, golf and supervised children's activities.

$$$ The View, 9 Hillside Rd, Amanzimtoti, T039-903 1556, www. theviewguestlodge.com. Smart small modern hotel high on the hillside with sweeping ocean views, 20 sea-facing individually decorated rooms with patios, 2 pools, spa, excellent terrace restaurant with an Italian-inspired menu, relaxing tropical gardens.

$$$-$$ Pumula Beach Hotel, 67 Steve Pitts Rd, Umzumbe, T039-684 6717, www.pumulabeachhotel.com. Surrounded by indigenous coastal vegetation with direct access to the Blue Flag beach, 63 neat a/c rooms, many for families, good range of holiday facilities including pool, gym, beach shop, pub and restaurant and you can rent mountain bikes.

$$ Blue Marlin Hotel, 180 Scott St, Scottburgh, T039-978 3361, www. blue marlin.co.za. Large resort on a hill overlooking the beach in spacious gardens with large pool, 120 functional rooms with TV, the rates inclusive of buffet meals are very good value, games room, 2 bars, tour desk for arranging activities.

$$ Cutty Sark, beachfront, Scottburgh, T039-976 1230, www.cuttysark.co.za. Slightly dated but good-value family hotel in a lovely beachside location, 55 rooms with TV, 2 restaurants, bar, swimming pool, tennis and squash courts, gym, in 14 ha of well-kept tropical gardens. Horse riding and diving can be arranged.

$ Mantis & Moon, Station Rd, Umzumbe, T039-684 6256, www.mantisandmoon.net. Rustic backpackers set in lush tropical forest, with dorms and doubles in wooden cabins or treehouses, and camping spots dotted between wild banana trees. Pool table, candlelit bar, home-cooked food, free use of surf boards, outdoor hot tub, rooftop deck. Have their own vehicle for local tours including to Oribi Gorge.

$ Nyengelezi Hutted Camp, Vernon Crookes Nature Reserve (page 64), on the R612, 12 km inland from the N2 between Scottburgh and Pennington, T039-974 2222, www. kznwildlife.com. Tucked away in the forest here are 5 2-bed huts sharing communal bathrooms and a kitchen with crockery, cutlery, cooking utensils, fridges and stove, plus a delightful self-contained 7-bed tree house built around an impressive wild fig. Peaceful spot full of butterflies and birds.

Camping

Scottburgh Caravan Park, beachfront, Scottburgh, T039-976 0291, www. scott burghcaravanpark.co.za. Giant camping and caravan park with good facilities including a swimming pool, laundry, playground with trampolines, shop and TV room, 265 sites stretching along 1 km of beach, designed to cater for families during school holidays when it gets very busy, but a great setting out of season.

Port Shepstone *p64, map p62*
$$ Kapenta Bay, 11-12 Princess Elizabeth Dr, T039-682 5528, www. kapentabay.co.za. Bland modern block with 50 typical holiday 3-bed self-catering units, but good value for families or groups (rates are for up to 6 people) and right on the beach, large

swimming pool, buffet restaurant, can organize diving and fishing.

Oribi Gorge Nature Reserve
p65, map p62

$$$$ The Gorge Private Game Lodge & Spa, on the D251 22 km from the N2 towards Kokstad, T039-687 0378, www.thegorge.co.za. Luxury lodge built on sandstone cliffs overlooking the Oribi Gorge, with 5 very large uniquely designed stone-clad chalets raised 3-5 m off the ground on columns, with outdoor showers, DSTV and contemporary decor. Spa and pool with stunning views into the gorge, excellent food. Game-drives and hikes can be arranged to see the plains game on the property.

$$$-$$ Oribi Gorge Hotel, on the D251, 11 km from the N2 towards Kokstad, T039-687 0253, www.oribigorge.co.za. Small family hotel with 18 comfortable rooms with DSTV, restaurant, country pub, curio shop, and pool, set in a 1870s colonial building encircled by a veranda. The gorge can be seen from viewpoints accessed by dirt roads on farmland adjoining the hotel, which is only 17 km from the hutted camp below. The **Wild Fig Café**, is an ideal stop for lunch, and a number of activities can be arranged from here with **Wild 5 Adventures** (see page 73).

$$-$ Lake Eland Game Reserve (see page 65), on the D251 28 km from the N2 towards Kokstad, T039-687 0395, www.lakeeland.co.za. There's a variety of simple accommodation here including

attractive 2-person self-catering wooden cabins with patios on stilts over the water's edge, a 6-bed self-catering house, and neat B&B rooms in a chalet near the reserve entrance, plus a scenic lakeside campsite with electricity. There's also a swimming pool, and fishing, mountain biking and horseriding can be arranged.

$ Oribi Gorge Camp, T039-679 1644, reservations through **Ezemvelo KZN Wildlife**, T033-845 1000, www.kznwildlife.com. Lovely setting with impressive views of the Oribi Gorge, 6 2-bed self-catering chalets with fridge and equipment and sharing a communal kitchen, plus 2 cottages sleeping 6-7 and 5 rustic campsites, and a swimming pool with sundeck. The camp gate is open 24 hrs to allow guests to eat out at restaurants on the coast or at the Oribi Gorge Hotel.

Shelly beach and around
p66, map p62

$$ Ayton Manor, 2.5 km inland from Shelly Beach, after driving under the N2, take the 1st right, T039-685 0777, www.aytonmanor.co.za. B&B and self-catering guest lodge with 6 rooms and 2 family suites set in a fine country house on a sugar estate, bar, pool, dinners on request, children will like the working farmyard and fishing on the farm dam can be arranged.

Margate *p66, map p62*
$$ Ingwe Manor Guesthouse & Spa, 38 Hibiscus Rd, T039-317 1914, www.ingwemanor.com. Located a couple blocks back from the beach on a hill with broad ocean views from

the house's wraparound balconies, 8 smart and spacious rooms, bar and lounge, swimming pool, and a long menu of spa treatments.

$$ Margate Hotel, 71 Marine Dr, T039-312 1410, www.margatehotel. co.za. Set in mature gardens overlooking the beach, 69 a/c standard rooms with TV, **Keg** pub and restaurant, pool, tennis, comfortable but run-of-the-mill family 3-star hotel but good discounts in low season.

$$-$ Dumela Holiday Resort, St Patrick's Rd, T039-317 3301, www. dumelamargate.co.za. Simple self-catering 2-bed cabanas overlooking Margate's Blue Flag beach, with balcony with *braai* and DSTV, café and takeaway, pool, thatched bar. Good value for groups/families up to 6, especially in low season.

Southbroom *p67, map p62*
$$$-$$ Mondazur Hotel, Marina Beach, signposted off the R61, T039-313 0011, www.mondazur.com. On the San Lameer Golf Estate, 40 modern rooms with a/c, DSTV and Wi-Fi, some with balconies and sea views, restaurant and bar, large pool, squash and tennis courts, 18-hole golf course (page 74), lovely sandy beach with tidal pool, nature walks through the dune belt and coastal forest.

$$ Sunbirds, 54 Outlook Rd, T039-316 8202, www.sunbirds.co.za. An award-winning B&B and an alternative to the large resorts with friendly owners and a 3-min stroll from the beach, 4 modern rooms with private entrances, DSTV and DVD, bar, large

12-m heated pool, gourmet breakfast, no children under 15.

Port Edward *p67, map p62*
$$$-$$ Estuary Country Hotel, Rennies Beach, 1 km north of Port Edward on the R61, T039-313 2675, www.estuaryhotel.co.za. A Cape Dutch-styled hotel with 44 comfortable a/c rooms with DSTV, most with balcony overlooking the estuary, bar, pool, spa, close to a safe swimming beach. The **Fish Eagle Restaurant** is open to non-residents and has a varied South African and Continental menu.

$ Ku-Boboyi River Lodge and Backpackers, Leisure Beach, 4 km north of Port Edward on the R61, T039-319 1371, www.kuboboyi.co.za. A bright hilltop budget lodge with good views over the ocean and beach, with singles, doubles, triples, quads with en suites or shared bathrooms, decorated in an African theme, plus plenty of space for camping in the tropical garden. Kitchen, pool, sunny veranda, meals available.

❷ Restaurants

Good restaurants on the south coast are mostly limited to the hotels and resorts, although most of the towns have the usual takeaways and family restaurants such as **Spur**.

Amanzimtoti to Scottburgh *p61, map p62*
$$-$ Dodo Bistro, 18 Cordiner St, Scottburgh, T039-978 3550. Mon-Sat 1200-1400, 1830-2100. Housed in a

cottage on a side street, this is owned by a family from Mauritious and offers tasty and inexpensive Mauritian/creole curries and prawns alongside seaside favourites like beer-battered hake and chips. Also famous in town for its crème brûlée.

Port Shepstone *p64, map p62*
$ Fish on the River, Spiller's Wharf, Old Sugar Mill Rd, Port Shepstone, T039-682 3814. Mon-Tue and Sun 1000-1700, Wed-Sat 1000-2000. Simple rustic tin shack selling fresh fish and seafood, with a deck overlooking the Mzimkhulu River estuary for delicious fresh fish and calamari and chips and perhaps a Greek salad. The wharf complex here has also got a clutch of decor and collectible shops.

Margate and Ramsgate
p66, map p62
$$ The Bistro, 2450 Marine Dr, Ramsgate, T039-314 4128. Open 1200-1500, 1800-2200, closed Sun lunch out of season. Friendly restaurant on 2 levels serving traditional bistro cuisine, such as rack of lamb, roast duck, grilled seafood and curries, comprehensive wine list and comfortable bar.
$$ La Capannina, 206 Marine Dr, Ramsgate, T039-317 1078, www. lacapannina.co.za. Wed-Sat 1200-1400, Tue-Sat 1800-2100. Authentic family-run Italian with a bustling trattoria-style atmosphere, a full range of pizza and pasta, and known for its tasty traditional soups, roast lamb and fried prawns.

$$-$ Larry's, corner of O'Connor Dr and Panorama, beachfront, Margate, T039-317 2277, www.larrys.co.za. Daily 1000-2200. Family restaurant offering breakfasts, pizza and pastas, roast dinners at Sun lunch, and specials like chicken and prawn curry or liver and onions, with seating on a busy terrace overlooking the beach.

Cafés
The Waffle House, Marine Dr, Ramsgate, T039-314 9424, www.waffle house.co.za. Daily 0800-1700. A south coast landmark that first opened in 1957, delicious sweet and savoury authentic Belgium waffles on a terrace next to Ramsgate Lagoon, breakfast waffles until 1100, beer and wine by the glass or good milkshakes.

O Shopping

Amanzimtoti to Scottburgh
p61, map p62
Galleria Mall, on the N2, Amanzimtoti, T031-904 2233, www.galleria.co.za. Mon-Sat 0900-1900, Sun 0900-1700. Large mall serving Durban's southern suburbs, with 198 shops, restaurants, and numerous entertainment facilities including an 11-screen **Nu Metro** cinema, 10-pin bowling, and an ice-skating rink (T031-904 1156, www. skategalleria.co.za; Mon-Fri 1230-2100, Sat-Sun 1000-2230).

Hibiscus Coast *p64, map p62*
Southcoast Mall, Old Main Rd (R61), Shelly Beach, T039-315 7515, www. southcoastmall.co.za. Mon-Fri 0830-1730, Sat 0800-1700, Sun 0830-1530.

Has the usual chain stores, a **Checkers** supermarket (open daily 0800-2000), and restaurants.

◐ What to do

Amanzimtoti to Scottburgh
p61, map p62
Diving
Aliwal Dive Centre, 2 Moodie St, Umkosaas, T039-973 2233, www. aliwalshoal.co.za. PADI 5-star dive centre, courses, snorkelling and whale- and dolphin-watching trips. Good-value accommodation for divers above dive centre with dorms, en suite doubles and meals.

Golf
Scottburgh Golf Club, corner Taylor and Williamson streets, T039-976 0041, www.scottburghgolf.co.za. Attractive 18-hole course set in coastal forest with ocean views. Well used to visitors with midweek special rates on green fees.

Oribi Gorge Nature Reserve
p65, map p62
Wild 5 Adventures, at the **Oribi Gorge Hotel** (see page 70), T0825-667424, www.wild5adventures.co.za. Daily 0830-1700. Offers **whitewater rafting** (0800-1400; R550) in conventional rafts or large inner tubes on the Umzimkulu River, and **abseiling** (R350) from Lehr's Waterfall, the last 66 m being a free abseil during which you can feel the spray of the falls on your back. Also has the **Wild Swing** (R490), a 75-m freefall and a 100-m outward swing over the falls, and the **Wild Slide** (R220), a

120-m steel cable slide over Lehr's. You can easily spend a day here and have lunch at the hotel; with the exception of rafting which requires 1 day's notice, no need to book.

Shelley beach and around
p66, map p62
Aqua Planet, corner of Marine Dr and Kings Rd, T039-315 7524, www. aquaplanet.co.za. Organizes dives to Protea Banks, which is the habitat of several species of shark – it's not uncommon to see 3-4 species in a single dive. Humpback whales may also be spotted Jun-Nov. A PADI centre, they offer a number of courses.

Margate *p66, map p62*
As the main tourist centre on the south coast, Margate is a good place to organize activities. Fishing is allowed off the pier and off Margate Rocks and there are plenty of tackle shops in town. Designated surfing and boogie-boarding areas are on Main Beach and at Lucien Point. Boards can be hired from shops in town. Main Beach is shark-protected and therefore the safest and most popular for swimming.

Diving
2nd Breath Scuba Diving, corner Bank and Berea sts, T039-317 2326, www.2ndbreath.co.za. Dives at the Protea Banks (see above), and a PADI centre for courses.

Golf
Margate Country Club, Wingate Av, T039-312 0571, www.margatecountry club.co.za. Pleasant 18-hole golf

course surrounded by palms and banana trees, visitors welcome.

Southbroom *p67, map p62*
San Lameer Country Club, Marina Beach, signposted off the R61, T039-313 514, www.sanlameer.co.za. Attractive 18-hole championship course sculptured around an indigenous wetland forest that is home to 195 species of birds and small antelope such as impala and bushbuck. There's a clubhouse as well as **The Halfway House** restaurant on the 9th hole. Visitors welcome or stay at the **Mondazur Hotel** (see Where to stay, page 71).

⊖ Transport

South of Durban *p61, map p62*
Baz Bus, reservations Cape Town T021-422 5202, www.bazbus.com, has a daily service between **Durban** and **Port Elizabeth** in 1 day before continuing on to **Cape Town** the next day, dropping off at the backpackers' hotels along the south coast. **Greyhound**, www.greyhound.co.za; and **Translux**, www.translux.co.za, tickets can be booked through **Computicket**, T011-340 8000, www.computicket.com, or at their kiosks at the larger shopping malls, as well as in **Checkers** and **Shoprite** supermarkets. Both run between **Durban** and **Cape Town** and stop in resorts along the N2. **Margate Mini Coach**, reservations T039-312 1406, www.margatecoach.co.za, runs between **King Shaka International Airport** and the **Wild Coast Sun** in the Eastern Cape. There are at least 3 daily services in each direction via **Durban**, **Amanzimtoti**, **Scottburgh**, **Hibberdene**, **Port Shepstone**, **Margate** and **Port Edward**. For more information, see Planning your trip, page 9.

North Coast and Zululand

The Dolphin Coast between the Tongaat and Umhali rivers is only 30 minutes away from Durban proper and features a clutch of attractive resorts popular with the well-heeled. The coastal part of Zululand extends from the northern bank of the Tugela River up to Hluhluwe, and this region was the homeland of the early 19th-century Zulu King Shaka, and there are dozens of sites linked to this great warrior and his legacy. Today the Zulu number over nine million, with the majority living in KwaZulu-Natal, and their language, isiZulu, is the most widely spoken in South Africa. For the visitor, Zululand offers a chance to experience one of the more traditional areas of South Africa, as well as long, unspoilt beaches and excellent game reserves. Hluhluwe-Imfolozi is Big Five territory, while iSimangaliso Wetland Park, a World Heritage Site, is characterized by untouched coastal lakes and dunes, subtropical forests, and wetlands teeming with birdlife.

Dolphin Coast → *For listings, see pages 93-103.*

The area is known as the Dolphin Coast, thanks to the bottlenose dolphins that frolic in the waves year-round. It is also known as the Sugar Coast, due to the rolling sugar plantations backing the sea. Like the coastline to the south of Durban it is possible to miss many of the sights and small coastal settlements if you remain on the N2 highway. The old coast road, however, runs parallel to the sea passing through the beach resorts of Umhloti, Ballito and Salt Rock. These are less developed and more upmarket than those found on the south coast with crowds thinning out the further you get from Durban. The beaches are beautifully wild stretches of soft sand, pounded by impressive waves, and they have lifeguards and are shark protected. Away from the water, locals flock to the impressive golf courses, although quieter choices are the numerous nature reserves.

Dolphin Coast

To St Lucia & Hluhluwe
Richards Bay Airport — Richards Bay
Enselini Nature Reserve
Empangeni — R34
R34
N2
Umhlatuzi Lagoon
Umlalazi — Mtunzini
Umlalazi Nature Reserve
Umlalazi
To Eshowe, Melmoth & Thula Thula Private Game Reserve
R66
KwaGingindlovu
2 Amatigulu Nature Reserve
7
aMatikulu
R102
Mandini
To Eshowe, Melmoth, Shakaland & Ithala Game Reserve
6
Tugela Mouth
Harold Johnson Nature Reserve
Thukela River
Fort Pearson
Darnall
Shaka's Memorial — Zinkwazi Beach
R74
KwaDukuza-Stanger
Blythdale Beach
To Greytown & Ladysmith
Sheffield Beach
Salt Rock **5**
Shaka's Rock
R102
i **1** Ballito **1**
R614
3 **2**
Tongaat — Zimbali Country Club
King Shaka International Airport
To Pietermaritzburg
Umhloti
Verulam
Umhloti Beach
Umhlanga Lagoon Nature Reserve
N2
Umhlanga
KZN Sharks Board — Umhlanga Lighthouse
To Pietermaritzburg
Durban
N3
To South Coast

N

10 km
10 miles

Where to stay
Boathouse 1
Dolphin Holiday Resort 2
Fairmont Zimbali Lodge 3
The Ridge Guesthouse 4
Salt Rock 5
Simunye Zulu Lodge 6

Zangozolo Tented Camp 7

Restaurants
The Galley Beach Bar & Grill & Al Pescatore 1
The Prawn Shak 2

Ballito

The N2 heads north past King Shaka International Airport, before reaching Ballito, 29 km from Umhlanga. Ballito was established as a holiday resort in the 1950s and was originally the beach on part of a sugarcane farm. Ballito has expanded significantly in recent times and today has hotels and self-catering apartments nestled in lush vegetation stretching up the hillside, three shopping malls, and a promenade of about 2.5-km long allowing easy access to the long beach. At the entrance of town is the **Dolphin Coast Publicity Association** ① *Ballito Dr, 032-946 1997, www. thedolphincoast.co.za, Mon-Fri 0830-1700, Sat 0900-1300, Sun in season,* which can help book accommodation.

Salt Rock and Shaka Rock

Just 6 km north of Ballito, and joined by a ribbon of development, the resort of **Salt Rock** is named after a rock where the Zulus used to collect salt. There's a large tidal pool here, and offshore a couple of interesting reefs for diving. Nearby **Shaka's Rock** is named after the lookout cliff from which Shaka is said to have thrown his enemies to their foamy deaths. Many of his own warriors were also required to prove their courage by leaping from the rock into the sea. There is good snorkelling at Sheffield Beach, but neither resort holds much appeal other than for those after a sand and sea holiday.

Tongaat, Verulam and KwaDukuza-Stanger

The inland towns of Verulam, Tongaat and KwaDukuza-Stanger are tucked between vast rolling sugar plantations and collectively form the heart of KwaZulu-Natal's sugar processing industry. They have large Indian populations – descendants of indentured labourers who were brought here from India in the 1860s – which give the region a distinct Indian atmosphere. The Hindu temples and Indian markets are interesting, but these industrial towns have few attractions for tourists, and while accommodation is available, the coastal beach resorts are more pleasant places to stay.

In **Tongaat**, the **Juggernath Puri Temple** is 23 m high and can be seen from miles away. There are no windows in the tower, but inside, as the eye adjusts to the darkness, the Vishnu statue gradually becomes visible. **Shri Gopalal Temple** is just outside of Verulam on the road to the Packo food factory. The temple was opened by Gandhi in 1912, and catered for wealthier and more educated Gujurati immigrants. **Subramanyar Alayam Temple** is set in a beautiful tropical garden just north of town as you reach the railway bridge. A good time to experience the atmosphere of the temple is at weekends when many weddings are held. It is customary to remove your shoes before entering the temple buildings.

KwaDukuza-Stanger is a busy commercial centre surrounded by sugar plantations. It has recently had a name change from just Stanger to include KwaDukuza; the original settlement here founded by Shaka as his capital. At its height there were up to 2000 beehive huts surrounding Shaka's royal kraal. It was here that his half-brothers Dingaan and Umhlangana murdered Shaka in 1828 and a monument was erected in his memory in 1932 on the site of his grave. Adjacent to the monument is the rock on which Shaka was alleged to be sitting on at the time of his assassination. These now stand in the centre of town on King Shaka Street.

Harold Johnson Nature Reserve

① *T031-486 1574, www.kznwildlife.com, 0600-1800, office 0700-1600, R20, children (under 12) R10.*
Just over 20 km north of KwaDukuza-Stanger on the N2, a signposted dirt track leads through sugar plantations up to the entrance of this 100-ha reserve, where there is a parking area and a picnic site. Wildlife includes zebra, red and grey duiker, bushbuck, impala, vervet monkey and over 110 species of butterfly, which can be sought out on 7 km of walking trails. The **Muthi Trail** gives an interesting insight into the medicinal uses of various traditional plants

used by the Zulu people; a booklet can be bought at the entrance. There's a peaceful campsite here (see page 94).

Zululand → *For listings, see page 93-103.*

The route into Zululand on the N2 crosses the Thukela River and the wide sweep of coastal sugarcane plantations almost immediately makes way for the rolling hills and green folds of grassland and forested valleys typical of the Zululand landscape. Modern commercial agriculture is replaced by traditional African farmsteads, dotted with traditional thatched houses, small patches of crops and grazing cattle. The Hluhluwe-Imfolozi Game Reserve and the iSimangaliso Wetland Park are both world-class conservation areas, but there are also private reserves in the region offering luxury accommodation, while scuba-diving and deep-sea fishing are available in the coastal resorts. As you travel north, you will notice the change of climate as it becomes more subtropical; it is hot and humid from December to March and warm and dry from April to November.

Arriving in Zululand

North from KwaDukuza-Stanger, the N2 first passes the turning to KwaGingindlovu and then continues up the coast to Mtunzini, Empangeni and then the turn-offs to Richards Bay, Hluhluwe-Imfolozi, and St Lucia. From KwaGingindlovu (7 km inland from the N2) the R66 goes inland to Eshowe (23 km) and Melmoth (70 km). From Melmoth the R68 goes 164 km through the interior of the province to Dundee in the battlefields (see page 135). Greyhound is the only long distance bus that has a service up the north coast. From Durban it goes via Ballito, KwaDukuza-Stanger, and Empangeni and Richards Bay, and then turns inland via Melmoth and Vryheid to re-join the N2 again at Piet Retief and continues to Johannesburg and Pretoria.

KwaGingindlovu and around

The Zulu name of KwaGingindlovu is said to mean 'place of the big elephant' or, more possibly, 'swallower of the elephant'. It was originally a military kraal of Zulu King Cetshwayo during the Battle of Gingindlovu in the Anglo-Zulu War. During this battle in 1879, Cetshwayo's 10,000-strong army was defeated and his kraal destroyed by the British. It was crucial for the British to win to relieve the small town of Eshowe close to the Zulu capital Ulundi and guarantee victory against the Zulu Kingdom. Today it is a small commercial centre surrounded by farmland and sugarcane plantations.

On the coast 15 km south of KwaGingindlovu and 3 km off the N2 is the **Amatigulu Nature Reserve** ① *T032-453 0155, www.kznwildlife.com, gates*

☐ Maputaland & Zululand game reserves

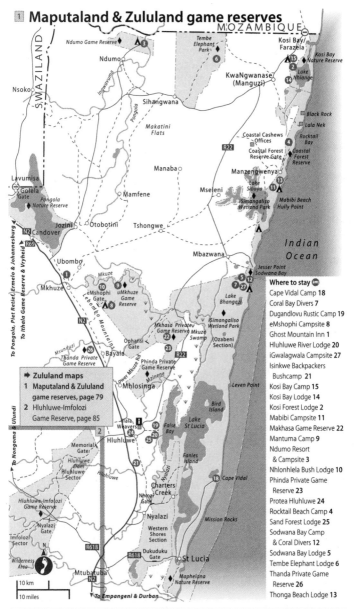

Where to stay

Cape Vidal Camp 18
Coral Bay Divers 7
Dugandlovu Rustic Camp 19
eMshophi Campsite 8
Ghost Mountain Inn 1
Hluhluwe River Lodge 20
iGwalagwala Campsite 27
Isinkwe Backpackers
  Bushcamp 21
Kosi Bay Camp 15
Kosi Bay Lodge 14
Kosi Forest Lodge 2
Mabibi Campsite 11
Makhasa Game Reserve 22
Mantuma Camp 9
Ndumo Resort
  & Campsite 3
Nhlonhlela Bush Lodge 10
Phinda Private Game
  Reserve 23
Protea Hluhluwe 24
Rocktail Beach Camp 4
Sand Forest Lodge 25
Sodwana Bay Camp
  & Coral Divers 12
Sodwana Bay Lodge 5
Tembe Elephant Lodge 6
Thanda Private Game
  Reserve 26
Thonga Beach Lodge 13

➡ Zululand maps
1 Maputaland & Zululand
  game reserves, page 79
2 Hluhluwe-Imfolozi
  Game Reserve, page 85

0530-2100, office 0800-1600, R20, children (under 12) R10. The reserve is 100 km from Durban and covers approximately 2000 ha of forested dunes overlooking the ocean. Unlike other small reserves in this area, Amatigulu does have some large mammals including giraffe, zebra, kudu and waterbuck, and is one of the few places to see these animals grazing close to the sea. The Nyoni and Amatigulu rivers attract the elusive African finfoot and other unusual waterbirds, and there is a whale-watching tower built on the dunes.

Eshowe and inland

Eshowe is a town 23 km inland from KwaGingindlovu and is named after the sound of a breeze passing through bushes. Situated on a hill, it has pleasant views over Dlinza forest and is an administrative centre for the surrounding sugarcane-growing region. The historical origins of Eshowe are based around a Zulu kraal called Eziqwaqweni. In 1860 the Norwegian missionary, Reverend Oftebro, was allowed to open a mission station here which was occupied by the British in 1879 while they planned an attack on Ulundi. The Zulus briefly gained the upper hand here when they laid siege to the garrison for 10 weeks. Eshowe was relieved by Lord Chelmsford in April 1879, but not before the Zulus had managed to burn the mission station down.

Dlinza Forest ① *Kangella Rd near Eshowe High School, T035-474 4029, www.kznwildlife.com, Sep-Apr 0600-1800, May-Aug 0800-1700, free*, is a 250-ha area of dense hardwood forest where Shaka supposedly hid his wives and children during attacks. The orchids, wild plum and milkwood trees, and knarled vines in turn attract a number of birds and butterflies, and 65 species of bird have been recorded in the forest, including the endangered spotted thrush and Delegorgue's pigeon. There are three short walking trails and the Royal Drive is a gravel road for cars that was specially cleared for the British royal family's visit to Eshowe in 1947. Additionally, a 125-m aerial timber boardwalk takes you through the treeline to a 20-m viewing platform that overlooks the canopy of the forest.

On Fort Nongqai Road is the **Fort Nongqayi Museum Village** ① *T035-474 2281, www.eshowemuseums.org.za, daily 0900-1600, R20, children (under 16) R10, tearoom.* With its high towers on each corner, the gleaming white Fort Nongqai was built in 1883 and served as a residence for the Natal Native Police who acted as bodyguards for Sir Melmoth Osborn, the Resident for British Zululand. This interesting cluster of attractions includes the Zululand Historical Museum (in the fort itself), the Vukani Zulu Cultural Museum, plus an art gallery, arboretum, restaurant and curio shop. Inside the Zululand Historical Museum there are displays on John Dunn and his 49 wives and on the Bambata rebellion, as well as a number of Zulu items. John Dunn was the first European settler in what is now KwaZulu-Natal. He became an honorary chief and was granted land by the Zulus, ruled at the time by King Cetshwayo.

His 49 wives gave him 117 children. Given this statistic, not surprisingly the surname Dunn is still very common in this region. **The Vukani Zulu Cultural Museum** has quite probably the largest display of Zulu art in existence with some 3000 to 4000 pieces on display. While there are antique items on display, some of the exhibits are by award-winning contemporary artists and include carvings, pottery, colourful basketry and the famous Zulu beadwork.

North of Eshowe

From Eshowe the R66 heads north through the Nkwalini Valley to Melmoth (52 km). On the way **Shakaland** ① *signposted off the R66, 14 km north of Eshowe, T035-460 0912, www.shakaland.com, 3-hr tours at 1100 and 1200, R420, children (6-11) R210, under 6s free*, is a very popular Zulu theme park with daily cultural shows, which include Zulu dancing and tours of a traditional village where tribal customs such as spearmaking, the beer ceremony and Sangoma rituals are explained. This is a reconstruction of a 19th-century village but it doesn't give a very authentic insight into how the Zulu people live today. However, the food isn't bad and a lunch in the **Shisa Nyama Restaurant** is included. You can also stay overnight here (see page 94).

The **Simunye Zulu Lodge** is about 45 km north of Eshowe on the way to Melmoth; look out for a left turning, marked with a wagon wheel and a large 'S', on to the D256 about 25 km north of Eshowe on the R66. This lodge hosted by the Biyela clan, offers a marginally more authentic introduction to Zulu culture. Follow the gravel road for 10 km until you reach an old trading store. This is the assembly point and car park for guests who want to be taken down to the lodge on horseback or ox wagon, or alternatively you can drive the last 3 km. Only overnight guests can visit (see page 94).

Melmoth itself, although a tiny town, lies on the Piet Retief Road on the route from Johannesburg and Pretoria and sees a fair amount of traffic heading to the north coast during holiday periods. As such there are petrol stations with fast-food restaurants on the main road. From Melmoth, the R68 heads northwest through the picturesque interior of central Zululand to Dundee in the battlefields region (see page 135), while the R64 heads northeast to Vryheid and the Ithala Game Reserve.

Ithala Game Reserve → *For listings, see pages 93-103.*

① *74 km east of Pongola, T034-983 2540, www.kznwildlife.com, gate Oct-Mar 0500-1900, Apr-Sep 0600-1800, the office is at Ntshondwe Resort, 0700-1930, R40, children (under 12) R20, car 40.*

Ithala Game Reserve lies in the extreme north of KwaZulu-Natal and is close to both the borders with Swaziland and Mpumalanga province. It was established in 1972 after the Natal Parks Board bought up farmland that had seriously deteriorated and where very little wildlife remained. Since then it has been restocked with numerous large species of game and has reverted back to its natural state. The reserve is also historically important having been occupied during major events such as the reign of Shaka, the arrival of the Voortrekkers in Natal, and the Anglo-Zulu and Anglo-Boer wars. Ithala's terrain is extremely rugged, rising from 400 m above sea level in the north to 1400 m above sea level in the south near Louwsburg. Several rivers rise in or near the reserve, winding down steep river valleys to the Pongola River which forms the northern boundary.

Arriving in Ithala Game Reserve
The park entrance is near the village of Louwsburg on the R69. Given its location in the north of the province, Ithala is both isolated and far from other popular destinations, but equally approachable from a number of directions. The shortest route from Durban (385 km) is via Eshowe, Melmoth and Vryheid on the N2, R66, R34 and then the R69. Other routes include from Ladysmith and Dundee in the battlefields via Vryheid, and from Maputaland via Pongola on the N2.

The reserve office and main facilities are at Ntshondwe Resort, which is 8 km from the gate. Petrol and diesel is available and the shop sells curios, books and maps, charcoal and firewood, ice, drinks and basic provisions. The nearest supermarkets are in Vryheid, 69 km away. The restaurant complex at Ntshondwe is situated beside a waterhole where a variety of animals come to drink and also has a takeaway kiosk and coffee shop. Morning or afternoon game-drives, R190, children (3-12) R95, no under threes, and game walks with an armed ranger, R170 per person, no children under 12, can be booked at the office and must be arranged on arrival.

Wildlife
Although game-viewing here pales compared to Hluhluwe-Imfolozi, the steep terrain has created several different ecosystems from deep narrow valleys and boulder outcrops to cliff faces, with an interesting diversity of wildlife. There is a network of dirt roads looping around the reserve and animals commonly seen include eland, kudu, blue wildebeest, zebra and, notably giraffe, which are so numerous that they have been selected as Ithala's logo. The following animals are also present but are rarely seen: cheetah, white rhino, elephant, tsessebe, klipspringer, leopard, nyala and black rhino.

Some 320 species of bird have been recorded here, including black eagle, bathawk, bald ibis, martial eagle and brown-necked parrot. Some interesting plants to look out for in season are the flowering aloes trees, unmistakable in June and July when they come into bloom. Their large orange flowers are an important source of nectar at this time of year and they attract birds and insects.

Empangeni and around → *For listings, see pages 93-103.*

Back on the coast, Empangeni is on the N2, 170 km north of Durban, and is named after the Zulu word of *pangaed* meaning grabbed – due to many people being taken by crocs on the banks of the Mpangeni River, on which the town is situated. King Shaka grew up in this area before the Norwegian Missionary Society mission station opened in 1851.

The town has developed into a busy industrial centre and has been pulping wood since the first eucalyptus plantations were established in 1905. While many visitors pass through, there is nothing to merit a stop and the N2 allows a quick escape north to St Lucia (82 km) and Hluhluwe-Imfolozi (80 km).

Thula Thula Private Game Reserve
ⓘ *T0822-599732, www.thulathula.com, breakfast and 2-hr game-drive 0900-1200, R800; lunch and 2-hr game-drive 1000-1430, R850; 2-hr game-drive and dinner 1600-2100, R900; half price for children (under 8), pre-booking essential.*
West of Empangeni, this reserve makes an excellent stopover for those who have missed the larger parks further north. To get there, take the R34 for 8 km before turning right for 10 km to Heatonville; from here, Thula Thula is 11 km on a well-signposted gravel road. This 4500-ha reserve is in the Enselini Valley and was originally part of King Shaka's hunting ground – although by contrast, Thula Thula means peace and tranquillity in isiZulu. It was converted from farmland in 1964, and the present owners offer exclusive accommodation (see page 95), game-drives and bush walks through rolling, acacia-covered thornveld, and there is a comprehensive day visitor's programme. Some of the larger mammals you can expect to see are white rhino, elephant, cheetah, giraffe, kudu, nyala and other antelopes.

Richards Bay
The R34 goes east from Empangeni and, crossing the N2, ends at Richards Bay (18 km). Although it began as a makeshift harbour established by Commodore of the Cape, Sir Fredrick Richards, in 1879 during the Anglo-Boer War, today it's a modern rash of a town, focused entirely on its enormous industrial port. This exports mineral ores and coal, and massive tankers arrive here to discharge oil for Gauteng through the oil pipeline; it is the first port of call for ships coming from Asia and Suez. Characterized by a series of vast industrial plants and featureless highways (albeit skirting around a pretty series of canals and a lagoon), the only reason for coming here is to use the small airport (see page 103), and then hire a car to speed up the coast to the parks.

Hluhluwe-Imfolozi Game Reserve → *For listings, see pages 93-103.*

ⓘ *Gates Oct-Mar 0500-1900, Apr-Sep 0600-1800, Imfolozi office T035-550 8476, 0700-1800, Hluhluwe office T035-562 0848 0700-1930, www.kznwildlife.com, R130, children (under 2) R65, per 24-hrs.*

This is one of Africa's oldest game reserves and the best place in KwaZulu-Natal to see the Big Five – lion, elephant, buffalo, leopard and rhino. What were traditionally two reserves, in 1989 Hluhluwe-Imfolozi was proclaimed as one joint reserve, along with the corridor between the two, and today covers some 96,000 ha. Hluhluwe is named after the *umHluhluwe* or 'thorny rope', a climber which is found in the forests of this area. Their aerial roots hanging from the sycamore figs where the Black Imfolozi and the White Imfolozi rivers meet give the area its name. Imfolozi is named after *uMfula walosi* or the 'river of fibres'. The reserve has a variety of landscapes – thick forests, dry bushveld and open savannah – that are home to a number of species of game, including healthy populations of rhino and the rare nyala. What is unusual about the park is the hilly terrain, which provides a great vantage point for game viewing.

Arriving in Hluhluwe-Imfolozi Game Reserve

Hluhluwe-Imfolozi is roughly 250 km or a three-hour drive from Durban via the N2. For the Imfolozi sector, turn off the N2 at Mtubatuba on to the R618 towards Hlabisa and travel for 27 kms to the Nyalazi Gate. For the Hluhluwe sector, turn off the N2 opposite the exit to Hluhluwe village, which leads 14 km to the Memorial Gate. This is an easy park to visit on a day trip if you are staying in the Maputaland or St Lucia regions, and some of the Durban tour operators (page 56) offer long (10-12 hours) excursions from the city.

   The best time for wildlife viewing is in the drier winter months from May to September, when the vegetation thins out and animals congregate around water sources. These cooler winter months are also considered the low season and the park tends to be less busy. The reserve's vegetation is lush during the summer months from October to April, when the weather is hot and humid, but this makes it more difficult to see the game. Like other parts of KwaZulu-Natal, Hluhluwe-Imfolozi is at its most crowded during the South African school holidays. Accommodation within the park maybe fully booked and the heavy traffic on the roads can detracts from the wilderness experience.

Background

The confluence of the Black and White Imfolozi rivers was once the exclusive royal hunting ground of King Shaka, and game was driven into large pits, where it was speared by young warriors eager to prove their courage. Consequently, the two separate reserves of Hluhluwe and Imfolozi were established as protected areas as long ago as 1895. In 1947 the newly formed **Natal Parks**

Board took control of the reserves and reintroduced locally extinct species such as lion, elephant and giraffe. Since then there have been a number of other conservation initiatives, especially with rhino. It is estimated that in the late 1800s when the reserves were proclaimed, the entire world population of white rhino was only 20, all of them living in this area. The rhino's early protection from hunting in Hluhluwe and Imfolozi allowed numbers to grow to such an extent that by the 1950s, this number had grown to around 500. By the 1960s there were so many that the Natal Parks Board launched 'Operation Rhino' – an ambitious project to move rhino from Hluhluwe and Imfolozi to other wildlife protected areas in the country. As such the reserve is credited for bringing the species back from the brink of extinction.

Today Hluhluwe-Imfolozi has about 1600 white rhino and 400 black rhino, which is the highest population of rhino per hectare in the world. Nevertheless, the reserve has not escaped the tragic scourge of rhino-poaching that is one of the biggest threats to the species today. When driving around the park, it's

▣ Hluhluwe-Imfolozi Game Reserve

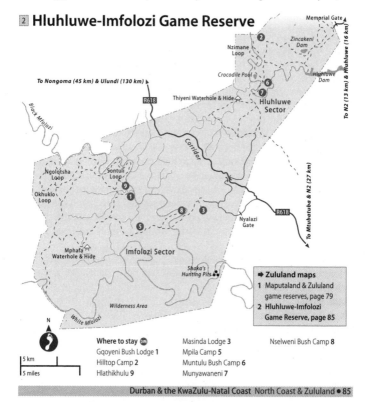

Memorial Gate

Zincakeni Dam

Nzimane Loop

Crocodile Pool

To N2 (13 km) & Hluhluwe (16 km)

Hluhluwe Dam

To Nongoma (45 km) & Ulundi (130 km)

Thiyeni Waterhole & Hide

R618

Hluhluwe Sector

Black Mfolozi

Corridor

To Mtubatuba & N2 (27 km)

Ngolqtsha Loop

Sontuli Loop

Okhuklo Loop

R618

Nyalazi Gate

Mphafa Waterhole & Hide

Imfolozi Sector

Shaka's Hunting Pits

Wilderness Area

White Mfolozi

N

5 km
5 miles

Where to stay 🛏️
Gqoyeni Bush Lodge **1**
Hilltop Camp **2**
Hlathikhulu **9**

Masinda Lodge **3**
Mpila Camp **5**
Muntulu Bush Camp **6**
Munyawaneni **7**

Nselweni Bush Camp **8**

➡ **Zululand maps**
1 Maputaland & Zululand game reserves, page 79
2 Hluhluwe-Imfolozi Game Reserve, page 85

not uncommon to bump into heavily armed anti-poaching patrols – a sad necessity in all wildlife areas in South Africa.

Wildlife

Hluhluwe-Imfolozi is one of the best reserves in KwaZulu-Natal for seeing wildlife. The Big Five are present and there are large populations of white and black rhino, lion and the nyala antelope. However despite the thriving hippo populations in nearby St Lucia, there are few hippo in this park because the rivers flow too fast. The Hluhluwe sector has a hilly and wooded landscape where elephant are often seen around the Hluhluwe Dam, and the thick forests are inhabited by the rare samango monkey. Imfolozi, in the south, is characterized by thornveld and semi-desert, and the grasslands here are the best places to see large populations of impala, kudu, waterbuck, giraffe, blue wildebeest and zebra. Over 300 species of bird have been recorded in Hluhluwe-Imfolozi and bird lists are available from the camp offices.

What to do

Game-viewing The majority of game viewing in Hluhluwe-Imfolozi is undertaken independently from a vehicle. Since you are left to your own devices (and may never have been on safari before) it's a good idea to arm yourself with some identification guides for animals, and if you're interested, birds and trees. The camp shops sell a wide choice. The best times for game-viewing are after dawn and just before dusk, as animals tend to rest during the heat of the day. The reserve is only open to self-drivers during daylight hours, so plan your drives to start at first light and to return to camp or the gates as it gets dark. An extensive network of over 300 km of well-maintained gravel roads link the camps and loop through the best game-viewing areas, which can easily be negotiated in a saloon car. A map can be bought at the reserve's offices and at Hilltop and Mpila camps, which also have frequently updated maps of where animals have recently been spotted (which you can add to if you like). Good areas for viewing game are the Sontuli Loop, the corridor linking Imfolozi to Hluhluwe and the areas around the Hluhluwe River.

Game-drives and walks Even if you drive yourself to and around Hluhluwe-Imfolozi, an additional game-drive or walk with an experienced guide can increase your chance of seeing animals and provides a deeper understanding of the wilderness. These must be booked at Hilltop or Mpila as soon as you arrive. Two and a half hour morning game-drives, R270, children (4-12, no under 4s) R135, leave at 0500 (October-March) and 0600 (April-September) so accommodation must be booked for the previous night in the reserve as they depart before the gates officially open. Night drives (same prices) are an added attraction as private vehicles are not allowed outside the camps after sundown, and these usually depart around 1700. Make sure you have warm clothing as temperatures drop in the evenings. There are also three-hour game walks in the morning, R215 per person (no children under 12), that leave at 0500 (October-March) and 0600 (April-September). Accompanied by an armed game ranger, groups are kept small – up to eight people – and these provide an excellent way of getting close to smaller animals and are a thrilling way of exploring the bush. Again like the game-drives, they depart before the gates officially open so accommodation must be booked for the previous night. Remember if you're staying at the private lodges, you'll have your own game guard for wildlife activities.

Wilderness trails There is little that can compare with the excitement of tracking wildlife through areas which are totally undisturbed by man – there are no roads and access is only allowed on foot. Several guided wilderness trails cross the reserve and run from mid-March to December. They are limited to a maximum of eight people and are extremely popular, so should be booked well in advance. Food, drinks, water bottles, cutlery and cooking equipment, bedding, towels, day packs, backpacks and donkey bags are all provided by Ezemvelo KZN Wildlife. The trails cover about 15 km per day and cost from R2250 to R3700 per person for up to three nights (accommodation is in tented camps in the wilderness area). Reservations can be made up to six months in advance through **Ezemvelo KZN Wildlife** ① *T033-845 1000, www.kznwildlife.com.*

Hluhluwe

On the R22, Hluhluwe is a small village 16 km from Hluhluwe-Imfolozi's Memorial Gate and 3 km from the N2. It is in an area surrounded by both (conversely) pineapple and game farms – the region produces about 90% of South Africa's pineapples and an international game auction is held here annually by Ezemvelo KZN Wildlife. It is also a tourism hub as it is within easy reach of many of the local game reserves, and also the principal point where traffic leaves the N2 and heads along the R22 to KwaZulu-Natal's Maputaland in the extreme northeast (see page 104). Formerly a rough gravel road, the R22 has now been tarred all the way to the Kosi Bay/Farazela border (open 0800-1700) with Mozambique.

Around the village is a clutch of places to stay, and along Main Street are coffee shops and takeaways (including a KFC), Zulu craft stalls, and an Engen petrol station where there's the office for the **Hluhluwe Tourism Association** ① *T035-562 0353, Mon-Fri 0800-1700, Sat 0900-1300,* which acts as a booking agent for the area.

iSimangaliso Wetland Park → *For listings, see pages 93-103.*

A UNESCO World Heritage Site since 1999, the area now known as the iSimangaliso Wetland Park consists of a number of formerly separate nature reserves and state forests. These are still referred to locally under a bewildering array of old and new names, but the greater area is considered to be South Africa's third largest park and protects the largest estuarine lake system in Africa. The 328,000-ha reserve starts south of the St Lucia Estuary, stretches north to the border with Mozambique and is about 280 km in length. The terrestrial section of the park varies from 1 km to 24 km wide, and the marine section extends 5 km out to sea, protecting 155 km of coastline.

Arriving in iSimangaliso Wetland Park

Getting there and around In the southern region, accessible from the town of St Lucia, the park falls into three main areas: **St Lucia Public Resort and Estuary**, which is a good area to see crocodile and hippo, and provides access to the public beaches around the town of St Lucia; the coastline up to **Cape Vidal**, 32 km north of St Lucia, with the beautiful Cape beach; and the **Western Shores Section** of the lake, which is accessed from either St Lucia or further north up the N2 and is the newly opened region for game driving. The iSimangaliso Wetland Park also encompasses all the coastal parks to the north, from Sodwana Bay to Kosi Bay Nature Reserve on the border of Mozambique. ➙ *For further details, see Maputaland, page 104.*

Tourist information For information about the iSimangaliso Wetland Park, visit the St Lucia office of **Ezemvelo KZN Wildlife** ① *Pelikan Rd, near Eden Park campsite, T035-590 1340, daily 0800-1630.* It has a small selection of brochures and can help with accommodation and trail information. Advance reservations for accommodation and wilderness trails should be made through **Ezemvelo KZN Wildlife** ① *T033-845 1000, www.kznwildlife.com.* For more information on the park also visit www.isimangaliso.com.

Background

St Lucia was named by the Portuguese explorer Manuel Perestrello in 1575, although European influence in the area was minimal until the 1850s. Up to that time the area was inhabited by a relatively large population of Thongas and Zulus who herded cattle and cultivated the land.

Professional hunters began visiting the lake in the 1850s in search of ivory, hides and horns, which were at one point the Colony of Natal's main source of income. So successful were these hunters that within 50 years the last elephant in this region had been shot. Among the big game hunters here were William Baldwin, Robert Briggs Struthers, 'Elephant' White and John Dunn who recorded having shot 23 seacows in one morning and a total of 203 seacows in the following three months. Hunting parties would kill hundreds of elephants, crocodiles and hippos on each expedition.

During the 1880s the British government annexed St Lucia in a move that would foil the Boers from the New Republic in their search for access to the sea. It was after this that land was distributed to settlers and that missions were founded at Mount Tabor, Cape Vidal and Ozabeni.

St Lucia Lake, along with Hluhluwe-Imfolozi, was one of the first game reserves to be established in Africa in 1895. Further moves to protect wildlife also took place in 1944 with the addition of False Bay Park to the protected areas, and in 1975 South Africa signed the international RAMSAR Convention to protect wetlands. It was then that the Greater St Lucia Wetland region was declared. Many more conservation initiatives were introduced when St Lucia won World Heritage status in 1999. One of the most important of these was the controversial national ban on beach driving in February 2002, enraging many South African 4WD owners. In 2008 it went under a name change to iSimangaliso Wetland Park – iSimangaliso is isiZulu for 'miracle'. The most exciting development in recent years has been the opening of the Western Shores Section in 2013 on the opposite side of the lake and its tributaries to St Lucia town. This has been restocked with numerous species of historically occurring game including elephant, rhino and giraffe, and now allows visitors to go on game-drives as well as enjoy the wetland environment.

Wildlife

The Mkhuze, Mzinene, Hluhluwe and Nyalazi rivers flow into the northern end of the lake system. The lakes are shallow and interspersed with islands and reedbeds and are bounded by papyrus, mangrove and forest swamps. The other inland areas in the park are grasslands with zones of thornveld, coastal and dune forest. The animals that are most often seen in these environments are large populations of common reedbuck, hippopotamus and Nile crocodile (there are an estimated 2000 crocs in the entire lake system). Depending on where you are in the park, there is also the chance of seeing impala, waterbuck, kudu, wildebeest, zebra, elephant and buffalo.

From November to March, giant leatherback and loggerhead turtles nest on the park's beaches up to 10 times each season (see box, page 105). They are protected by Ezemvelo KZN Wildlife who monitor them and protect them from predators such as honey badgers and jackals.

The birdlife is the main attraction, and more than 520 species have been recorded. The fish eagle, easily spotted, has become the unofficial symbol of the area. Other species often seen around the water include kingfishers and weaverbirds, and large numbers of unusual migrant birds can also be spotted. The St Lucia waters are high in nutrients and support large populations of pink-backed and white pelicans, greater and lesser flamingos, ducks, spoonbills and ibises.

St Lucia

The holiday resort of St Lucia lies to the south of the lake and is surrounded by the iSimangaliso Wetland Park. It is the largest seaside holiday destination on this part of the coast and is particularly popular during the South African school holidays. Although it can get very busy around Christmas, it remains a sleepy provincial town off season, making a pleasant base from which to explore both the wetlands and the nearby wildlife reserves.

Many visitors come for a day trip, to explore the narrow reaches of the estuary leading up to the lake. Boats leave regularly from the jetty at the far end of McKenzie Street, usually seating around 20 people and taking a two-hour tour upriver. These provide an excellent introduction to the wetlands, with chances of seeing large pods of hippo and crocodile, and prolific birdlife.

Arriving in St Lucia The end of the R618 leads directly into the centre of town on McKenzie Street, which is lined with supermarkets, banks, restaurants, curio shops and boat charter companies. Continuing down past the end of McKenzie Street, the road leads to the large Ezemvelo KZN Wildlife office to the left, and the jetty from which river cruises leave to the right.

The best source of local tourist information is **Advantage Tours & Charters** ⓘ *McKenzie St, next to the Dolphin Supermarket at the entrance of town, T035-590 1259, www.advantagetours.co.za, Mon-Fri 0800-1700, Sat 0800-1400, Sun 0800-1200*, who act as a booking agent for all local activities and accommodation, and run their own boat excursions (see page 101).

Beaches The beaches lying to the east of St Lucia are large swathes of pristine white sand backed by dune forest, which stretch all the way to Cape Vidal. The vegetated sand dunes here can exceed 180 m in height and, estimated to be over 30,000 years old, they are considered to be some of the highest vegetated coastal dunes in the world. Visitors can swim here but do so at their own risk as there are dangerous currents, no shark nets and no lifeguards.

St Lucia Public Resort and Estuary These areas directly surround St Lucia town. There is a 12-km network of self-guided trails, which start in the area near the Crocodile Centre (see below). They cross several different habitats such as dune forest, grasslands, mangroves and swamps, and close to the estuary take you to some good hippo-viewing spots. However, avoid the water's edge – hippos kill more people than any other mammal in Africa. If you come across one on land, retreat slowly and quietly. Swimming in the estuary is prohibited due the presence of crocodiles.

The **Crocodile Centre** ⓘ T035-590 1386, www.kznwildlife.com, Mon-Fri 0800-1600, Sat 0830-1700, Sun 0900-1600, R35, children (under 12) R20, crocodile

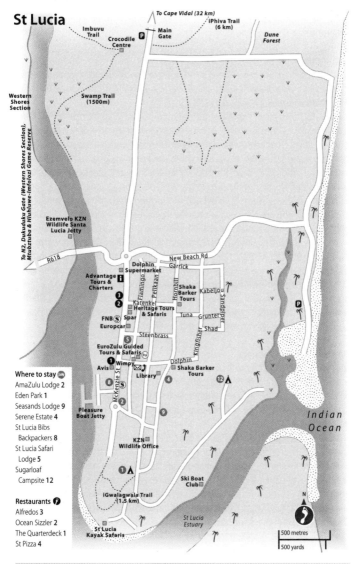

St Lucia

Imbuvu Trail

To Cape Vidal (32 km)

Main Gate

iPhiva Trail (6 km)

Dune Forest

Crocodile Centre

Swamp Trail (1500m)

Western Shores Section

To N2, Dukuduku Gate (Western Shores Section), Mtubatuba & Hluhluwe-Imfolozi Game Reserve

Ezemvelo KZN Wildlife Santa Lucia Jetty

R618

New Beach Rd
Garrick

Dolphin
Supermarket

Advantage Tours & Charters

Flamingo

Pelikaan

Hornbill

Shaka Barker Tours

Kabeljou

Katenkel

Heritage Tours & Safaris

Tuna

Grunter

Sandpiper

FNB
Europcar

Spar

Steenbrass

Kingfisher

Shad

EuroZulu Guided Tours & Safaris

Avis

Wimpy

Dolphin

Shaka Barker Tours

Library

McKenzie St

Pleasure Boat Jetty

KZN Wildlife Office

Indian Ocean

Where to stay
AmaZulu Lodge **2**
Eden Park **1**
Seasands Lodge **9**
Serene Estate **4**
St Lucia Bibs
  Backpackers **8**
St Lucia Safari
  Lodge **5**
Sugarloaf
  Campsite **12**

iGwalagwala Trail (1.5 km)

Ski Boat Club

St Lucia Estuary

Restaurants 🍴
Alfredos **3**
Ocean Sizzler **2**
The Quarterdeck **1**
St Pizza **4**

St Lucia Kayak Safaris

N

500 metres
500 yards

feeding Sat 1500, restaurant, is next to the entrance gate to Cape Vidal, where a small display highlights the important role crocodiles play in the ecosystem of the park. The Nile, long-snouted and dwarf crocodiles that are kept here in pens, are all endangered in the wild and are part of an international breeding programme to protect them.

Cape Vidal

ⓘ *32 km north of St Lucia, T035-590 9012, www.kznwildlife.com, gates Nov-Mar 0500-1900, Apr-Oct 0600-1800, office Mon-Fri 0800-1630 Sat-Sun 0800-1530, R35, children (under 12) R25, car R45.*

Cape Vidal, an area of vegetated dunes along what must be one of the most spectacular beaches in KwaZulu-Natal, makes an easy and pleasant day trip from St Lucia. A road heads north from the park gates (near the crocodile centre), passing through an area that was until recently pine forest but is now returning to indigenous wilderness. The area is home to reedbuck, waterbuck, kudu and buffalo, and in the lake to the west of the road, crocodile and hippo.

Mission Rocks is 16 km from St Lucia, signposted off the dirt road. Snorkelling and scuba-diving are allowed here and tours can be arranged from St Lucia (see page 102). The rock pools here are full of life and are best seen at low tide.

At Cape Vidal the sand is pure white and the Indian Ocean is warm and inviting; the rocks just off the beach are teeming with tropical fish and the shallow water is safe to swim and snorkel in. The beach is never crowded even at the busiest of times. The camp has facilities for launching powerboats and is popular for game fishing, but, as Cape Vidal marks the beginning of a marine reserve that stretches north to the Mozambique border, anglers require permits and many fish are on a tag-and-release system.

Western Shores Section

ⓘ *Dukuduku Gate is on the R618 2 km before reaching St Lucia town, Nhlozi Gate is off the N2 20 km north of Mtubatuba or 32 km south of Hluhluwe, then 13 km on a tarred road, 035-562 0425, www.kznwildlife.com, gates Nov-Mar 0500-1900, Apr-Oct 0500-1900, office at Dukuduku Gate 0800-1630, R35, children (under 12) R25, car R45.*

A new 25,000 ha section of the park was opened to visitors in 2013 on the western shores of the lake for self-drive or guided tour game viewing. Developments include two new entry gates – Dukuduku and Nhlozi gates – a network of game-viewing gravel roads, and hides and picnic sites. Much of this area was formerly under forestry plantations and over the last decade or so thousands of hectares of alien trees have been removed and the natural landscape has been rehabilitated. This has enabled the reintroduction of historically occurring game including elephant, tsessebe, giraffe, nyala, white and black rhino, buffalo, zebra, red and grey duiker, and wildebeest. Some of the park's largest herds of waterbuck, reedbuck and kudu are found here, and the numerous pans and wetlands host not only hippos and crocodiles but a plethora of birdlife, particularly waterfowl. The Kwelamadoda Pan is especially good to see spurwing and pygmy geese, white-faced duck, shovellers, egrets and dabchicks. The uMdoni loop takes you to the uMthoma boardwalk where you can park and stroll to the end for a magnificent view across the lake to Cape Vidal.

False Bay

ⓘ *Off the R22, 16 km east of Hluhluwe, T035-562 0425, www.kznwildlife.com, gates Oct-Mar 0500-2000, Apr-Sep 0600-2000, office 0830-1230, Sun 1400-1630, R25, children (under 12) R18.*

This is the northernmost accessible point on Lake St Lucia, and the 2247 ha reserve is mostly sand forest, woodland and mixed patches of open shoreline. It's a good place to see flamingos and pink-backed pelicans on the lake during the breeding season from December to April, and the sand forests are inhabited by the rare suni antelope and nyala. As its not home to large mammals, there are two self-guided trails – Dugandlovu and the Mphophomeni – which are both 8 km long, and a viewing platform at Lister Point looks over the lake, but swimming is prohibited because of crocs.

◉ North Coast and Zululand listings

For hotel and restaurant price codes and other relevant information, see pages 12-16.

◉ Where to stay

Dolphin Coast *p75, map p76*
Ballito and Salt Rock on the Dolphin Coast have hundreds of holiday apartments; these can be expensive in the height of the summer season but out of season renting an apartment is excellent value for families or groups. Contact **Ballito Accommodation**, 29 Sandra Rd, Ballito T032-946 0180, www.ballitoaccommodation.co.za.
$$$ Boathouse, 33 Compensation Beach Rd, Ballito, T032-946 0300, www.boathouse.co.za. Upmarket guesthouse on the beach, 22 a/c

beautifully decorated rooms with balconies and DSTV, the bar is a great place to have a sundowner and spot dolphins, lovely pool on wooden deck, restaurant specializing in seafood.
$$$ Fairmont Zimbali Lodge, just off the coast road, 2 km south of Ballito, T032-538 5000, www.fairmont.com/zimbalilodge. 1 of 3 luxurious hotels set in the grounds of the massive 700-ha Zimbali country club and golf estate, where golf carts ferry guests between the sport facilities, spa and restaurants. The 76 opulent rooms have polished wooden floors, huge beds, balconies and all mod cons, all set in beautiful tropical forest, stunning pool area and direct access to 3 km of beach.

$$ Salt Rock Hotel, Basil Hluett Dr, Salt Rock, T032-525 5025, www.saltrock beach.co.za. A big uninspiring block but a family-friendly hotel in a beautiful location right on the beach, with buffet restaurant, bar and swimming pool, all rooms are sea facing and have DSTV, fridge and balcony. Caravan and camping park attached (**$**).

$$-$ Dolphin Holiday Resort, Ballito, T032-946 2187, www.dolphinholiday resort.co.za. Pleasant resort with shady caravan and camping sites and 10 self-catering log cabins sleeping 2-6, swimming pool, games room, kiosk, trampolines for kids and volley ball court. You can't see the sea from here but it's only a couple of mins' walk to the beach.

Harold Johnson Nature Reserve
p77, map p76
Campsite, T032-486 1574, www.kzn wildlife.com. 6 shady sites with tap, *braai* pit and ablution block with hot water. Come fully prepared as there are no other facilities.

KwaGingindlovu and around
p78
$ Zangozolo Tented Camp, Amatigulu Nature Reserve, Ezemvelo KZN Wildlife, T033-845 1000, www. kznwildlife.com. Simple camp with 6 2-bed tents connected by wooden walkways on raised platforms overlooking the sea, a shared ablution block, dining area and fully equipped kitchen with stoves, fridge and freezer. There's also a **campsite** here, T035-340 1836, with 5 shady sites, ablutions and thatched kitchen area.

Eshowe and inland *p80*
$$$ Shakaland, T035-460 0912, www.shakaland.com. If you are staying the night the Shaka experience continues in the adjacent **hotel**, where Zulu dancers escort you to your beehive-shaped hut. The evenings are spent sampling the local brew *tshwala* around the campfire while being entertained with dancing and storytelling. The 53 rooms are huge and have all mod cons and there's a swimming pool, bar and restaurant.

$$$ Simunye Zulu Lodge (page 81), T035-450 0103, www.simunyelodge. co.za. You can drive to the lodge or park up at the trading post by 1530 to go by horseback or ox wagon. There are 24 rooms in the formal lodge or simple and traditional thatched stone huts lit by candles and oil lamps. The programme includes meeting the chief of the village, a traditional dinner, and performances of Zulu music, singing and dancing. Rates include all meals, guides and demonstrations.

$$ George Hotel, 116 Main St, Eshowe, T035-474 4919, www. eshowe.com. Friendly country hotel with a Zulu theme and 27 rooms with DSTV, in a historical building adjacent to the Dlinza Forest (see page 80). **Quarters Restaurant**, **Happy George Pub**, which serves home-brewed Zulu Blond ale, and there's a swimming pool. Runs excellent tours (see What to do, page 101). Also has 7 B&B rooms in a Victorian guesthouse in town (same contacts).

$ Zululand Backpackers, 38 Main St, at the back of the **George Hotel**, T035-474 4919, www.eshowe.com.

Dorms, double rooms and camping, lounge with DSTV, bar with pool table, internet, swimming pool, kitchen, meals available at the hotel, close to shops and banks. Again organizes excellent local tours, such as visits to traditional Zulu weddings.

Ithala Game Reserve *p81*
Reservations through **Ezemvelo KZN Wildlife**, T033-845 1000, www.kznwildlife.com. The private bush camps and lodge here have their own game ranger for walks.
$$$$ Mhlangeni Bush Camp. Set on high granite boulders overlooking the Ncence River and well away from the busier areas of the reserve, sleeps 10 in 5 rooms with a central open-plan lounge, kitchen and sundeck. Must be booked as a single unit.
$$$$ Ntshondwe Lodge. Suspended on the edge of a cliff with sweeping views, this ingeniously designed private lodge is set on tiers in a jumble of boulders. Sleeps 6 in 3 en suite rooms, jacuzzi, viewing deck, self-catering but with a cook to prepare food brought by guests. Must be booked as a single unit.
$$$ Mbizo Bush Camp. Overlooking the rapids on the Mbizo River where you can swim, this sleeps 8 in 2 chalets, each with 2 bedrooms and its own bathroom, lounge, kitchen and viewing deck. Must be booked as a single unit.
$$$-$$ Ntshondwe Resort. In a beautiful setting at the base of sandstone cliffs, the main camp has a total of 39 units including chalets with fully equipped kitchen sleeping 2-7 and 2- to 3-bed rest huts sharing a kitchen and ablution block. Restaurant and bar with a game-viewing deck overlooking a small pan, and swimming pool built around a giant rock.
$$ Thalu Bush Camp. On the edge of the Thalu River next to rapids and clear pools where you can swim, this sleeps 4 in 2 bedrooms separated by a lounge kitchen and viewing deck. Must be booked as a single unit.

Camping
Droonkraal Campsite, T034-983 2540. Close to Ntshondwe Resort, this rustic campsite has 20 sites with simple ablution block with only cold showers. Animals can be seen wandering around and it's a great place for wilderness camping.

Empangeni and around *p83*
$$$$ Thula Thula Private Game Reserve (see page 83), T035-792 8322, www.thula thula.com. Luxury safari lodge with 8 thatched chalets and 8 safari tents decorated in an ethnic style, set on rolling lawns and surrounded by forests full of birds. Excellent food served in an outside boma, with tables set around a fire, thatched bar area overlooking the pool. Rates are inclusive of meals and game-drives.

Richards Bay *p83*
$$ The Ridge Guesthouse, 1 Jack's Corner, Davidson Lane, Meerensee, T035-753 4312, www.theridge guesthouse.co.za. Good choice if you're passing through Richards Bay, this upmarket guesthouse has

14 tasteful rooms with a/c, DSTV and Wi-Fi set around a pool, with views of the ocean and harbour, and a restaurant and bar.

Hluhluwe-Imfolozi Game Reserve *p84, map p85*

All reservations through **Ezemvelo KZN Wildlife**, T033-845 1000, www.kznwildlife.com.

$$$-$$ Hilltop Camp. This, the largest and most accessible of the camps, has a fabulous hilltop location in the Hluhluwe sector, with sweeping views over much of the park and parts of Swaziland. Although it doesn't have the exclusivity of the smaller bush camps, the central lounge, restaurant, bar, pool and veranda are welcome at the end of the day. The shop stocks curios, cold drinks, beers and wines, ice, firewood and charcoal and some food, and there's a petrol station. Game-drives and guided walks can be arranged here. The main camp offers 4 types of accommodation. At the top end are 22 **4-bed chalets ($$$)** with 2 bedrooms, 2 bathrooms and fully equipped kitchen; slightly cheaper are the 7 **2-bed chalets ($$)**, with fully equipped kitchen, and the 20 2-bed rest huts (not self-catering) with fridge and kettle. The cheapest options are the 20, **2-bed rest huts ($$)**, with communal kitchen and ablution block.

$$$-$$ Mpila Camp. This is the main camp in the Imfolozi sector and commands magnificent views over the wilderness area to the east and the Msasaneni Hills to the west. The shop stocks curios, cold drinks, beers and wines, ice, firewood and charcoal and some food, and there's a petrol station but no restaurant. Game-drives and guided walks can be arranged here. Accommodation is in 2 self-contained **3-bed cottages ($$$)** sleeping 7 (cook on hand to prepare food supplied by guests); 6 self-catering **2-bed chalets ($$$)**, sleeping up to 5, with fully equipped kitchen; tented camp with 9 walk-in en suite tents **($$)**, self-catering with a communal kitchen and dining area; and 12 **1-bed self-catering thatched cottages ($$)**, sleeping 4 with a communal kitchen and ablutions.

Private lodges and camps

The private lodges and camps are only available for single group bookings. Codes refer to minimum charge.

$$$$ Gqoyeni Bush Lodge, Imfolozi sector. Expensive 8-bed bush lodge with 4 thatched cottages, each with 2 bedrooms, on stilts connected by raised wooden walkways to the living area with lounge, dining area and kitchen, the camp has its own viewing platform overlooking the Mfolozi River. Bring your own food but in residence are a cook and a game guard for bush walks.

$$$$ Hlathikhulu, Imfolozi sector. 8-bed mid-range bush camp, rustic decor, lovely setting overlooking the Black Mfolozi. 4 2-bed chalets, a central lounging area and kitchen linked by wooden boardwalks, cook (bring your own food) and game guard for bush walks.

$$$$ Masinda Lodge, Imfolozi sector. Luxury 6-bed self-catering lodge, with lounge and dining room with Zulu decor. Beautiful setting with good views of the bush, cook (bring your own food) and game guard for bush walks.

$$$$ Muntulu Bush Camp, Hluhluwe sector. Four 2-bed units in this rustic mid-range bush lodge, linked by wooden walkway to a central lounge and dining area, all overlooking the Hluhluwe River, verandas, cook (bring your own food) and game guard for bush walks

$$$$ Munyawaneni, Hluhluwe sector. 8-bed mid-range bush lodge on the banks of the Hluhluwe River in a good area for seeing the elephant and nyala that come to drink at the secluded waterhole in view of each of the 4 rooms. Boardwalks link the units to a central lounge and kitchen, cook (bring your own food) and game guard for bush walks.

$$$ Nselweni Bush Camp, Imfolozi sector. A wonderfully atmospheric reed and thatch bush lodge raised on stilts just above the floodplain of Mfolozi River, with four 2-bed units, shared ablutions, lounge, dining area, cook (bring your own food) and game guard for bush walks.

Hluhluwe *p87, map p85*

$$$$ Hluhluwe River Lodge, 15 km from Hluhluwe village off the road to False Bay, T035-562 0246, www.hluhluwe.co.za. With sweeping views of False Bay, 12 attractive and spacious a/c A-frame thatched chalets with wooden decks set well apart under indigenous trees. Central lodge has dining area, bar, lounge, curio shop, library and pool. Mid-range rates are

fully inclusive of meals and a game-drive into Hluhluwe-Imfolozi.

$$$$ Phinda Private Game Reserve, 23 km northeast of Hluhluwe off the R22, the gate to the reserve is 6 km to the west of the road, reservations T011-809 4300, www.andbeyond.com. One of KwaZulu-Natal's most renowned private Big Five reserves covering 23,000 ha and sandwiched between the iSimangaliso Wetland Park and uMkhuze Game Reserve, with 6 luxury 5-star lodges, each with its own unique atmosphere and bush or wetland views. The very expensive rates are all-inclusive of game-drives and fine cuisine, and other activities include rhino tracking on foot, canoeing on the Mzinene River, horse riding or beach excursions.

$$$$ Thanda Private Game Reserve, 23 km north of Hluhluwe, 6 km to the left of the N2, T035-573 1899, www.thanda.com. A very expensive 7800-ha Big Five reserve, with 9 bush suites and 15 spacious colonial-style tents, plus Zulu themed dining and lounge areas, decks overlooking a waterhole, library, wine cellar and spa. Other than game-drives, there are visits to Zulu villages and the beach at Sodwana Bay.

$$$ Makhasa Game Reserve, 32 km northeast of Hluhluwe off the R22 towards Sodwana Bay, T033-345 6531, www.makhasa.co.za. Secluded bush lodge on a 2000-ha community-run reserve adjacent to Phinda, with 6 rustic thatched cabins on stilts in the sand forest linked by boardwalks lit by flaming lanterns in the evening, central eating boma and bar overlooking a waterhole, game-drives, walks to track rhino and buffalo.

$$ Protea Hotel Hluhluwe, 104 Main Rd, T035-562 4001, www.proteahotels.com. Smart modern hotel decorated with African motifs, 76 a/c rooms with DSTV, swimming pool, 2 restaurants serving an à la carte menu or a buffet, performances of Zulu dancing in the evenings. Offers good value daily 3-hr safaris to Hluhluwe-Imfolozi.

$$-$ Sand Forest Lodge, off the R22 towards False Bay, 10 km from Hluhluwe T0824-176484, www.sandforest.co.za. Simple rustic self-catering camp in an ancient sand forest, with 4 en suite simple thatched cottages or 2 huts on stilts with verandas which share ablutions with the campsite, bar, pool and thatched lapa, game-drives into Hluhluwe-Imfolozi and visits to Zulu villages. Good value and peaceful setup.

$ Isinkwe Backpackers Bushcamp, 2 km east of the Bushlands exit off the N2, 36 km north of the St Lucia/Mtubatuba turning and 14 km south of Hluhluwe, T0833-383494, www.isinkwe.co.za. A rustic set-up with 40 beds in dorms, doubles and camping, swimming pool, bar, great home-made meals and kitchen. Day trips to Hluhluwe-Imfolozi, transfers to Sodwana Bay, and delightful evening guided walks to see bushbabies.

St Lucia *p90, map p91*
There are dozens of B&Bs and guesthouses in St Lucia aimed at the domestic family holiday market or fishermen, and out of season it's possible to drive around and take your pick.

$$$-$$ Serene Estate, 119 Hornbill St, T072-365 2450, www.serene-estate.com. Upmarket and architecturally interesting guesthouse, 5 rooms with a/c, DSTV and Wi-Fi, unusual black and white minimalist decor, roof garden with good views over the wetlands, 12-m rim-flow pool.

$$ AmaZulu Lodge, 107 McKenzie St, T035-590 1026, www.amazululodge.com. Attractive thatched complex with earthy ethnic decor using local materials, 16 stylish B&B a/c rooms modelled on Zulu huts with DSTV and patio, built around a tropical garden and pool, bar and lounge, and can organize local tours.

$$ Seasands Lodge, 135 Hornbill St, T035-590 1082, www.seasands.co.za. Fairly large modern lodge, 28 a/c rooms with DSTV, balconies or terraces, some with kitchenettes, dotted around extensive tropical gardens with a swimming pool and pleasant wooden sundeck, restaurant and bar with pool table.

$$-$ St Lucia Safari Lodge, 103 McKenzie St, T035-590 1133, www.stlucia-safari-lodge.co.za. Close to shops and restaurants with 15 simple brick self-catering chalets sleeping 2-6 or 12 comfortable B&B rooms with a/c and DSTV, large pool, thatched *braai* and bar, popular with tour groups but a good budget family option.

$ St Lucia Bibs Backpackers, 310 McKenzie St, T035-590 1056, www.bibs.co.za. Dorms, doubles, chalets with kitchenette sleeping 2-4, and some space for tents. Kitchen, relaxing gardens with hammocks, rock swimming pool, *braai* and bar area, Zulu dancing on Sat nights, Wi-Fi. Well-organized day trips to Hluhluwe-Imfolozi and other local sights.

Camping
Sugarloaf Campsite, close to the beach and estuary, **Ezemvelo KZN Wildlife**, reservations T035-590 1340, www.kznwildlife.com. 92 sites with power points, swimming pool and children's playground. The other **Ezemvelo KZN Wildlife** campsite is Eden Park, in a small forest to the south of town, and has another 20 sites, but this is only open in high season as an overflow for Sugarloaf.

Cape Vidal p92, map p79
$$ Cape Vidal Camp, Ezemvelo KZN Wildlife, T033-845 1000, www.kzn wildlife.com. 18 5- to 8-bed self-catering log cabins with verandas and *braais* set under trees on the dunes 200 m from the beach. There's a small shop selling firewood but limited provisions; stock up in St Lucia.

Camping
Cape Vidal Camp, T035-590 9012. 50 sites with power points set among the pines. It gets overcrowded with fishermen here during high season, but being so close to the lovely beach is definitely a bonus.

False Bay p93, map p79
$ Dugandlovu Rustic Camp, Ezemvelo KZN Wildlife, T033-845 1000, www.kzn wildlife.com. A peaceful spot but you need to be self-sufficient, 4 huts sleeping 4, basic kitchen equipment, cold showers, paraffin lamps, gas cookers, freezer, *braais*, firewood, bring your own bedding. The elevated viewing platform here has great sunset views across the lake.

🍴 Restaurants

Ballito and around p76, map p76
$$$-$$ Al Pescatore, 14 Edward Pl, Ballito, T032-946 3574 www. alpescatore.co.za. Mon 1800-2100, Tue-Sun 1130-2130. An elegant Mediterranean and seafood restaurant with smartly dressed tables and white linen, serving excellent but pricey seafood, with good prawn curries and fresh line-caught fish. The less formal deck overlooking the beach serves light lunches including generous pizzas.
$$ The Galley Beach Bar & Grill, 17 Compensation Beach Rd, Ballito. T032-946 2546. Daily 1000-2200. Great sunny balcony overlooking the main beach just a few metres from the waves, long menu from seafood platters to Mexican nachos, extensive choice of beers, wines and cocktails. Family friendly with kids' menu and childminders on the beach during the day.

KwaGingindlovu and around p78
$$ The Prawn Shak, 5 km from the KwaGingindlovu turn off on the N2, go in the opposite direction on a gravel road under the N2 to the beach, T084-737 6493, www.shak.co.za. Sat-Sun 1130-1900. Perched on a dune with great ocean views and possibly whales in season, tables in the sand and

rustic bar and only open for weekend lunches of delicious piri-piri prawns and Durban prawn curry cooked over hot coals. People from Durban will make the 110-km drive here for a long leisurely lunch.

Richards Bay *p83*
Dockside Shack, corner Pioneer and Newark Rds, T035-788 0320. Mon-Sat 1000-2200, Sun 0900-1700. Informal thatched restaurant and café in a good location with broad open deck, views of the harbour, offers seafood, grills, pizza and beer on tap. An alternative to the usual South African chain restaurants found elsewhere in Richards Bay.

St Lucia *p90, map p91*
$$ Alfredos, 54 McKenzie St, T035-590 1150. Mon-Sat 1200-2200. Good traditional Italian food at this affordable and cheerful set-up, run by an Italian chef, with a good range of pasta, seafood and veal dishes, and tables inside and out. Fun, easy-going atmosphere.
$$ The Ocean Sizzler, 37 McKenzie St, T035-590 1554 www.oceansizzler. co.za. Daily 1000-2130, bar stays open until late. Hugely popular local restaurant serving steaks, seafood and a couple of Greek specials to tables spilling out onto the pavement. There's also a good wine and cocktail list.
$$-$ The Quarterdeck, 166 McKenzie St, T035-590 1116. Daily 1100-late. Great wooden deck overlooking the road, with a large (more beery) interior. Good selection of fresh grilled seafood, as well as burgers, ribs and salads. Popular cocktail bar downstairs.

O Shopping

Dolphin Coast *p75, map p76*
Ballito Lifestyle Centre, Main Rd, Ballito, T032-946 3923 www. ballitolifestylecentre.co.za. Mon-Sat 0900-1800, Sun 0900-1700. Nicely designed mall with plenty of al fresco lanes with cafés and stalls and shops aimed at holidaymakers. The **Spar** supermarket here is usefully open daily 0700-2000 to pick up self-catering provisions or takeaway meals.

Richards Bay *p83*
Boardwalk Inkwazi Shopping Centre, Kruger Rand Rd, T035-789 7251, www.boardwalkinkwazi.co.za. Mon-Thu 0900-1800, Fri 0900-1800, Sat 0900-1700, Sun 0900-1500. The largest mall north of Gateway in Umhlanga with 150 shops, banks, supermarkets, restaurants and a 5-screen **Ster-Kinekor** cinema.

Hluhluwe *p87, map p85*
Ilala Weavers, 3 km north of the village just after the turning to False Bay, T0878-021792, www.ilala. co.za. Daily 0800-1730. A quality handicraft shop selling traditional Zulu basketwork and beadwork. There's a café and children's playground. By contrast it's also a good spot for birdwatching and there's an identification bird board.

St Lucia *p90, map p91*
Zulu curios like baskets, mats, carvings, walking sticks and clay pots, and in season, fresh tropical fruit are sold from stalls along McKenzie St.

Spar, 40 McKenzie St, T 035-590 1007. Mon-Sat 0800-2000, Sun 1000-1530. Well-stocked supermarket for self-catering supplies.

⚙ What to do

Dolphin Coast *p75, map p76*
Zimbali Country Club, 2 km south of Ballito, T032-538 1040, www. zimbali.co.za. An 18-hole Par-72 championship course designed by Tom Weiskopf, lovely clubhouse with sea views from the broad wooden deck. Golf clubs and carts can be hired.

Eshowe and inland *p80*
Zululand Eco-adventures, based at the **George Hotel** and **Zululand Backpackers**, T035-474 4919, www. zululandeco-adventures.com. Run by Graham Chennells, a registered guide and a former mayor of Eshowe who has intimate knowledge of the Zulu people and has been involved in community projects for many years. Unusual cultural tours of the surrounding countryside moving from village to village; no shows are visited. Tours take in Zulu weddings and ceremonies, traditional healers, and visit historical battlefield and cultural sites as well as showing contemporary traditional life as it is today. Highly recommended for more of an insight into the Zulu people than the usual all-singing all-dancing tourist traps.

Hluhluwe *p87, map p85*
Most of the hotels and lodges in the region organize full- and ½-day guided game-drives into Hluhluwe-Imfolozi and uMkhuze game reserves. Alternatively try **Dinizulu Safaris**, T035-562 0025, www.dinizulu.co.za; or **Isinkwe Tours & Safaris**, at **Isinkwe Backpackers Bushcamp**, see page 98.

St Lucia *p90, map p91*
Boat trips
Advantage Tours & Charters, McKenzie St, next to the **Dolphin Supermarket** at the entrance of town, T035-590 1259, www.advantagetours. co.za. Mon-Fri 0800-1700, Sat 0800-1400, Sun 0800-1200. A wide choice of boat cruises, including 2-hr estuary trips, 1000, 1200, 1400 and 1600, R180, children (2-12) R90, under 2s free. Whale-watching trips run Jun-Nov when humpback, mink and occasional southern right whales travel along the coast heading for the warmer breeding waters of Mozambique. Trips cost R950 per person, 40% of which is refundable if no whales are spotted after 2 hrs at sea. This, the only licensed whale-watching operator in St Lucia, is permitted to get within 50 m of the whales. Can also arrange sightseeing boat trips outside of whale season and deep-sea fishing.
Ezemvelo KZN Wildlife Santa Lucia, T035-590 1340, www.kznwildlife.com. The 80-seater double-storey Santa Lucia departs from the jetty next to the bridge at 0830, 1030 and 1430, R155, children (under 12) R75. The tour lasts for 1½ hrs and travels around 8 km up the estuary past thick banks of vegetation as far as the Narrows. There is a good chance of seeing hippo and waterfowl.

St Lucia Kayak Safaris, T035-590
1233, www.kayaksafaris.co.za. Relaxing
2½-hr paddles on the estuary (up to
the bridge), with a good chance of
spotting hippos and crocs, R295 per
person (no children under 12). The
slipway is on Honeymoon Bend on
the estuary in the south of town. Can
also organize a day trip up to Cape
Vidal with snorkelling and kayaking
at Mission Rocks and lunch on the
beach, R525 per person (no children
under 12).

Horse riding
Bhangazi Horse Safaris, T083-792
7899, www.stlucia-adventureactivities.
com. Daily 1- to 3-hr horse trails along
the beach (departure times depend
on low tide) and inland through the
dune forest. Suitable for novices, no
children under 8, from R350 per hr.

Tour operators
There are a number of day tours
on offer from St Lucia. A full day to
Hluhluwe-Imfolozi including lunch
cots in the region of R900, children
(under 12) R720. Day trips to Cape
Vidal, which include a game-drive,
snorkelling at Mission Rocks and lunch
on the beach, costs R625, children
(under 12) R500.

The new Western Shores Section of
the iSimangaliso Wetland Park is not
accessible to self-drivers after dark,
but the tour operators have been
granted concessions to operate night
drives. With spotlights, this is a great
way to search for creatures like genets,
hyena, jackal, and perhaps the elusive
leopard, and hippo may well be seen

out of the water grazing. Departures
are from town at 1600-1700 for a 3-hr
sunset game-drive and 1900-2000 for
a 3-hr spotlight game-drive and cost
in the region of R400 per person.

Turtle-watching trips are between
Nov-Feb (see box, page 105). As the
turtles only come on to the beach
at night, tours usually depart town
around 2200 and return around 0300
and supper or a midnight picnic on
the beach is included. The tours go
first to Cape Vidal, from where there
is a beach drive for about 25 km to
a restricted area in the iSimangaliso
Wetland Park wilderness. A 6-hr tour
costs from R1000 per person and
advance booking is essential.
Advantage Tours & Charters
(see above) can book all these
excursions, or contact:
EuroZulu Guided Tours & Safaris,
Wimpy Centre, McKenzie St, T035-
590 1635, www.eurozulu.com.
Heritage Tours & Safaris,
53 McKenzie St, T035-590 1555,
www.heritagetoursandsafaris.com.
Shaka Barker Tours, 4 Hornbill St,
T035-590 1162, www.shakabarker.co.za.

⊖ Transport

Dolphin Coast *p75, map p76*
Greyhound, www.greyhound.co.za,
buses stop in Ballito at the **Shell**
petrol station on Ballito Dr, just
off the N2. In KwaDukuza-Stanger,
they stop at the **Shell** petrol station
on King Shaka St. The service runs
between **Durban** and **Johannesburg**
and **Pretoria** via **Empangeni** and
Richards Bay, and then turns inland

via **Melmoth** and **Vryheid** to re-join the N2 again at Piet Retief.

Empangeni and around *p83*
Greyhound, www.greyhound.co.za, buses stop at the museum in Turnbull St, to **Durban**, **Johannesburg** and **Pretoria**.

Richards Bay *p83*
Air
There is a small airport located at the northern edge of town, around 5 km from the centre on **Fish Eagle Flight Crescent**, T035-789 9630. SAA, T011-978 1111, www.flysaa.com, operates daily flights to/from **Johannesburg** (90 mins).

Bus
Greyhound, www.greyhound.co.za, buses stop on Premium Promenade outside **McDonalds** to **Durban**, **Pretoria** and **Johannesburg**.

Car hire
All offices are located at the airport: **Avis**, T035-789 6549, www.avis.co.za; **Budget**, T035-786 0986, www.budget.co.za; **Europcar**, T035-786 0896, www.europcar.com; **First Car Rental**, T035-786 0001, www.firstcarrental.co.za; **Tempest**, T035-786 1519, www.tempestcarhire.co.za.

St Lucia *p90, map p91*
Avis, Ponta Lucia Centre, McKenzie St, T035-590 1634, www.avis.co.za; **Europcar**, St Pizza Building, McKenzie St, T035-590 1555 www.europcar.com.

❶ Directory

Richards Bay *p83*
Medical services Netcare The Bay Hospital, Kruger Rand Rd, T035-780 6111, www.netcare.co.za.

Maputaland

Named after the Maputa River, Maputaland is bordered by the Lebombo Mountains in the west and the Indian Ocean in the east. It covers an area of about 10,000 sq km, stretching from the town of Hluhluwe and the northern section of Lake St Lucia to the border of Mozambique. One of South Africa's least developed regions, Maputaland has preserved a traditional African atmosphere. The land is unsuitable for intensive modern agriculture, and small farmsteads and fishing communities dot the landscape.

The climate is tropical in the north, subtropical in the south, creating a fascinatingly diverse range of ecosystems, from the forested Lebombo Mountains at 700 m to the low-lying expanses of coastal plain. Maputaland's predominant feature is the dune and riverine forests, lakes, mangrove swamps and estuaries that make up the northern reaches of the remarkable iSimangaliso Wetland Park. The ocean too has its attractions, and South Africa's most northern coral reefs offer superb diving at Sodwana Bay and loggerback and leatherback turtles nest on the isolated beaches.

Arriving in Maputaland

Maputaland is well connected by road on the N2 from either Durban or Johannesburg. From the south leave the N2 at the Hluhluwe exit, and follow the R22, which runs along the southern boundary of uMkhuze Game Reserve and the turn-off to its western gate, and passes a number of luxury private game lodges. This tarred road continues on via Mbazwana to Sodwana Bay (95 km from Hluhluwe), and then on to Kosi Bay (163 km) and the Mozambique border at Kosi Bay/Farazela (185 km).

Coming from the north on the N2, you can either follow the route along the tarred R22 from Hluhluwe above, or take the exit to the village of Mkhuze, which is 53 km before or north of Hluhluwe. From here it is 18 km to the eastern gate of uMkhuze Game Reserve. From Mkhuze there is also an alternative northern route on a good gravel road to Sodwana Bay (95 km), passing through Ubombo, Tshongwe and Mbazwana.

Maputaland turtles

The coastline of the iSimangaliso Wetland Park is the only nesting site in Africa where loggerhead and the leatherback turtles lay their eggs. The turtles arrive between November and February migrating vast distances from as far afield as Madagascar, Kenya and the Cape.

After mating offshore, the female turtle, which can weigh up to 900 kg, struggles through the surf and up the beach above the high tide mark. Egg laying takes place at night and after digging a hole in the beach down to 1 m in depth, the female will lay a batch of 80-100 eggs. She then carefully covers the nest with sand and makes the cumbersome journey back to sea.

Incubation takes around 70 days, and then from January to March, the tiny turtles hatch together and then dig their way to the surface and scramble to the sea, which again happens at night. Few hatchlings live to become adults and the threat of being eaten by predators begins immediately with ghost crabs and jackals waiting to catch them before they can reach the sea. Only about four out of 1000 hatchlings are estimated to survive.

Most of the coastal lodges in Maputaland, and the tour operators in St Lucia (page 102), offer night-time turtle-watching trips. This is a very special wildlife experience and in the dark with spotlights, it's not uncommon to see other creatures like jackals, crocodiles and snakes on the beach, and nightjars, bush babies and chameleons in the coastal bush.

Another approach if coming from the north to northern Maputaland – Ndumo, Tembe and Kosi Bay reserves and the Kosi Bay/Farazela border with Mozambique – is to take the Jozini exit off the N2, which is 10 km north of Mkhuze and 54 km south of Pongola. From this exit a tarred road (though beware of potholes and cattle in the road) goes northeast via Jozini and crosses the Lebombo Mountains and the Maputaland coastal plain past the access roads to Ndumo and Tembe and joins the R22 just before KwaNgwanase, also known as Manguzi, which is 130 km from the N2 turn-off. From KwaNgwanase (Manguzi) there is access to Kosi Bay Nature Reserve and the Kosi Bay/Farazela border with Mozambique is another 20 km north.

Note The extreme northern KwaZulu-Natal coast towards the border with Mozambique lies in what is considered a seasonal low-risk malarial area (December-April). However, malaria is not a serious threat and is very rarely contracted by anyone in this region, but the situation could change depending on the amount of rainfall. Take local advice and precautions if necessary.

uMkhuze Game Reserve → *For listings, see pages 112-114. See map, page 79.*

ⓘ *T035-573 9004, www.kznwildlife.com, gates Nov-Mar 0500-1900, Apr-Oct 0600-1800, the office and shop is at Mantuma Camp 0800-1600, R35, children (under 12) R25, car R45.*

This 40,000-ha reserve was proclaimed a protected area in 1912, and constitutes the northwestern spur of the iSimangaliso Wetland Park. It has an astonishing diversity of natural habitats, from the eastern slopes of the Lebombo Mountains, to broad stretches of acacia savannah, swamps and a variety of woodlands and riverine forest. The Mkhuze River curves along the reserve's northern and eastern borders with a fine stretch of fig forest along its banks. Mkhuze is not visited as often as Hluhluwe-Imfolozi (see page 84) as there are not as many rhino, but it offers opportunities to go on guided bush walks and see some of Maputaland's more unusual animals.

Arriving in uMkhuze Game Reserve

There are two gates into the reserve; the eastern entrance is clearly signposted off the N2 at the turn-off to the village of Mkhuze. From there follow a gravel road 17 km to the eMshophi Gate. For the western entrance, follow the R22 northeast from Hluhluwe for 50 km then turn left onto the D820. The Ophansi Gate is a further 14 km along this road. If you're coming from the north on the R22, the turn-off onto the D820 is 28 km southwest of Mbazwana.

The office and shop are at Mantuma Camp, which is in the northeast of the park, 10 km from eMshophi Gate. Reservations for camping should be made here. The shop sells cold drinks, ice, some basic supplies, curios, and is also a good place to pick up some informative leaflets on birds, trees, walks and drives. The **Rhino-Dine-O** ⓘ *0700-0930, 1130-1400 and 1700-1900*, restaurant and takeaway and a petrol pump are also at Mantuma.

Wildlife

uMkhuze is an excellent place to see some of Maputaland's big game. Elephant, hippo, crocodile, giraffe, blue wildebeest, impala, kudu, suni, black and white rhino, cheetah, leopard, wild dog and hyena are all present in the reserve. It is also one of the best places to see the shy nyala antelope – nearly 8000 live here. Over 420 bird species have been recorded, and as part of the Mozambique coastal plain, uMkhuze attracts many tropical birds often only seen further north. Look out for Neergard's sunbird, the yellow-spotted nicator and the African broadbill. Many aquatic birds visit the pans here during the summer when you can see woolly-necked storks, herons, flamingos, pink-backed and white pelicans, ibises, spoonbills and jacanas from the hides overlooking the pans. Bird checklists are available from the shop.

Game-drives

A 100-km network of roads crosses the reserve, but some pass through areas of thick bush, which are not ideal for game viewing; the grasslands, however, are more open and animals are easier to see. The best game-viewing areas are the **Loop Road**, the **Nsumo Pan** and the **airstrip**. There are four game-viewing hides next to the Kubube, Kumasinga, Kwamalibala and Kumahlala pans. The viewing here is excellent and you can watch the game coming down to drink. There are also two bird-viewing hides next to the Nsumo Pan, where a myriad of waterfowl can be seen. There are car parks nearby where you can leave your car and walk to the hides. Day and night drives, R200, children (under 12) R100, which last about two hours, and two- to three-hour game walks, R110 children (under 12) R55, must be booked at the Mantuma Camp office as soon as you arrive.

Sodwana Bay → *For listings, see pages 112-114. See map, page 79.*

ⓘ *Gate 24 hrs, office and shop Mon-Thu 0800-1630, Fri-Sat 0700-1630, Sun 0700-1500, T035-571 0051, www.kznwildlife.com, R25, children (under 12) R20.*

Some 360 km northeast of Durban, and 620 km east of Johannesburg, Sodwana Bay is South Africa's premier scuba-diving destination – and is the site of the world's southernmost tropical coral reefs. The reserve is part of the iSimangaliso Wetland Park's area that protects the coast from Sodwana Bay north to Kosi Bay Nature Reserve on the border of Mozambique and 5 km out to sea. Around 80% of South Africa's 1200 species of fish can be found in the waters off Sodwana; ragged-toothed and whale sharks, humpback whales, black marlin and turtles are some of the major attractions. Diving has become so popular here that over 100,000 dives a year are made on these reefs.

Arriving in Sodwana Bay

From the south, turn off the N2 at the Hluhluwe exit on to the tarred R22 and its 97 km via Mbazwana. From the north, turn off the N2 at the Jozini exit and its 79 km on a gravel road via Mbazwana. Mbazwana village itself has a colourful market selling fruit and handicrafts, as well as a petrol station and ATM. From the village it's 16 km to the Sodwana gate. Once there, the shop at the office sells limited groceries, fishing tackle and beach gear, and petrol is available.

Sodwana is popular with visitors all year round and the weather is typically subtropical. Diving conditions are good throughout the year, but the best diving is from April to September, when on a good day visibility can reach up to 30 m, and water temperatures are usually above 20°C and can reach 29°C in summer. Fishermen tend to congregate here in November and December, and December and January are the best times to see the turtles laying their eggs. Sodwana gets very crowded during the school holidays when the accommodation is fully booked months in advance.

Diving

The coral reefs at Sodwana lie just offshore and teem with colourful tropical fish. Among some of the more unusual sightings are the loggerhead, leatherback and hawksbill turtles, honeycomb moray eels, dolphins, whale sharks, stingrays, humpback whales and black marlins. **Two Mile Reef** is very popular with divers. It is 1.5 km long and nearly 1 km wide, with depths ranging from 9 m to 34 m. There are numerous dive sites to explore here and anemones, triggerfish, sponges and fan-shaped gorgoniums can be seen in this area of overhangs and caves. The dives at **Five Mile Reef** and **Seven Mile Reef** are at around 22 m, and both are renowned for their corals. Access to Five Mile Reef is limited, but it is worth trying to get on a dive to see this protected area with its delicate miniature Staghorn Coral Gardens. **Nine Mile Reef** is only open for a limited number of dives and is well known for its soft corals. There are some large caves which can shelter pyjama sharks. Depths range from 5 m to 24 m.

The closest snorkelling site to Sodwana is on **Quarter Mile Reef**, 500 m off Jesser Point. Further south are **Algae Reef** (5 km) and **Adams Reef** (10 km). These are shallow rocky reefs with good visibility inhabited by tiny tropical fish.

Coastal Forest Reserve and Lake Sibaya → For listings, see pages 112-114.
See map, page 79.

ⓘ *Gate 0600-1800, office 0700-1600, information from Kosi Bay Camp T035-592 0235, www.kznwildlife.com, R25, children (under 12) R15, car R20.*
Lake Sibaya, about 20 km north of Sodwana as the crow flies, is the largest freshwater lake in South Africa and was previously connected to the sea. It now lies within the iSimangaliso Wetland Park and covers around 70 sq km and is surrounded by swampy reed beds and patches of forest. Although its clear blue waters may look cool and appealing, Lake Sibaya is not a good place to swim and crocodiles and hippos paddle about in numbers second only to those in Lake St Lucia.

Arriving in the Coastal Forest Reserve

From Mbazwana go north for 18 km on the R22 and you'll see the Coastal Forest Reserve sign on the right. From there it's 24 km to the gate; you will see the signs to either **Rocktail Beach Camp** or **Thonga Beach Lodge** (see page 113). Once in the reserve, the sandy coastal track heads south to Lake Sibaya and Mabibi Beach, and north to Rocktail Bay and Black Rock. However because of deep sand, the reserve is only accessible by 4WD. For visitors in 2WD vehicles staying in the lodges, it's possible to park at the Coastal Cashews offices which are 4.7 km along this road and where the lodges pick up from. For those who are able to drive into the reserve, there is a simple rustic campsite here, **Mabibi Campsite**, see page 113, close to Thonga Beach Lodge. Once back on the R22, it continues north to KwaNgwanase (Manguzi) and Kosi Bay, Tembe and Ndumo reserves.

Wildlife and activies

A long strip of thickly forested dunes runs between the Indian Ocean and the lake, and here you can find 279 species of birds, including the rare palmnut vulture, Pel's fishing-owl, pygmy goose, bat hawk, yellow white-eye, the rufous-bellied heron and Woodward's batis. Kingfishers, cormorants and fish eagles are often seen on the lake itself. Apart from the more or less unmissable crocodiles and hippos, keep an eye out for smaller creatures like the samango monkey, red squirrel and blue duiker.

A little further north, the sandy track running parallel to the coast leads to the beautiful secluded beaches of Mabibi, Rocktail Bay and Black Rock. These are renowned for being among the ultimate game-fishing sites in South Africa. The clear waters also offer spectacular opportunities for snorkelling, with good chances of seeing turtles and sharks as well as hundreds of colourful tropical fish.

Ndumo Game Reserve → For listings, see pages 112-114. See map, page 79.

ⓘ *T035-591 0098, www.kznwildlife.com, gate Apr-Sep 0600-1800, Oct-Mar 0500-1900, office and shop 0800-1200, 1300-1600, R40, children (under 12) R20, car R40.*
Ndumo is a low-lying and humid tropical floodplain lying along the border of Mozambique and is renowned for its magnificent birdlife and large numbers of crocodiles and hippos. This is one of the wildest and most beautiful reserves in South Africa. The area had been heavily hunted since the 1850s, and a reserve was established in 1924 to protect the hippos. Over time, some species that had been hunted out were reintroduced. Today the varied flora of the reserve, which includes numerous pans and reedbeds interspersed with patches of riverine forest and mixed woodland, provides habitats for a good cross-section of game that favours wetlands.

Arriving in Ndumo Game Reserve

The most direct route is to take the Jozini exit on the N2 from where it's 93 km north to Ndumo. Ndumo is also 98 km northeast of Mbazwana via the R22. The roads in the reserve are in good condition and visitors can drive around the reserve in their own cars or travel by 4WD with a guide. There are five game-viewing hides to stop at and a leaflet is available for a self-guided car trail. The shop sells ice, soft drinks, beer and wine, but no food.

Wildlife

The pans at Banzi and Nyamithi are fascinating areas to experience the atmosphere of an African tropical swamp. There are many waterbirds to look out for on the pans including some rare tropical species at the southern limit of their habitats. Thousands of birds congregate here in the evenings and it is possible to see flocks of flamingos, geese, pelicans and storks. Special ticks for birders include Pel's fishing owl, the broadbill and southern-banded snake eagle.

Buffalo are occasionally seen in the swampy areas of the reserve, but nyala, bushbuck, impala, grey and red duiker, hippo and crocodiles are present in large numbers. The vegetation in the rest of the reserve is quite thick and makes game viewing difficult. Black and white rhino, leopard and suni antelope thrive in these thickets but they are very rarely seen. A good way to see Ndumo is on one of the morning or afternoon game-drives, R220, children (under 12) R155, or game walks with an armed game ranger, R110, children (under 12) R55. These must be arranged with the office on arrival.

Tembe Elephant Park → For listings, see pages 112-114. See map, page 79.

ⓘ *T035-592 0001, www.kznwildlife.com, gate Apr-Sep 0600-1800, Oct-Mar 0500-1900, office 0700-1600, R40, children (under 12) R20, plus R40 vehicle.*
Tembe lies on the border with Mozambique between Ndumo Game Reserve and Kosi Bay and was established in 1983 to protect this area's elephant population, which had declined to just 130. The South African Defence Force had erected an electrified fence between South Africa and Mozambique during the Mozambique civil war (1977-1992), which blocked a natural elephant migration path. The fences have now been removed and the elephants' range has expanded again. In this area, approximately 1200-1500 elephants move between Tembe and Ndumo and the Maputo Special Reserve in Mozambique – known on that side of the border as Reserva Especial de Maputo. The 30,000-ha protected area at Tembe is a vast impenetrable wilderness of sand forest, thick bush and the Muzi Swamp. This is a very special place to visit, but you will need to plan well in advance, given the strict access controls.

Arriving in Tembe

Tembe is 87 km from the Jozini exit on the N2, or alternatively its 65 km north of Mbazwana on the R22. Although the road is tarred as far as the entrance to the park, the roads inside are so rough that only 4WDs are allowed in. If you are staying at the **Tembe Elephant Lodge** (the only accommodation within the park, see page 114) you can leave your car at the gate and arrange for a 4WD transfer. In addition to overnight visitors staying in the lodge, only a further

10 groups of day visitors in a 4WD are allowed into the park each day, and each group is accompanied by a game ranger.

Wildlife

Some of the more common species to be seen include giraffe, elephant, waterbuck, zebra, nyala and buffalo. If you are lucky you may see the small, shy, suni antelope and leopard. There are two hides in the reserve: one at Ponweni by Muzi swamp, this overlooks an elephant crossing point; the second overlooks Mahlasela Pan. There is also a self-guided walk within the Ngobazane enclosure area.

Kosi Bay Nature Reserve → *For listings, see pages 112-114. See map, page 79.*

ⓘ *T035-592 0236, www.kznwildlife.com, gate 0600-1800, office and shop 0800-1600, R30, children (under 12) R15, car R40.*
Kosi Bay is one of South Africa's favourite wilderness destinations. The protected area covers 11,000 ha and is over 25 km long and consists of four lakes separated from the sea by a long strip of forest-covered dunes. Lakes Amanzimnyama, Nhlange, Mpungwini and Sifungwe are part of a fascinating tropical wetland environment. Lake Amanzimnyama is a freshwater lake with darkened water due to decomposing plants. The shores of the lakes are bordered with reedbeds, ferns, swamp figs and umdoni trees. Five species of mangrove thrive in the estuary. Kosi Bay is home to South Africa's only remaining estuarine hunter-gatherer tribe, the Tembe-Thonga, whose traditional fishing traps you can see across the estuary.

Arriving in Kosi Bay Nature Reserve

From the Jozini exit on the N2 follow directions to Ndumo and Tembe but stay on the road through to the village of KwaNgwanase (Manguzi); this is 138 km from the N2. Alternatively, it's 75 km from Mbazwana to KwaNgwanase (Manguzi) on the R22. From KwaNgwanase (Manguzi) the entrance gate to Kosi is around 10 km to the north on the way to the Mozambique border. The last 5 km and most of the tracks in the reserve are deep sand for which a 4WD is needed. The shop sells maps, ice, soft drinks, beer and wine, but no food, and the day visitor area has *braais* and shades.

Wildlife

The lakes are inhabited by hippos and crocodiles, which can be seen basking in the sun around Lake Amanzimnyama. There are no large mammals here but you are likely to see samango and vervet monkeys, bushbuck and duiker. The tropical climate is a boon to reptiles and two species of monitor lizard, the rock monitor and the Nile monitor, are often seen. Many of the snakes that live here are poisonous. The gaboon adder, boomslang, green mamba and forest cobras are all found here.

Many aquatic birds are attracted to the lakes and over 250 species have been spotted here. Rarities include the palmnut vulture and Pel's fishing owl, while the fish eagle and purple and reed kingfishers are commonly seen.

The research station at Bhanga Nek has been tagging turtles and protecting nesting sites since 1963. Leatherback and loggerhead turtles arrive on these beaches in December and January to lay their eggs after lengthy journeys from as far away as Madagascar and the Cape, see box, page 105.

◉ Maputaland listings

For hotel and restaurant price codes and other relevant information, see pages 12-16.

🛏 Where to stay

uMkhuze Game Reserve
p106, map p79

$$$ Ghost Mountain Inn, Fish Eagle Rd, Mkhuze, T035-573 1025/7, www.ghostmountaininn.co.za. With easy access to the eastern gate of uMkhuze Game Reserve, this is one of the most popular country hotels in Maputaland, 50 a/c rooms with DSTV and patios leading to indigenous gardens and rolling lawns, restaurant serving excellent food, spa and 2 swimming pools. Good-value safari packages and Zulu cultural experiences – a good option if you don't want to self-cater in the reserve.

$$$ Nhlonhlela Bush Lodge, reservations Ezemvelo KZN Wildlife, T033-845 1000, www.kznwildlife.com. Luxury lodge sleeping 8 looking out over fever trees and Nhlonhlela Pan. The 4 en suite rooms are connected by boardwalks branching out from the communal lounge and kitchen, where a cook will prepare meals and there's a ranger for guided game walks. Must be booked as a single unit.

$$$-$$ Mantuma Camp. The main camp, the buildings are set among natural gardens and are not fenced off so game does sometimes wander through. 15 cottages sleeping 4-6 with fully equipped kitchen, 10 2- to 3-bed tents raised on wooden decks with en suite bathrooms and communal kitchen, and 6 2-bed rest huts with communal kitchen and ablution block. There's a restaurant and takeaway, swimming pool and shop.

Camping
eMshophi Campsite, 1 km from the eMshophi Gate, 9 km from Mantuma. Located at the western entrance of the reserve in the foothills of the Lubombo Mountains, has 55 sites and a swimming pool and children's playground. There's electricity for lights and hot showers 0500-0800 and 1700-2200.

Sodwana Bay *p107, map p79*
$$$-$$ Sodwana Bay Camp, reservations Ezemvelo KZN Wildlife,

T033-845 1000, www.kznwildlife.com. 10 8-bed and 10 5-bed self-catering fully equipped log cabins set in dune forest close to the beach. A supermarket is across the road from the main office and fuel is also available.

$$ Sodwana Bay Lodge, T035-571 6010, www.sodwanabaylodge.com. 20 twin-bedded reed and thatch huts on stilts overlooking woodland, restaurant serving seafood (what else), bar, pool, game-fishing trips available. The lodge offers a number of all-inclusive diving package deals plus a full range of PADI courses, with a fully equipped PADI dive shop and learning pool run by the **Sodwana Bay Lodge Scuba Centre**, T035-571 0117, www.sodwanadiving.co.za.

$ Coral Divers, T035-571 0290, www.coraldivers.co.za. PADI dive centre with accommodation in either en suite wooden cabins or pre-erected dome tents that share ablutions with the **Ezemvelo KZN Wildlife** campsite above. Each cabin/tent must have at least one diver. The camp has its own *braai* area with a boma, bar, restaurant, deck, TV room with DSTV and internet, and swimming pool. Again offers diving package deals plus a full range of courses.

Camping

iGwalagwala Campsite, T035-571 0051/3, www.kznwildlife.com. In the main section there are 64 sites with power points and 286 sites without, and it can become very crowded, plus there are 33 more expensive sites in a more secluded area with their own taps and power points. Freezer drawers can be hired and should be booked in advance, and there's a supermarket at the entrance.

Coastal Forest Reserve and Lake Sibaya *p108, map p79*
Access is by 4WD only. Guests can leave their 2WD cars at the Coastal Cashews offices where the lodges pick up from (see page 108).

$$$$ Rocktail Beach Camp, Rocktail Bay, reservations T011-883 0747, www.wilderness-safaris.com. Secluded bush camp with 17 comfortable A-frame chalets set on stilts among dunes, central dining area, bar and lounge with raised wooden deck and ocean views, pool, a wide range of activities including birdwatching walks, diving, snorkelling, 4WD trips to Lake Sibaya, and turtle excursions.

$$$$ Thonga Beach Lodge, Mabibi Beach, 6 km north of Lake Sibaya, T035-474 1473, www.thongabeach lodge.co.za. Remote luxury lodge with 24 spacious a/c thatched suites with stone bathrooms, reed walls, large open windows, built on stilts on a strip of forested dunes, each very private, bar and restaurant with ocean views, pool and spa. Activities include excursions to see turtles, kayaking on Lake Sibaya, diving and snorkelling, and Tsonga village visits.

Camping

Mabibi Campsite, Mabibi Beach, 6 km north of Lake Sibaya, T035-474 1473 www.mabibicampsite.co.za. Next to and run by **Thonga Beach Lodge** in a lovely spot overlooking Hulley Point with 10 sites on the top of a forested dune, each has tap, *braai* and shade and access to the beach is via a long wooden stairway. Only accessible by 4WD through thick sand.

Ndumo Game Reserve
p109, map p79

$$ Ndumo Resort, Ezemvelo KZN Wildlife, T033-845 1000, www.kzn wildlife.com. 7 2-bed rest huts with and verandas in a lovely setting overlooking the Pongola floodplain, surrounded by tropical vegetation. Shared bathrooms and well-equipped communal kitchen and a cook is on hand to prepare meals (guests must bring their own food).

Camping
Reservations, T035-591 0058. 14 shady sites with power points and *braais*. Campers share the communal ablutions and kitchen used by guests in the resort.

Tembe Elephant Park
p110, map p79

$$$ Tembe Elephant Lodge, T031-267 0144, www.tembe.co.za. Bush camp with 9 comfortable tents raised on wooden platforms tucked away in secluded areas. There are hot showers with glass walls that look out over the bush, small pool, dining boma with fire and relaxing veranda. Rates include meals and game-drives, which are also available to day visitors by prior arrangement.

Kosi Bay Nature Reserve
p111, map p79

$$$$ Kosi Forest Lodge, reservations T035-592 9239, www.isibindiafrica.

co.za. Set on the banks of Kosi Lake with 8 secluded reed and thatch suites, with hardwood floors and delightful open-air bathrooms, restaurant, bar, swimming pool. Activities include turtle-watching trips, canoeing and diving. Beautiful setting, and popular with honeymooners. Non-4WD drivers can park cars at the Total garage in KwaNgwanase (Manguzi) and prearrange a pickup.

$$$-$$ Kosi Bay Camp, Ezemvelo KZN Wildlife, T033-845 1000, www. kznwildlife.com. Set on the western shore of Lake Nhlange with 3 thatched cabins with either 6, 5 or 2 beds, fully equipped for self-catering. The strictly 4WD sandy track to the camp is spectacular with views across the fish kraal-dotted lake to the sea as you crest huge coastal dunes.

$$ Kosi Bay Lodge, access from the approach road to the reserve, T035-592 9561, www.kosibaylodge.co.za. The cheapest option in the region with a collection of Tsonga/Zulu-style reed and thatch rustic en suite huts on stilts with 2-4 beds, plus A-frame chalets with kitchen and *braai*, and tents with communal ablution block. Restaurant and pub with deck, swimming pool. Normal cars can reach here, only the last 3 km are sand on a well-used road, and it's another 2 km to the reserve gate.

Camping
Reservations, T035-592 0236. 16 sites with power points and an ablution block among the trees near **Kosi Bay Camp** at Lake Nhlange.

Contents

116 Pietermaritzburg and the Midlands
116 Arriving in Pietermaritzburg and KwaZulu-Natal Midlands
117 Pietermaritzburg
121 KwaZulu-Natal Midlands
124 Listings

129 Battlefields
129 Ladysmith and around
135 Dundee and around
138 Listings

142 uKhahlamba-Drakensberg Park
142 Arriving in uKhahlamba-Drakensberg Park
143 Background
147 Northern Drakensberg
150 Central Drakensberg
157 Southern Drakensberg
161 Listings

Footprint features

130 Visiting the battlefields
132 The siege of Ladysmith
134 Ladysmith Black Mambazo
136 Blood River
144 Cave paintings
156 Lammergeyers

The Midlands, Battlefields & Drakensberg

Pietermaritzburg and the Midlands

Pietermaritzburg was named after the Voortrekker leaders Gert Maritz and Piet Reteif, who settled here in 1838 after the Battle of Blood River. The British arrived in 1843 and established a garrison here. It became a prosperous Victorian town and many of its most attractive buildings date from this period and, despite its largely African population and bustling street life, its red-brick buildings do give it a strikingly similar look to a provincial English town.

The KwaZulu-Natal Midlands has a well-watered, fertile landscape and is the province's most prosperous farming region. It can be explored by following the Midlands Meander route, which is reminiscent of a Sunday afternoon drive through English countryside. It is one of South Africa's local tourism success stories.

Arriving in Pietermaritzburg and KwaZulu-Natal Midlands

Pietermaritzburg is only 80 km from Durban on the N3 and can easily be visited in a day. **King Shaka International Airport** (see page 24) is about a one-hour drive, and **Peitermaritzburg/Oribi Airport** is 7 km south of the centre of town on Oribi Road and has daily flights to/from Johannesburg operated by SAA. The **railway station** is on the corner of Church and Pine streets. This is a rough part of town, so arrange to be collected in advance if you're arriving by train. Long-distance buses and the **Baz Bus** stop here on the route between Durban and Johannesburg. The **Underberg Express** runs regular shuttles to the Southern Drakensberg on its route to and from Durban. » For more information see Transport, page 128.

Pietermaritzburg Tourism ① *Publicity House, 177 Chief Albert Luthuli Rd, T033-345 1348, www.pmbtourism.co.za, Mon-Fri 0800-1700, Sat 0800-1300*, is conveniently situated and has a comprehensive range of maps and leaflets, as well as an accommodation and bus booking service. The original building was completed in 1884 and used to be the local police station. In the Queen Elizabeth Park Nature Reserve, about 8 km northwest of Pietermaritzburg, is the headquarters and central reservations office for **Ezemvelo KZN Wildlife** ① *T033-845 1000, www.kznwildlife.com, Mon-Fri 0800-1630, telephone reservations until 1700 and Sat 0800-1300*. To get here, follow Chief Albert Luthuli Road out of town and follow the Old Howick Rd (R103) towards Hilton, then take the right hand fork to Montrose (be careful not to go onto the N3) on to Duncan Mckenzie Drive, and carry on for 4 km past Victoria Country Club.

Places in Pietermaritzburg

City Hall and around Dominating the city centre is the grand **City Hall**, which looms on the corner of Chief Albert Luthuli Road and Church Street. Built on the site of the Volksraadsaal (people's council) in 1900, it is supposedly the largest all-brick building in the southern hemisphere and is decorated with stained-glass windows. The **Supreme Court Gardens** are opposite the City Hall and are the site of several war memorials. The **Memorial Arch** is flanked by two field guns captured from the Germans by South African forces in Southwest Africa in 1915. The **Zulu War Memorial** has a cannon next to it, which was cast in Scotland in 1812 and used to be fired to let the citizens of Pietermaritzburg know that the mail had arrived.

The **statue of Gandhi**, commemorating the centenary of his arrival in South Africa (1893), is just below the gardens on Church Street, and across the street is the old **Colonial Building**, built in 1899, decorated with Natal's coat of arms, featuring a wildebeest, and Pietermaritzburg's coat of arms, featuring an elephant.

Tatham Art Gallery ① *60 Chief Albert Luthuli Rd, T033-342 2801, www. tatham.org.za, Tue-Sun 1000-1800, free, café and museum shop,* opposite the City Hall is a similarly imposing red-brick structure, completed in 1879 and used as a post office until 1906, when it became the site of the Supreme Court. In 1990, it was inaugurated as the new home for the Tatham Art Gallery. Inside is a fairly ramshackle selection of modern and Victorian art; the original collections are of French and British Victorian artists, and although the landscapes are fairly pleasant there is nothing particularly striking about them. The **South African Gallery** is the most interesting, with a collection of contemporary art including beadwork of Zulu and Xhosa origins. There is a large, highly ornate ormolu late Victorian clock at the top of the stairs on the first floor. When chiming, a screen is raised to reveal a clockwork blacksmith and some bellringers moving in time with the chimes. The gallery shop stocks some fine Zulu baskets and ceramics.

Msunduzi Museum ① *351 Langalibalele St, T033-394 6834, www.voortrekker museum.co.za, Mon-Fri 0900-1600, Sat 0900-1300, R8, children (under 12) R2, museum shop.* Formerly known as the Voortrekker Museum, this is on the site of the original Church of the Vow and has a collection of period farm machinery, furniture and other Voortrekker relics. There is an interesting display that ponders the subject of Kruger's war chest, which disappeared en route to Lorenço Marques (today's Maputo – capital of Mozambique) and has never been recovered. Another item to look out for is a pair of enormous Voortrekker trousers. The former Longmarket Street Girls' School building is incorporated into the site, and houses more culturally significant exhibitions on the peoples of KwaZulu-Natal including a reproduction of a traditional Zulu home, filled with household goods, and a small replica of a Hindu Shiva temple surrounded by beautiful herb garden.

KwaZulu-Natal Museum ⓘ *237 Jabu Ndlova St, T033-345 1404, www.nmsa. org.za, Mon-Fri 0815-1630, Sat 0900-1600, Sun 1000-1500, R10, children (4-17) R2050, under 4s free.* The KwaZulu-Natal Museum has a more diverse collection

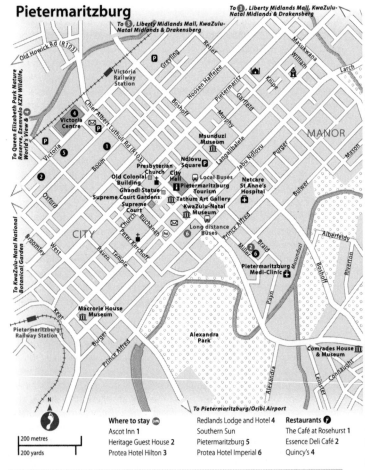

Pietermaritzburg

Where to stay 🛏
Ascot Inn **1**
Heritage Guest House **2**
Protea Hotel Hilton **3**

Redlands Lodge and Hotel **4**
Southern Sun
Pietermaritzburg **5**
Protea Hotel Imperial **6**

Restaurants 🍴
The Café at Rosehurst **1**
Essence Deli Café **2**
Quincy's **4**

than many other South African museums. The natural history gallery has a considerable collection of stuffed creatures that date from the foundation of the museum, including the last wild elephant shot in Natal in 1911. The first treasure chest of the Colony of Natal can be found here; an old iron chest that used to travel around the colony by wagon and was used to collect the Native Hut Tax. The colony's finances were at times so desperate that the chest held less than a pound. There are also a number of archaeological displays, with examples of San rock art in a reconstructed cave, and the final gallery focuses on Portuguese shipwrecks.

Saki Pacific Grill 5
Traffords 6

Comrades House Museum ① *18 Connaught Rd, T033-897 8650, www. comrades.com, Mon-Fri 0830-1300, free.* To the east of the city in Scotsville in an old restored Victorian house is the Comrades House Museum, which is dedicated to the Comrades Marathon between Durban and Pietermaritzburg held in May or June; it is also its headquarters. Established in 1921 to commemorate South African soldiers killed during the First World War, this is the world's oldest and most gruelling ultra-marathon as it tackles both distance and gradient. The direction of the race alternates each year between the 'up' run (87 km) starting from Durban and the 'down' run (89 km) starting from Pietermaritzburg. It attracts more than 20,000 runners and international competitors are welcome (register and book accommodation well in advance). The museum has trophies and shields, memorabilia, historic photos and a to-scale (1:25000) model of the route showing the 'big five' hills; Cowies, Fields, Botha's, Inchanga and Poly Shorts. This may either inspire new Comrades runners or stir painful memories for past participants.

Outside the city centre Four kilometres east of the centre is the attractive **KwaZulu-Natal National Botanical Garden** ① *2 Swartkops Rd, Mayors Walk, T033-344 3585, www.sanbi.org, May-Sep 0800-1730, Oct-Apr 0800-1800, restaurant Tue-Sun, R20, children (6-16) R12, under 6s free*, which was established in 1874 and following a fine Victorian tradition has a collection of plants from the northern hemisphere including camphor, plane and magnolia trees. The most interesting feature is the **Zulu Muthi Garden**, created with the help of local healers and including a traditional beehive-shaped healer's hut. The garden is rich in birdlife, with over 150 species recorded, and is ideal for a leisurely stroll or afternoon tea next to the ornamental lake. A farmer's market is held here every Saturday morning where you can buy items to make up a picnic.

Situated on the northern slopes of Pietermaritzburg is the **Queen Elizabeth Park Nature Reserve** ① *8 km northwest of Pietermaritzburg follow the Old Howick Rd (103) and take the right hand fork to Montrose (be careful not to go onto the N3) on to Duncan Mckenzie Dr, carry on for 4 km past Victoria Country Club, free*. It is small but has a network of short walking trails from which you can see blesbock, impala and zebra, and the flora here is particularly interesting; the park has been a wild flower reserve since 1960 and has stunning displays of colour in the spring. The headquarters of **Ezemvelo KZN Wildlife** (see page 116) are located within the park. Before you get here, stop at **World's View** on World's View Road near the Victoria Country Club on the Old Howick Road (R103). There's a plaque that marks the route taken by the early Voortrekkers in 1837-8, when they brought their ox-wagons down the slopes of the Drakensberg into Natal. There are magnificent views of Pietermaritzburg from the top of this hill.

Butterflies for Africa ① *Willowton Rd, T033-387 1356, www.butterflies.co.za, Tue-Fri 0900-1600, Sat 0930-1530, Sun 1030-1530, R38, children (3-16) R24, under 3s free, Kestrel Café and curio shop*, is clearly signposted from the N3 towards Durban. It incorporates a large enclosed butterfly house, a butterfly garden and nursery with a maze, a craft and coffee shop, an art gallery and museum, and audio-visual presentations on the life of a butterfly.

The African Bird of Prey Sanctuary ① *Camperdown, 18 km south of Pietermaritzburg on the N3 take Exit 65 (Lynnfield Park) and follow signs east for 4 km, T031-785 4382, www.africanraptor.co.za, Tue-Sun 0900-1600, flying displays Tue-Fri 1030, Sat-Sun 1030 and 1500, R50, children (3-16) R30, under 3s free, Kestrel Café and curio shop*, is set in a scenic 60-ha bushveld valley. A rehabilitation centre for orphaned, sick or injured birds of prey from throughout KwaZulu-Natal, visitors can walk around the spacious enclosures to see what is considered South Africa's largest collection of owls, raptors and vultures; around 180-200 individuals from more than 50 different species. Try to be here for the aerial display, which demonstrates how big and powerful some of these birds are.

KwaZulu-Natal Midlands → *For listings, see pages 124-128.*

The KwaZulu-Natal Midlands cover the region between Greytown and Richmond, Pietermaritzburg and Estcourt. The fertile landscape that originally supported a large population of Zulu cattle herders and farmers in the lowlands. San migrated between here and the Drakensberg, following the herds of eland according to the changes of the seasons. Later the fertile territory attracted first the Voortrekkers and then British immigrants in the 1850s, all of whom fought for control of the land.

Today, the farms here cultivate wattle for tanning and paper pulp, and there are large horse-breeding studs, cattle and sheep ranches. The N3 bisects the Midlands and the majority of traffic passes through on its way between Gauteng and Durban. However, by taking the alternative R103, the Midlands towns and countryside can be explored by following the Midlands Meander route, which extends over 80 km between Pietermaritzburg and Mooi River.

Arriving in KwaZulu-Natal Midlands

There is an excellent map and brochure available in the region's tourist information offices for the **Midlands Meander**① *T033-3308195, www.midlands meander.co.za*, which promotes a series of routes for visiting the KwaZulu-Natal Midlands by car. Over 400 places are marked on the map and include a selection of country hotels, B&Bs, galleries, craft outlets and restaurants; the antique shops, potteries and weavers are especially good places to buy gifts. The symbol of the Midlands Meander (seen on road signs marking the routes) is the endangered Karkloof blue butterfly, which is only 'on the wing' for a couple of weeks in autumn and is indigenous to this region of KwaZulu-Natal.

Howick

The small and quiet town of Howick 25 km northwest of Pietermaritzburg has grown up around what was originally a fording point across the Umgeni River on the wagon route to the interior. The original settlement was named by the colonial secretary Earl Grey after his English home of Howick in Northumberland. The 95-m-high **Howick Falls** are a popular stop off for a break while travelling on the N3. To the Zulu people the waterfall is known as kwaNogqaza, 'the place of the tall one', local legend has it that the pool at the bottom of the falls is the residence of the Inkanyamba, a giant serpent-like creature. There is a path to the bottom of the falls but beware of the slippery rocks, but the best views are above the falls where there is a viewpoint with carpark, curio stalls and an open-air café. The **Howick Umgeni Museum** ① *T033-239 9240, www.howickmuseum.co.za, Mon-Fri 0845-1230, 1330-1530, Sat-Sun 1000-1300, R10 per person*, is just next to the falls and reveals how farming, the timber industry and village life developed from the 1850s.

Howick is most famous for being the place where Nelson Mandela was arrested on 5 August 1962, which was the catalyst for a series of trials, culminating in the Rivonia Treason Trial that would ultimately see him spend 27 years in prison. At the time of his arrest he had been on the run from the South African Apartheid government for 17 months, a feat that had earned him the name 'Black Pimpernel'. He was disguised as a driver named David Motsamay for a white friend and it is thought the police waved down the car on this lonely country road in KwaZulu-Natal because of a tip off. The actual spot where the police arrested him is about 5 km north of town on the R103, on a road heading towards Tweedie Junction. If you are coming from the N3, take the Tweedie turn-off to Lions River and turn right on to the R103. Once an unassuming spot in a field next to the road with a plaque, this is now the impressive and moving **Nelson Mandela Capture Site** ① *www.thecapturesite. co.za, daily 0900-1600, R25, children (under 18) R15, Truth Café, Fri-Sun 0800-1600 which has a swimming pool and children's playground,* which was unveiled by President Jacob Zuma in 2012. The unique sculpture by artist Marco Cianfanelli is made up of 50 steel columns between 6.5 m and 9.5 m tall, which create something of an optical illusion. From a distance, the structure simply looks like a random collection of poles, but as you approach down the Long Walk to Freedom Garden to within 35 m, they merge to form a portrait of Nelson Mandela's face. The site also features a museum where his capture in 1962 is documented along with more information about South Africa's political history.

The Karkloof range of hills is famed for its extensive mist belt forests and excellent birdwatching and it's not unheard of to see 80-100 species in a day including Cape parrot, emerald cuckoo, Knysna loerie and a number of raptors. Of great significance, is the isolated population of crested guinea fowl, which belong to a subspecies that is believed to be endemic to the Karkloof. The **Karkloof Canopy Tour** ① *Karkloof Nature Reserve, 17 km north of Howick towards Rietvlei, T033-330 3415, www.karkloofcanopytour.co.za, departure on the hour 0800-1400, R495 per person, no children under 7,* is one of many canopy tours now around South Africa (see www.canopytour.co.za for the other locations). It's a great way to see birds, and if you're lucky, samango monkeys, in the forest canopy from platforms in the trees some 40 m above the ground, which are connected by steel cables that you swing across on a harness; allow about two hours for the excursion.

Midmar Dam

① *7 km west of Howick on the R617 towards Bulwer, T033-330 2067, www. kznwildlife.com, gates 24 hrs, office 0800-1600, day visitors R20 per person, for accommodation, see page 125.*

This attractive dam formed by the Umgeni River is a hugely popular holiday resort for power boating, jet-skiing, windsurfing and yachting. It's surrounded by a 1000-ha game park that is home to red hartebeest, blesbok, reedbuck, black wildebeest, oribi and zebra, which can be seen from a network of gravel roads. There are also *braai* and picnic spots along the 15-km shoreline of the dam and a small shop open at weekends and peak periods rents out bikes, windsurfs and canoes. First swum in 1973, the **Midmar Mile** (www.midmarmile. co.za) swimming contest is held here every February and is now the world's largest inland swimming race that attracts more than 20,000 entrants.

Towards Estcourt

The fastest route north from Howick to Mooi River (41 km), Estcourt (74 km) and Harrismith (197 km) in the Free State is on the N3. An alternative scenic route is to take the R103 through Nottingham Road (35 km) to Mooi River (53 km).

The Nottingham Regiment gave their name to the small farming settlement of **Nottingham Road** after being stationed near here in the 1870s. This is a quiet, rural area, known for its trout fishing and holiday farms. The **Nottingham Road Brewery Company** ① *Old Main Rd, Rawdons Estate, T033-266 6728, www.nottsbrewery.co.za, tastings and shop 0800-1700*, is a rustic brewery with enticingly named beers that are hand-brewed using spring water: Tiddly Toad Lager, Pie-eyed Possum Pilsner, Pickled Pig Porter.

Further northwest, the **Mooi River** flows through a small farming community en route from the Drakensberg Mountains to the Tugela River. The area around Mooi River is well known for stud farming. The Drakensberg reserves at Kamberg (55 km; see page 156) and Giant's Castle (88 km; see page 155) are well signposted from here.

Estcourt

Estcourt is a thriving industrial town, site of South Africa's largest sausage factory and a Nestlé factory, both of which can be visited on a factory tour, if you're that way inclined. Factories aside, there's no reason to stop other than to stock up if you're on the way to self-catering accommodation in the Drakensberg.

Fort Durnford ① *T033-352 3000, open 0900-1200, 1300-1600, R5 per person*, has interesting displays on military history, a good section on fossils and, rather oddly, one of Africa's most complete bird egg collections, donated by a local collector. In the grounds you can look around a reconstructed Amangwane Zulu kraal. The fort itself was built in 1874 in order to protect local residents from feared Zulu attacks. It was named after Major Anthony Durnford who commanded the Natal Carbineers and was killed during the heroic last stand at Isandlwana.

For hotel and restaurant price codes and other relevant information, see pages 12-16.

⊜ Where to stay

Pietermaritzburg *p117, map p118*

$$$ Protea Hotel Hilton, 1 Hilton Av, Hilton, 500 m off the N3 12 km north of Pietermaritzburg, T033-343 3311, www.proteahotels.com. Tudor-style country hotel built in 1936, period furnishings like grandfather clocks and chandeliers, 60 comfortable rooms with DSTV and Wi-Fi, neat pool with wooden decks, bar with fireplace and cosy restaurant.

$$$ Redlands Lodge and Hotel, 1 George Mcfarlane Lane (off the Old Hilton Rd), T033-394 3333, www.redlandshotel.co.za. A smart red-brick hotel set in a quiet suburb, 22 comfortable country-style pastel-coloured rooms with balconies, DSTV and Wi-Fi, bar with a good choice of fine wine and whiskies, excellent restaurant, pool.

$$$ Southern Sun Pietermaritzburg, 45 New England Rd, Scottsville, T033-395 8500, www.tsogosunhotels.com. Part of the **Scotsville Racecourse** and **Golden Horse** casino complex (see page 127) where there are several restaurants and bars, this glitzy block has little atmosphere but will appeal to those wanting a modern hotel with good standards, 96 plush rooms, DSTV and Wi-Fi, pleasant swimming pool and terrace.

$$ Ascot Inn, 210 Woodhouse Rd, Scottsville, T033-386 2226, www. ascot-inn.co.za. Good value B&B or self-catering cottages with DSTV and Wi-Fi in converted stables of a former racehorse stud set in a lovely garden with ponds, paths, benches and swimming pool, friendly **Gallop Inn Pub & Grill**.

$$ Protea Hotel Imperial, 224 Jabu Ndlova St, T033-342 6551, www. proteahotels.com. Historical and atmospheric building with 70 good a/c rooms with DSTV, restaurant and bar. It's the oldest hotel in town; the Imperial Crown Prince of France, Louis Napoleon, stayed here during the Anglo-Boer War.

Howick *p121*

$$$ Old Halliwell Country Inn, 10 km north of Howick on Curry's Post Rd, T033-330 2602, www.oldhalliwell. co.za. A traditional English-style country hotel built in 1830 as a wagon stop. 15 rooms with fireplaces, DSTV, private garden patios, some have jacuzzis. **Lemon & Lavender** restaurant, and swimming pool set in lovely gardens with rolling lawns.

$$$-$$ Fern Hill Hotel, in Tweedie, 6 km west of Howick on the R103, T033-330 5087, www.fernhillhotel. co.za. Close to the Nelson Mandela Capture Site (see page 122) and Midmar Dam, this 3-star family-run country hotel is also a hotel school, 27 neat rooms, some with balconies, and the **Snooty Fox** à la carte restaurant which is open to passing trade and does an excellent Sun carvery lunch and curry buffet on Fri evening.

$$ Shafton Grange, 12 km north of Howick towards Rietvlei, T033-330 2386, www.shaftongrange.co.za. A fine old farmhouse built in 1852, with 5 rooms, some with Victorian baths and washstands, lounge, country meals, swimming pool. The 52-ha property is a Lipizzaner stud farm; horse riding and trout fishing can be arranged and there are lots of walks on the farm, which has a number of antelope. It's 5 km from **Karkloof Canopy Tour** (see page 122).

$$-$ Howick Falls Hotel, 2 Main St, T033-330 2809, www.howickfallshotel. co.za. Historic and atmospheric hotel built in 1872 – former guests include Mark Twain and Cecil Rhodes, 18 rooms with a/c, DSTV, some sleeping 4, bar, lounge and the **Victorian Café**, for all meals which is also worth stopping at for afternoon tea.

Midmar Dam *p122*

$$ Midmar Resort, Ezemvelo KZN Wildlife, T033-330 2067, T033-845 1000 (reservations), www. kznwildlife.com. 32 fully equipped self-catering chalets with DSTV sleeping 2-6 overlooking the dam, plus 16 rustic twin huts with fridge and stove and communal ablutions, and 3 campsites, 2 of which are on the shoreline. Gets very crowded during school holidays but otherwise a pleasant and well-managed resort.

Towards Estcourt *p123*

$$$$ Fordoun, Nottingham Rd, T033-266 6217, www.fordoun.com. Luxury country retreat, with 17 spacious and stylish rooms, overlooking a farm dam and rolling lawns. Excellent and intimate restaurant and an award-winning spa with indoor pool, flotation pool in the old silo tower and treatments using both international products and some created by a traditional African healer. Can organize fly-fishing in the area.

$$$ The Bend Country House, 14 km from Nottingham Rd towards Kamburg on the R103, T033-266 6441, www.thebend.co.za. Smart lodge set in a nature reserve with 16 spacious rooms with attractive decor and antique furniture, country meals, indoor swimming pool, horse riding and hiking, 5 km of the Mooi River runs through this reserve, trout fishing on 7 dams.

$$$-$$ Rawdons Hotel & Estate, Old Main Rd (R103), Nottingham Rd, T033-263 6044, www.rawdons. co.za. A thatched and whitewashed English-style country hotel that was established in 1954, 25 light and airy rooms decorated with antiques, **Boars' Head Pub & Restaurant**, swimming pool, lawn tennis, lots of walks around the 195-ha estate, also location of the **Nottingham Road Brewery** (see page 123).

$$ Sierra Ranch, on the R622 or Old Greytown Rd, 16 km from Mooi River, T033-263 1073, www.sierraranch. co.za. Good value Western-themed 935-ha resort with the Mooi River running through. Accommodation in 16 hotel rooms, 22 chalets sleeping 2-4, and 8 double rondavels. Restaurant, bar, pool, a wide range of activities, including tennis, bowls, river tubing and horse riding. Rates include dinner, bed and breakfast.

Estcourt *p123*
$$$ Blue Haze Country Lodge, 6 km from Estcourt on the Giant's Castle road, T036-352 5772, www. bluehaze.co.za. Thatched lodge in expansive grounds located on the way to the Battlefields and mountains, overlooking a peaceful lake, with 23 comfortable garden suites, swimming pool fringed by palms, cosy pub and restaurant.

❼ Restaurants

Pietermaritzburg *p117, map p118*
$$$-$$ Traffords, 43 Miller St, T033-39 443 64, www.traffords.co.za. Tue-Fri 1200-1500, Tue-Sat 1830-2100. Set in a lovely Victorian house, the menu is seasonal and uses fresh herbs and greens from their garden, expect the likes of duck, pork belly, lamb shanks or Durban seafood. Also has 6 comfortable rooms (**$$**) in the adjoining **Heritage Guest House**.
$$ Saki Pacific Grill, 137 Victoria Rd, T033-342 6999, www.saki.co.za. Daily 1200-2200. Asian-themed restaurant with informal atmosphere at long wooden tables, family orientated, a wide selection of affordable Thai, Indian, Japanese and Chinese food, something for everyone, Singapore and Indian beer to drink and, of course, saki.
$$-$ Quincy's, Victoria Centre, 157 Victoria Rd, T033-345 4339, www. quincys.co.za. Mon-Sat 0730-2130, Sun 0900-1430. Friendly and relaxed with a large shaded outdoor seating section,

this offers everything from breakfast and light meals to hearty Durban mutton curry and oxtail casserole. Holds regular quiz nights in the bar.

Cafés
The Café at Rosehurst, 239 Boom St, T033-394 3833. Mon-Fri 0830-1600, Sat 0830-1430. This 30-year-old Maritzburg institution is set in a Victorian cottage surrounded by stunning gardens influenced by the garden at Sissinghurst Castle in southeast England; it's divided into the pink lawn garden, the yellow sundial garden, the white gazebo garden and the mauve side garden. The delightful café serves breakfasts, light lunches and cream teas and the shop is filled with quirky bits and pieces from antiques and crafts, to books and home-made chocolates.
Essence Deli Café, 120 Victoria Rd, T033-342 9215, www.essencecafe. co.za. Mon-Fri 0700-1700, Sat-Sun 0800-1400. Bright white airy café with modern paintings on the walls, serving healthy breakfasts, excellent coffees, and the lunchtime buffet of home-made bakes and salads is priced per weight. Also sells a great collection of cookery and decor books.

Howick *p121*
$$-$ Yellowwod Café, 1 Shafton Rd, T033-330 2461, www.yellowwood. co.za. Tue-Sun 0930-2130. Beautiful historic farmhouse with rambling rooms and large veranda, varied menu using organic and local produce, breakfasts, light lunches, afternoon teas, dinners include the likes of lamb shank or steak and kidney pie.

Children will enjoy the delightful animal petting farm which is home to tiny miniature ponies and donkeys.

Cafés
Nutmeg Bistro, 1 Falls Dr, T033-330 8373. Daily 0800-1700. Pleasant café just 300 m from the top of Howick Falls in the historic agricultural hall with cottage decor and tables set outside beneath an oak tree.

O Shopping

Pietermaritzburg *p117, map p118*
Liberty Midlands Mall, 3 km north of the city off the N3, if coming from Durban take the Armitage Rd off-ramp, T033-341 9570, www.midlands mall.co.za. Mon-Sat 0900-1800, Sun 0900-1700. The regional shopping mall with 170 shops, restaurants and an open-air piazza-style food court.

Howick *p121*
Piggly Wiggly Country Village, on the R103, 11 km northwest of Howick, T033-234 2911, www.pigglywiggly. co.za. Daily 0800-1700. A good stop on the Midlands Meander with a café and 22 shops for arts and crafts, decor, ceramics, wine, books, an organic farm shop, and the **3 Fat Pigs** is a deli that can make up picnics. Plus **Piggly Putt**; mini-golf for kids.

Nottingham Road *p123*
Swissland Cheesery, Old Main Rd (R103), Balgowan, near the junction of Currys Post Rd, 11 km south of Nottingham Rd, T0782-393 975, www. swisslandcheese.net. Daily (closed

Wed) 0900-1630. Can sample and buy a range of goat's cheese including a smoked chevin and a mild blue cheese. You can also learn about the cheese-making process and picnic and feed the goats on lush green lawns.

O What to do

Pietermaritzburg *p117, map p118*
Casino and horse racing
Race meetings are held at **Scottsville Racecourse**, 45 New England Rd, Scottsville, T033-345 3405, operated by the **Golden Circle Turf Club**, www. goldcircle.co.za. Check the website for racing calendars. **Golden Horse**, T033-395 8136, www.goldenhorse. co.za, is casino and entertainment complex attached to the back of the Scottsville grandstand with easy access to both facilities. Apart from the 24-hr casino, there are several restaurants and bars, including **Rockafellas**, a buffet restaurant that overlooks the racecourse, and the **Southern Sun Pietermaritzburg** hotel (see page 124).

Tour operators
Meet us in Africa, T033-239 4607, www.meetusinafrica.co.za. Interesting tours for older (50+) travellers to some of the lesser-visited nature reserves near Pietermaritzburg, plus birding and flower trips to the Drakensberg.

O Transport

Pietermaritzburg *p117, map p118*
Air
Pietermaritzburg/Oribi Airport is located in Oribi 7 km to the southeast

of town, follow the R56 from the centre. **SAA**, T011-978 1111, www. flysaa.com, operates 2-3 daily flights to/from **Johannesburg** (1 hr).

Bus

Baz Bus reservations Cape Town T021-422 5202, www.bazbus.com, stops in Pietermaritzburg 3 times a week. **Greyhound**, www.greyhound.co.za; **Intercape**, www.intercape.co.za; and **Translux**, www.translux.co.za, tickets can be booked through **Computicket**, T011-340 8000, www.computicket. com, or at their kiosks at the larger shopping malls, as well as in **Checkers** and **Shoprite** supermarkets. They stop in Pietermaritzburg on the route between **Durban**, and **Johannesburg** and **Pretoria**. All of these long distance buses stop in front of **McDonalds** in the centre of town on the corner of Burger and Chief Albert Luthuli streets and each has a desk in the plaza/station here to buy tickets. **Underberg Express**, T033-701 2750, www.underberg express.co.za, also stops opposite **McDonalds** on its daily service between **Durban** and **Underberg** (see page 157). Fares and timetables can be found on the website.

For more information, see Arriving, page 116.

Car hire

At the airport: **Avis**, T033-346 6101, www.avis.co.za; **Europcar**, T033-386 2077, www.europcar.com; and **Tempest**, T033-346 2551, www.tempestcarhire.co.za.

Train

The main railway station is on the corner of Church and Railway streets. The service between **Durban** and **Johannesburg** stops here (Mon, Fri, Wed and Sun in both directions). Central reservations, **Shosholoza Meyl**, T0860-00888 (in South Africa), T011-774 4555 (from overseas), www. shosholozameyl.co.za, timetables and fares are published on the website.

❶ Directory

Pietermaritzburg *p117, map p118*
Medical services Pietermaritzburg Medi-Clinic, 90 Payne St, T033-845 3911, www.pietermaritzburgmc. co.za. **Netcare St Anne's Hospital**, 331 Burger St, T033-897 5000, www.netcare.co.za.

Battlefields

The vast, open landscapes of northern KwaZulu-Natal are as evocative as one would hope, with rolling plains and savannah grasslands stretching to the horizons and studded with flat-topped acacias, mysterious rock formations and granite koppies. This landscape forms the stage upon which three major wars have been fought, and the battlefields of the clashes between Boers, Britons and Zulus can all be visited. The 80 or so battlefield sites, museums, old fortifications and places of remembrance are accessed from a number of battlefields routes that criss-cross the countryside. Don't expect self-explanatory sights, however – many of the battlefields are marked by little more than small commemorative plaques, and the best way to really bring the history of the region to life is to be with a decent guide who can make the experience very moving.

Ladysmith and around → *For listings, see pages 138-141.*

On the banks of KwaZulu-Natal's Klip River, 245 km north of Durban, Ladysmith is a quiet rural town surrounded by cattle and sheep ranches. It's rather featureless and scruffy with little more than a couple of run-down shopping complexes and a handful of Victorian buildings, and lost its importance as a a stopover between Durban and Johannesburg in the 1980s with the completion of the N3. It was established in 1850 and named after the Spanish wife of Sir Harry Smith, the British governor of the Cape Colony, and is most famous for being besieged for 118 days during the most crucial stage of the Anglo-Boer War, when the British garrison of 12,500 men was cut off from the outside world. Ladysmith's Siege Museum is a good place to start a visit to the battlefields, and the region lying to the south of Ladysmith is where many of the Anglo-Boer War battlefield sites are located. The siege aside, Ladysmith is perhaps best known as being the origin town to Ladysmith Black Mambazo, the phenomenally popular South Africa band (see box, page 134).

Arriving in Ladysmith and around
Ladysmith is on the N11 and is well connected to the highway network. The N11 heads north to Newcastle (102 km), and Volksrust (152 km) which

Visiting the battlefields

Those with an interest in the battlefields should choose an era, war or campaign and then select the sites you want to visit. Of the wars fought between the Voortrekkers and the Zulus, the most interesting battlefield site is Blood River, east of Dundee. Two of the most interesting historical sites of the Anglo-Zulu War are Isandlwana and Rorke's Drift; the latter has a good museum, making it the best site to visit without a guide. The most interesting Anglo-Boer War sites to visit are Talana, the Siege Museum in Ladysmith and Spioenkop. Most visitors drive to accommodation near the sites they wish to visit and then either drive themselves or organise a guide to go with them. Alternatively there are a number of guided tours from Durban or Johannesburg. For more information visit www. battlefieldsroute.co.za.

is just over the KwaZulu-Natal border in Mpumalanga. Some 19 km west of Ladysmith, the N11 connects with the N3, which in turn leads north into the Free State and south to Durban. The N11 also connects at this junction with the R616 leading to the Northern Drakensberg. Greyhound and Translux buses deviate off the N3 between Durban and Johannesburg and stop in Ladysmith.

Ladysmith Tourism ① *Siege Museum, 151 Murchison St, T036-637 2992, www. ladysmith.co.za, Mon-Fri 0900-1600, Sat 0900-1300*, has a good selection of maps and leaflets on the battlefields, and is also very helpful with accommodation suggestions and advice on battlefield tours and guides. There is also an excellent bookshop with a wide variety of Anglo-Boer War related books.

Ladysmith

Ladysmith's historical monuments are on the main square by the town hall on Murchison Street. The **town hall**, on the corner of Murchison and Queen streets, is a classic Victorian municipal building which was completed in 1893. During the siege, it was converted into a hospital until a six-inch shell hit the clock tower. The **Siege Museum** ① *151 Murchison St, T036-637 2231, Mon-Fri 0800-1600, Sat 0900-1300, R15, children (under 14) R8*, is next to the town hall. This is a fascinating museum with one of the country's largest collections of South African military memorabilia, including reconstructions of scenes from the Siege of Ladysmith and the Boer War. There are displays of weapons, uniforms and household goods that were used during the siege, with explanations in English, Afrikaans and Zulu.

There are four field guns on Murchison Street just outside the museum: **Castor** and **Pollux** are the two guns sent from Cape Town at the outbreak of the Boer War for the defence of the town; **Long Tom** is a replica of the Creussot Fortress Guns, which were used by the Transvaal Republic to bombard Ladysmith from the surrounding hills. The Boers destroyed the original gun at

Haenertsburg when Kitchener's Fighting Scouts threatened to capture it. The last gun is a German **Feldkanonne**, which was captured in German Southwest Africa and sent back as a war trophy.

Walking south down Murchison Street will take you past two historical hotels. The **Royal Hotel** (see Where to stay, page 138) was built before the siege, at the time of the gold and diamond rushes of the interior. During the siege the press corps used it as a base. The **Crown Hotel** is the site of Ladysmith's first hotel, built of wattle and daub. The earliest battlefield tours, on horseback, could be booked here in 1904.

To the east of the town centre off Queen Street is the Hindu **Vishnu Temple** and, next to it, the 2.7-m-tall **Statue of Mahatma Gandhi**, which was erected in 1993 by the Hindu community in Ladysmith to celebrate the centenary of Gandhi's arrival in Natal. He was a stretcher-bearer during the Anglo-Boer War, and trained some 1100 other Indians in this dangerous task. To the south of town on the banks of the Klip River, the sight of the gleaming white **Soofi Masjid (mosque)** ① *41 Mosque Rd, T036-637-7837, daily 1300-1400, 1700-2100, free,* comes as quite a surprise against the backdrop of

Ladysmith

To Newcastle

Greyhound & Translux buses

Pick 'n' Pay

San Marco Shopping Centre

Central Mosque

La Verna Private Hospital

Shopping Mall

ABSA

Siege Museum

Town Hall

Oval Shopping Centre

Vishnu Temple & Ghandi Statue

Crown Hotel

Shell

All Saints

Old Toll House

To Harrismith & Durban (N3)

To Newcastle & Dundee (R602)

Klip River

To Avis & Europcar

To Durban (N3) & Bergville (R616)

To Soofie Mosque   *To Durban*

200 metres
200 yards

N

Where to stay
Bullers Rest Lodge 1
Nambiti Plains Private
  Game Lodge 6
Naunton Guest House 5

Royal 3

Restaurants
Guinea Fowl 3
Santa Catalina Spur 1

Tipsy Trooper 2
Wimpy 4

The siege of Ladysmith

The siege of the British in Ladysmith by Boer forces lasted from early in the Anglo-Boer War, October 1899, until February 1900, 118 days in total. Some 10,000 British troops in northern Natal, under General White, had been forced to withdraw into Ladysmith after a series of defeats at the hands of Boers from both the Free State and Transvaal. The Boers, under the command of Piet Joubert (ably assisted by his tactically minded wife), took up positions in a six-mile radius around the town and decided to starve out and shell them into submission, while they held off any British attempts to relieve the town from the south by securing defensive positions in the hills overlooking the Tugela River. For the besieged British troops the defence of Ladysmith required patience and organization, rather than heroics. In December 1899, British forces under General Buller were attempting an advance through Colenso. But details of the advance were never relayed to White and the first he knew of the attack was when he heard the artillery fire, and was unable to offer any support to Buller's forces in their attempts to relieve Ladysmith. All his troops could do was sit tight and survive the bombardment as best they possibly could. Conditions for the town's inhabitants, whether military or civilian, were harsh. The artillery bombardment of the town centre was relentless and there were many causalities. Food and other provisions were in short supply and what was available became exceptionally expensive; tins of condensed milk, for example, could fetch up to a pound and bottles of whisky seven pounds. Morale was low and many inhabitants and troops felt it was only a matter of time before they had to give in to the Boers. In February 1900 Buller's army at last had some success in its assaults on the Boer positions along the Tugela. On 27 February the British succeeded in taking Pieter's Railway and Terrace Hills overlooking the railway crossing of the Tugela at Colenso. Meanwhile, as news of the decisive defeat of General Conje's forces in the northern Cape filtered through to the Boer military lines, their resolve snapped and they fell back towards Elandslaagte, many in fact returning home, leaving the path clear for Buller's troops to at last relieve the beleaguered troops and citizens at Ladysmith on the 28 February.

green fields. Built in 1969, it is one of the finest mosques in the country with beautiful filigree stonework, scalloped archways, and distinctive minarets. Its origins date back to 1895 when Hadrat (also spelt Hazrath) Soofi Saheb, regarded as an important Muslim mystic, arrived in South Africa. He made it his mission to build 13 mosques along the eastern inland seaboard of

Durban and the first Ladysmith Soofi Mosque would have originally been built before his death in 1910. What was a ruin was then rebuilt in the 1960s, but the original mihrab, a semi-circular niche in the wall of the mosque that indicates the direction of Mecca, remains. To go inside, it goes without saying, you must be dressed respectively.

Weenen Game Reserve
ⓘ *20 km south of Colenso off the R74, from Durban take the N3 to Estcourt and follow the Colenso road for 25 km, T036-354 7013, www.kznwildlife.com, Oct-Mar 0500-1900, Apr-Sep 0600-1800, R40, children (under 12) R20, car R40.*
This 5000-ha reserve has succeeded in converting heavily eroded farmland into an area where the flora and fauna indigenous to the KwaZulu-Natal Midlands have been re-established. The vegetation is mostly grassland, interspersed with acacia woodland. One of the great attractions are the black and white rhino. More common species include giraffe, red hartebeest, eland, zebra, kudu, ostrich and common reedbuck. This is a good reserve for birdwatchers; more than 250 species have been recorded including korhaans, blue crane and the scimitarbilled woodhoopoe. There are some short walking trails from the campsite, picnic sites, and a 47-km network of game-viewing dirt roads.

Spioenkop Dam Nature Reserve
ⓘ *On the R600, 38 km west of Ladysmith and 14 km north of Winterton, T036-488 1578, www.kznwildlife.com, Oct-Mar 0600-1900, Apr-Sep 0600-1800, office and shop 0800-1200, 1400-1600, R20 per person.*
Although Spioenkop is closer to Winterton and Bergville on the opposite side of the N3 to Ladysmith and is usually visited en route to the uKhahlamba-Drakensberg Park, its listed here as its interest is more closely related to the battlefields. It covers 6000 ha of bushveld terrain and a number of wildlife species have been reintroduced and there is a good chance of seeing white rhino and buffalo. With this in mind visitors must be careful when walking in the open around their campsite. Other animals you can expect to see include giraffe, kudu, mountain reedbuck, waterbuck, blesbok, impala, zebra, eland, duiker and steenbok. The area is particularly rich in birdlife and more than 270 species have been recorded here. The dam itself is popular with boating although no boats can be hired to the casual visitor.

The **Battle of Spioenkop,** 24 January 1890, was yet another embarrassing defeat for the British at the hands of the Boers and had a marked impact upon British public opinion. In order to relieve the beleaguered British troops at Ladysmith (see box, opposite), General Warren attempted a direct assault on the Rangeworthy Hills to dislodge the Boer positions. He decided to occupy the highest peak on the ridge – 'Spion Kop'. However, this meant that the shallow British defences were exposed to Boer gunfire from all sides and soon suffered

Ladysmith Black Mambazo

Ladysmith Black Mambazo is one of the best-known South African musical groups of all time, outselling both the Beatles and Michael Jackson in their homeland. Over the years their music has been traditionally based on *isicathamiya* music and dance born in the gold mines of Johannesburg at the turn of the 20th century. The word itself does not have a literal translation; it is derived from the isiZulu verb *cathama*, which means walk softly, or tread carefully. Back then, blacks went to the mines from all over southern Africa as migrant workers, leaving their homes and families for 11 months a year. Poorly housed in overcrowded hostels, they would entertain themselves after a six-day week by singing songs into the early hours every Sunday morning, with dance steps that were choreographed softly so as not to disturb the hostel security guards.

As a child, founding member Joseph Shabalala worked as a simple herd boy in the Ladysmith area. In 1961 he formed the group Ladysmith Black Mambazo, meaning the 'Black Axe of Ladysmith'. At their first concert in Soweto the band was an immediate hit and each member received the princely sum of R5.28.

Internationally, Ladysmith Black Mambazo were relatively unknown until Paul Simon 'discovered' the band on a visit to Johannesburg in the mid-1980s. They collaborated with him on his album *Graceland*, released in 1986, which sold millions of copies worldwide and brought them instant fame. Joseph gave Paul Simon the Zulu nickname *Vulindlela*, 'he who has opened the gate'.

Rather astonishingly, the band has now been going strong since 1961. In January 2013 the group released a new album, *Live: Singing for Peace Around the World*, which was dedicated to Nelson Mandela. On 6 December 2013 it was announced that it was nominated for a Grammy award – the day after Mandela passed away. In January 2014 it won the award for Best World Music CD; the fourth Grammy award for the group. For more information visit www.mambazo.com.

heavy losses. A brigade under General Lyttelton came to Warren's assistance but General Buller disastrously reversed the decision, ordering all British forces to retreat down from Spioenkop and back across the Tugela. Some 1750 British troops were either killed, wounded or captured at Spioenkop compared to about 300 Boers. The famous battlefield overlooks the dam and can be reached on one of the self-guided trails in the reserve, and a booklet on the Battle of Spioenkop is available from the reserve shop.

Dundee and around → *For listings, see pages 138-141.*

The R602 leaves the N11 26 km north of Ladysmith and shortly passes the village of **Elandslaagte**, where there is a signpost leading to the site of the Battle of Elandslaagte. On 21 October 1899, British forces abandoned the village and the railway station. They had kept it open to enable the Dundee garrison to retreat to Ladysmith. The R602 continues to Dundee through a vast treeless plain with plateaux rising up in the distance. The small mining and farming town of **Glencoe**, just before Dundee, is named after the town in the Highlands of Scotland, from where some of the first miners originated.

The modern town of Dundee, 68 km from Ladysmith, grew up around the coal mining deposits that were first exploited here on a large scale in the 1880s. The town centre unfortunately fell victim to South Africa's town planners, and is today a rather dull grid of modern streets lined with sleepy shops. Although it provides a convenient base from which to explore the battlefield sites at **Isandlwana**, **Rorke's Drift** and **Blood River**, it might be preferable to stay at one of the more remote lodges away from town.

Arriving in Dundee
Tourism Dundee ① *Civic Gardens, Victoria St, T034-212 2121, www.tourdundee. co.za, Mon-Fri 0900-1630*, is another helpful office with advice on how best to view the battlefields depending upon your time, budget and level of interest. Contact them in advance to book a local personal battlefield guide.

Dundee
The **Talana Museum** ① *1 km north of town on the R33, T034-212 2654, www. talana.co.za, Mon-Fri 0800-1630, Sat and Sun 0900-1630, R25, children (under 16) R2, restaurant and shop*, has been built on the site of the Battle of Talana Hill, which took place on 20 October 1899 and was the first major battle of the Boer War. British forces had been sent to Dundee to protect the coal field from the advancing Boers. General Lucas Meyer, moving down from the Transvaal, took the hill and began bombarding the British. The counter attack succeeded in forcing the Boers off the hill but only at great cost to the British, who lost 255 soldiers including their commanding officer, General Penn Symons. A self-guided trail visits the remains of two British forts and the Boer gun emplacements, passing a cairn where General Penn Symons was wounded. The main building is a modern museum with good displays on the Zulu Wars and the Anglo-Boer War.

Many outlying buildings are original. The **Peter Smith Cottage** has been restored and decorated with period furniture, while the workshop and stables outside have a collection of original blacksmith's tools and several wagons. **Talana House** has historical displays on the lifestyles of the Zulus and the early

Blood River

The year 1838 had been a difficult one for the Voortrekkers in Natal. In February their leader Piet Retief was beaten to death at the Zulu king Dingane's kraal and shortly afterwards about 500 members of a Voortrekker party at Bloukrans River were killed in a Zulu ambush. It was only with the arrival later in the year of Andries Pretorius with his 468 men and three cannons that Voortrekker fortunes began to take a turn for the better.

On 15 December Pretorius' scouts reported a heavy Zulu presence nearby and he ordered the column to move their wagons into the tried and tested Voortrekker defensive laager. The method involved lashing all the wagons together into a ring and protecting all cattle, horses and stores in the centre. This allowed trekkers to hide in and under the wagons and fire out at any approaching attackers. Pretorius had formed his laager on the banks of the Ncome River with a deep gully to the rear and an open plain to the front. He placed the three cannons at points along the perimeter of the laager to give them a clear line of fire across the open ground. Early in the morning of 16 December the Zulu army, estimated at about 10,000, began its attack.

Wave upon wave of Zulu soldiers charged the laager but their short spears, so effective in hand-to-hand combat, were useless against the trekkers' rifles and the cannons. Finally the Zulu attack faltered and Pretorius sent out a party of mounted commandos to pursue the shattered Zulus. The trekkers were merciless and shot every Zulu in sight, including more than 400 hiding in a small ravine. No prisoners were taken and around 3000 people were killed. No trekkers had been killed and only three were injured – including Pretorius who was stabbed in the hand. So many Zulu soldiers were shot whilst trying to flee back across the Ncome River the waters ran red – hence the name Blood River.

settlers in Dundee, with interesting bead collections. Both these buildings were used as dressing stations during the Battle of Talana Hill. The **Miner's Rest** restaurant and curio shop in the gardens is housed in a typical miner's cottage of the 1920s.

Ncome-Blood River
ⓘ *43 km from Dundee, take the R33 northeast as far as Dejagersdrif, where there is a turning on the right leading to Blood River, the last section of the journey is on a dirt road, T034-271 8121, www.ncomemuseum.co.za, 0800-1630, free, café.* This is the site of a replica *laager* that commemorates the dreadful battle between the Zulus and the Boers on 16 December 1838 (see box, above).

The 64 wagons are made of bronze and include replica bronze spades, lamps and buckets, all slightly larger than life size, and there is a small museum, the **Ncome Museum**, which is dedicated to the Zulu role in the battle. It is designed in the shape of a pair of buffalo horns, which was the formation in which the Zulu army attacked. To the east of the complex is a mountain called **iNtaba kaNdlela** (Ndlela's Mountain). Ndlela was the chief commander of the Zulu army during the battle, and his warriors rested on this mountain before crossing the Ncome River to the iNtibane Mountain, which is west of the museum. iNtibane is known as Vegkop (Battle Hill) in Afrikaans.

Isandlwana

ⓘ *80 km southeast of Dundee, take the R68 west, passing through Vant's Drift and Nqutu; the dirt road leading to Isandlwana is clearly signposted south of Nqutu, T034-271 8165, Mon-Fri 0800-1600, Sat-Sun 0900-1600, R20, children (under 12) R10, curio shop.*

This is where the 24th Regiment was defeated by 25,000 Zulu warriors on 22 January 1879. It is the most epic of the great Zulu War stories: the Zulus sat silently in a valley watching a small British regiment (which thought the Zulus were elsewhere), waiting for the signal to attack. A British patrol stumbled across them, upon which the impis leapt to their feet and stormed over the lip of the hill, descending upon the small regiment in the characteristic 'horns of the buffalo' manoeuvre. Within two hours, 1329 of the 1700 British soldiers were dead. Today, it is an atmospheric spot, with white-painted cairns marking the places where British soldiers were buried, and a self-guided trail taking in the memorials, starting with the relatively new memorial to the Zulu dead, a giant bronze replica of a Zulu victory necklace.

Rorke's Drift

ⓘ *42 km from southeast of Dundee, clearly signposted off the R68 between Dundee and Nqutu, T034-642 1687, Mon-Fri 0800-1600 Sat-Sun 0900-1600, R20, children (under 12) R10.*

Made famous by Michael Caine and his memorable performance in the movie *Zulu*, this site was a Swedish mission next to a ford over the Buffalo River. In 1879, the mission consisted of two small stone buildings, a house and a storeroom, which was also used as a church, and these were commandeered by the British at the start of the war and converted into a hospital and a supply depot. Only 110 men were stationed there on 23 January 1879, when two survivors of Isandlwana arrived warning of an imminent attack. Four thousand Zulus arrived 1½ hours later and launched the assault on the mission station. The British refused to surrender, and succeeded in defending the mission from behind a makeshift barricade of grain bags and biscuit boxes. The ferocious attack was resisted for 12 hours before the Zulu impis withdrew, losing around 400 men;

17 British officers were killed. The mission station has been converted into a fascinating little **museum**, which illustrates scenes from the battle and outlines the lives of the men who were awarded the Victoria Cross. Just beyond the museum there is a cemetery and a memorial to those who died.

⦿ Battlefields listings

For hotel and restaurant price codes and other relevant information, see pages 12-16.

⦿ Where to stay

If you've got a thirst for the history of the Battlefields, and the cash, then there are no better places to stay than **Isandlwana Lodge** or **Fugitive's Drift Lodge**, which both offer outstanding tours. Both charge around R950 for combined day tours to Isandlwana and Rourke's Drift so allow 2 nights to enjoy the experience.

Ladysmith and around
p129, map p131
$$$$ Nambiti Plains Private Game Lodge, 25 km east of Ladysmith and 2 km after the turning off the N11 on to the R602 to Dundee, T071-680 4584, www.nambitiplains.com. An expensive private 20,000-ha Big Five game reserve and one of the few safari options in the battlefields region, with 5 secluded luxury bush suites with verandas and outside showers set in a tract of acacia trees, thatched bar and boma, pool and deck. Rates include all meals and 2 game-drives; the reserve has been stocked with a number of plains species, lion and cheetah and an expanding herd of elephant. They can also arrange battlefield tours or

recommend self-drive routes and provide packed lunches.
$$ Bullers Rest Lodge, 61 Cove Cres, T036-637 6154, www.bullersrestlodge. co.za. B&B with 12 rooms and DSTV in a family-run lodge, set in a thatched house with fine views of the mountains. The **Boer War Pub** on site has a fine collection of battlefield artefacts. Located near the site of the Naval Gun Shield.
$$ Naunton Guest House, 2 km from town centre off the N11 towards Newcastle, T036-631 3307, www. nauntons.co.za. Smart option with 10 rooms in thatched farmhouse outbuildings with crisp white linen, DSTV, Wi-Fi, a/c and coffee and tea trays, cosy pub with pool table, evening meals on request and swimming pool in neat gradens.
$$-$ Royal Hotel, 140 Murchison St, T036-637 2176, www.royalhotel. co.za. Central and cheap 3-star town hotel with an interesting history, but the 71 rooms with TV and a/c could do with a facelift. Good **Tipsy Trooper** pub and restaurant, and the town's major meeting place, **MacKathini's** sports bar, which has a pool table.

Weenen Game Reserve *p133*
$$ Cottage, T036-354 7013, www.kznwildlife.com. 5-bed self-catering modern bungalow and

12 pitches for caravans and tents (**$**) near the entrance, with electricity points and shared ablution block. There's also a game-viewing hide overlooking a waterhole.

Spioenkop Dam Nature Reserve
p133

$$$$ Spionkop Lodge, on the R600 between Winterton (14 km) and Ladysmith (35 km), T036-488 1404, www.spionkop.co.za. Delightful country lodge with 8 comfortable rooms, good farm food, pub and library, rates are inclusive of meals, also 2 family self-catering cottages (**$$**). Can arrange canoeing on the Little Tugela River, birdwatching and horse riding. Owners Raymond and Alistair Heron are vivid storytellers and excellent battlefield guides to nearby Spioenkop and the sites in Ladysmith.

$$ Iphika Tented Bush Camp, in the reserve, T036-488 1578, reservations **Ezemvelo KZN Wildlife**, T033-845 1000, www.kznwildlife.com. Self-catering camp sleeping up to 4 in 2 large 2-bed tents with a stone and thatch lounge area with fireplace and kitchen overlooking a small waterhole. Spioenkop battlefield is a short walk away up a steep slope. Next to the dam are 30 camping sites (**$**) with power points and *braais*.

Dundee and around *p135*

$$$$ Fugitive's Drift Lodge, approximately 50 km south of Dundee towards Greytown on the R33, T034-642 1843, www.fugitives drift.com. Home to the Rattray family, stylish and comfortable accommodation

is in the main lodge or cottages, the lounge and dining room is filled with Battlefields memorabilia. This was the base for the late David Rattray, the battlefields finest historian, and the guides here that he trained are equally superb storytellers and bring the history alive. Also has a 22-km river frontage on the Buffalo River and fishing, game walks, horse riding, mountain biking and hiking are also on offer. Rates include all meals.

$$$$ Isandlwana Lodge, Islandlwana, 74 km southeast of Dundee, accessed off the R68, T034-271 8301, www.isandlwana. co.za. Superbly constructed luxury lodge with awesome views over Isandlwana and the rolling grasslands. The stunning wood, thatch and stone double-storey building sensitively blends in with the landscape and is built into the rock that the Zulu commander stood on at the start of the Isandlwana battle. 12 tastefully decorated rooms, with stone bathrooms and balconies with views over the battle site. Rob Gerrard, the resident historian, offers excellent tours – his storytelling will provide a startlingly moving insight to the battles. Rates include all meals.

$$$ Penny Farthing Country House, 14 km south of Dundee on the R33 towards Greytown, 2 km off the main road on the right, T034-642 1925, www.pennyf.co.za. Offers 1 room in a restored old fort with its own lounge and fireplace, or 5 rooms in the colonial sandstone farmhouse, decorated with antiques and French doors leading to the garden. Meals are taken communally at the 16-seater table and battlefield tours are with resident guide Foy Vermaak, a descendent of a Voortrekker family who fought in the Zulu and Anglo-Boer wars.

$$$-$ Battlefields Country Lodge, overlooking Talana Hill battlefield site, T034-218 1641, www.battlefieldslodge. co.za. An excellent and affordable resort-like set up with 71 rooms in comfortable double-storey circular thatched bungalows, 25 are self-catering and there are 10 cheaper budget rooms in a long block, plus there's campsite with kitchen area under thatch and power points, and the **Warriors Arms** pub and restaurant, swimming pool and zebra and impala graze on the immaculate lawns. Organizes battlefield tours in English, French or German or, alternatively, takes a tour with a Zulu guide for a different perspective.

$$ Royal Country Inn, 61 Victoria St, T034-212 2147, www.royalcountryinn. com. The original inn was established in 1886, and today there are still somewell-preserved pressed-iron ceilings and wrought-iron fittings, opening onto a peaceful garden. 24 a/c rooms and 5 cheaper rooms with shared bathrooms, decent meals served in the à la carte restaurant, a bar decorated with Zulu and Boer War memorabilia, and a tea garden.

❼ Restaurants

Ladysmith and around
p129, map p131
$$ Guinea Fowl, San Marco Shopping Centre, corner of Harrismith and

Francis roads, T036-637 8163. Mon-Sat 1200-2130. Located in a shopping centre and might not seem like much from outside, but is the best of a limited choice in Ladysmith offering reasonable curries, chicken and steaks with inventive sauces and toppings. There's a **Wimpy ($)** and a **Pick 'n' Pay** supermarket in the centre too.

$$-$ Tipsy Trooper at the **Royal Hotel**, page 138, T036-637 2176. Daily 0700-1000, 1200-1400, 1800-2100. An old-fashioned carvery restaurant, serving a selection of steaks, pub lunches, and with the occasional large, good-value buffet dinner and a reasonable Sun lunch.

$ Santa Catalina Spur, Oval Shopping Centre, T036-631 1260. Daily 0900-2300. Usual family chain restaurant serving reliable if uninspiring steak, ribs and chicken, and there's a salad bar.

Dundee and around *p135*
$$-$ Royal Country Inn, see above. Daily 1200-1400, 1600-2200. The best place to eat in town is at the main hotel, with 2 dining rooms, tables outside in a courtyard and the **Garrulous Griffin Pub**, named after the 24th Welsh Regiment who fought at Rorke's Drift.

○ Shopping

Dundee and around *p135*
ELC Craft Centre, Rorke's Drift Museum, T034-642 1627, www. centre-rorkesdrift.com. Mon-Fri 0800-1600, Sat-Sun 0900-1600. Established in 1962, this cooperative

and workshop is well known for its excellent Zulu crafts and sells beadwork, baskets, ceramics, dyed cloth and replica spears.

⏺ What to do

Most of the lodges provide excellent battlefield tours and they can also be organized in advance by the tourist offices in Ladysmith, see page 130, and Dundee, see page 135, and at the **Talana Museum** in Dundee, page 135. These can recommend several characterful guides in the region. The website for the **Provincial Tour Guides of KwaZulu-Natal**: www.battlefieldsregionguides.co.za, is also a good resource for organizing a guide. Costs are in the region of R700-900 for a full-day guided tour in your own car.

Dundee and around *p135*
Dundee Heritage Tours, T034-212 4040, www.battleguide.co.za. One of the leading operators on the Battlefields Route, Evan Jones is a member of the International Guild of Battlefield Guides, tours with accommodation are tailor made.

⏺ Transport

Ladysmith and around
p129, map p131
Bus
Greyhound, www.greyhound.co.za; and **Translux**, www.translux.

co.za, tickets can be booked through **Computicket**, T011-340 8000, www.computicket.com, or at their kiosks at the larger shopping malls, as well as in **Checkers** and **Shoprite** supermarkets. They stop in Ladysmith on the route between **Pietermaritzburg** and **Durban**, and **Johannesburg** and **Pretoria**, at the **Caltex** petrol station on the corner of Murchison St and Alfred Rd.

Car hire
Avis, 70 Murchison St, T036-631 4447, www.avis.co.za; **Europcar**, 60 Murchison St, T036-631 0913, www.europcar.com. These are car hire agents so pre-book to ensure cars are available.

Train
The station is in the middle of town off Lyell St. Central reservations, **Shosholoza Meyl**, T0860-00888 (in South Africa), T011-774 4555 (from overseas), www.shosholoza meyl.co.za, timetables and fares on website. The service between **Durban** and **Johannesburg** stops in Ladysmith (Mon, Fri, Wed and Sun in both directions).

⏺ Directory

Ladysmith and around
p129, map p131
Medical services La Verna Private Hospital, 1 Convent Rd, T036-631 0065, www.lenmedhealth.co.za.

uKhahlamba-Drakensberg Park

South Africa's highest mountain range, the Drakensberg, rises to 3000 m along the western edge of KwaZulu-Natal and the border with Lesotho, and forms the backbone of the uKhahlamba-Drakensberg Park. This formidable mountain range known as *Drakensberge* in Afrikaans, meaning 'dragon mountains', or *uKhahlamba* by the Zulu, 'barrier of spears', is one of South Africa's most staggeringly beautiful destinations. It is a UNESCO World Heritage Site both for its diverse flora and fauna and its impressive San rock paintings. The 2428 sq km uKhahlamba-Drakensberg Park is 180 km long and up to 20 km wide and most of the South African parts have been designated as game reserves or wilderness areas managed by Ezemvelo KZN Wildlife (see page 147). This is a place to exercise the body, fuelled with crisp clean air, and hiking, rock climbing and fly-fishing are popular activities.

Arriving in uKhahlamba-Drakensberg Park

Getting there and around
There is little in the way of public transport, so the best way of exploring the area is by car. The most popular resorts are within two to three hours' drive of Johannesburg, Pretoria or Durban, accessed from the N3 and then a network of minor roads heading west into the mountains. The popular sights and resorts are well signposted. Those in the far south are best approached via Underberg on the R617 from either Pietermaritzburg or Kokstad. The Central Drakensberg reserves such as Kamberg and Giant's Castle can be reached from the N3 and the Midlands towns of Nottingham Road, Mooi River and Estcourt. The Northern Drakensberg resorts and reserves around Monk's Cowl and Cathedral Peak are signposted from Winterton and Bergville, off the N3, along either the R74, the R600 or the R616. These can also be reached by taking the N3 as far as Harrismith if coming from the Johannesburg direction and then following the R74 over the Oliviershoek Pass and on to the Royal Natal National Park and Bergville and Winterton. The battlefields lies to the northeast of this region (see page 129). The regular long-distance buses stick to the N3 on the route between Durban and Johannesburg. The Baz Bus stops in the northern/central Drakensberg at Winterton and the **Amphitheatre Backpackers** (see page 162) on its route between Durban and Johannesburg.

The Underberg Express runs to and from Underberg in the southern Drakensberg and Pietermaritzburg and Durban. ►► *For further details, see Transport, page 172.*

Best time to visit
Although the weather tends to be pleasant all year round, the altitude and the mountain climate shouldn't be underestimated. Climatic conditions can change rapidly and snow, fog, rain and thunderstorms can develop within minutes, enveloping hikers on exposed hillsides.

Winter (May to August) is the driest time of the year and also the coolest. There will always be some rain during the winter months which, when it's cold enough, will occasionally fall as snow. Daytime temperatures can be as high as 15°C, while at night temperatures will often fall below 0°C. Despite the risk of snow, this the best season for hiking. Summer (November to February) is the wettest time. The mornings tend to be warm and bright, but as the heat builds up clouds begin to collect in the afternoon. The violence of the thunderstorms when they break is quite spectacular, usually accompanied by short bursts of torrential rain. Daytime temperatures average around 20°C and the nights are generally mild with temperatures not falling much below 10°C. The summer is a less popular season for hiking, although then the landscape is greener and the wildlife more abundant.

Background

The earliest human inhabitants of the Drakensberg were the San who lived here as hunter-gatherers. Evidence of their time here is the rock art which can be seen throughout the range (see Cave paintings box, page 144). It is thought that groups of San would gather at certain points in the year at these sites to exchange goods, arrange marriages and carry out shamanic ceremonies. For the rest of the year they dispersed into smaller family groups moving slowly in search of food. The women gathered edible plants and looked after children while the men hunted. The few goods that they needed could be made from local materials – hides for clothing, bones, flint and wood for tools, and hunting poison from crushed insects and plants.

The San came under increasing pressure towards the middle of the 19th century as the first European hunters, missionaries and farmers began to arrive. The new immigrants shot such large numbers of game, that gradually the San were driven further and further into the mountains, and eventually abandoned their stone tools and hunting poisons in favour of horses and guns and became cattle rustlers. The last records of San being seen in the Drakensberg date from 1878, just before the Natal government began auctioning plots of land at the base of the mountains for themselves.

Cave paintings

The park is rich in rock art left behind by the San people, and contains some 550 known sites amounting to over 40,000 recorded individual images. They are estimated to be between approximately 200 and 3000 years old, and most are on the walls of rock overhangs or caves. They were painted with a mixture of red and yellow ochre, charcoal, manganese oxide and clay. These minerals were bound together with blood, fat, egg or plant extract, and artists used feathers, animal hairs or grass to paint the figures.

Many of the paintings seem to be merely pictorial journals of hunting trips and everyday life, such as scenes of the San collecting wild honey, hunting pigs or being chased by a leopard. More recent paintings dating 200-300 years old depict the likes of ox-wagons and mounted men with rifles and illustrate friendly interaction, as well as conflict, between the San and African and European migrant groups. In some, there is thought to be a deeper meaning to the art.

The most frequently depicted animal is the eland, the largest antelope of the uKhahlamba-Drakensberg and vital to the wellbeing of the San, providing meat, fat and skins. It was viewed as an animal of power, with supernatural potency, and it is thought that the eland in some way represented god. Other paintings show mysterious, elongated dancing figures – half-eland, half-human – which relate to the San spirit realm. These are thought to represent people taking part in shamanic rituals who are in a state of trance, and a lengthening of their bodies and the sense of becoming animal-like created a sense of 'oneness' with the natural world.

Whatever the explanation, there is no doubt that the San probably saw themselves as indistinguishable from their environment – before being exterminated in clashes with the Zulus and white settlers, they lived in the Drakensberg as hunters and gatherers for thousands of years. It was partly the significance of these rock art sites which led to the uKhahlamba-Drakensberg Park being declared a World Heritage Site in 2000.

The Drakensberg's natural resources were subject to the settler's rapacious exploitation. The timber and sheep farming industries were particularly successful in the short term, but their effects on the delicate ecosystem of the Drakensberg were eventually to lead to the creation of a national park. The first area of the park to receive protection was the Giant's Castle Game Reserve in 1903, and over the years more land was acquired and given protected status. One of the main reasons was that the Drakensberg escarpment is the source of many of the rivers which flow through KwaZulu-Natal. The indigenous vegetation of the Drakensberg was shown to play an essential role in holding water from torrential seasonal rain and preventing flash floods. The root systems in the soil release the water gradually throughout the year providing the region with a regular water supply. Today the Tugela, the Mkhomazi and the Mzimkhulu are three of the most important sources of water in the province.

Landscape

The Drakensberg are divided into two areas known as the High Berg and the Little Berg. The **High Berg**, covering the area which rises steeply up to the plateau, is the more interesting of the two with its spectacular scenery of high peaks and cliffs. The top of the escarpment averages an altitude of around 3000 m and forms the western boundary of the park along the watershed between KwaZulu-Natal and Lesotho. The **Little Berg** lies at lower altitude and consists of the spurs of sandstone, which stretch out towards the plains of KwaZulu-Natal. The landscape here is of rolling hills and grassland divided by forested ravines. The Little Berg is the most popular area for hiking and many of the Ezemvelo KZN Wildlife resorts are located here.

Wildlife and vegetation

The different habitats in the Drakensberg vary according to altitude, which can range from the subtropical at around 1000 m to the Afro-alpine at over 3000 m. The wealth of **plantlife** in the Drakensberg is quite staggering: over 1500 plant species have been identified here, among which 350 are endemic. By far the best time of year to see the veldt is during the spring, when the grass is green and lush and many of the orchids, irises and lilies are in flower. Plants on the high plateau are hardy, small alpine plants consisting mostly of grasses, shrubs and succulents.

The **wildlife** is not as easy to spot as in some of South Africa's other wildlife reserves. Numbers are relatively low, but the mammals you might see include eland, baboon, and some of the small antelope such as klipspringer and duiker. Red hartebeest, blesbok, bushbuck and oribi are present but are seen less often as they only inhabit certain areas. Leopard, lynx, serval, aardvark, aardwolf and porcupine are thought to be present but are almost never seen, even by park staff or regular hikers.

Birdlife in the Drakensberg is particularly rich, as it is possible to visit several different ecosystems within a relatively small area. Over 300 species have been recorded here, most of which live below 2000 m. The best time to see the birds is during the summer when they are courting and nesting. The rarest birds live at higher altitudes on the summit plateau, and include the orange-breasted rockjumper, the Drakensberg siskin, the bald ibis, the Cape vulture and the lammergeyer.

Hiking

Trails vary between short, well-marked strolls to challenging hikes at high altitude, lasting several days. The majority of visitors to the Drakensberg prefer to complete a number of day hikes and stay overnight in Ezemvelo KZN Wildlife camps. On some of the longer hiking trails several days are spent in wilderness areas at altitudes of up to 3000 m, crossing through isolated and challenging mountain passes. Planning ahead is essential for longer hikes as overnight caves and mountain huts have to be booked in advance.

Permits Permits are necessary on all longer walks and are available from camp offices for a fee of R25-75 per person. Maximum group size is 12 people and the minimum size is three. Hikers must fill in the **Mountain Rescue Register**, carry detailed maps and be equipped to deal with extreme weather. Mountain registers are located at all the trail heads and should be filled in even for short day walks.

Equipment and supplies Note that **camping stoves** are essential for overnight hikes as fires are not allowed in the park. Resort shops have a limited selection of tinned and dried **food**, but it's best to bring lightweight provisions and fresh produce from the supermarkets in the towns en route to the mountains. Some hikers choose not to carry a tent if they have booked accommodation in caves or mountain huts. However, these are not always marked accurately on maps and they can be difficult to find, so it's sensible to have a tent as a backup in case you get caught out at nightfall. On overnight hikes a **trowel** or a spade is necessary for digging toilets to prevent litter and pollution. Dig a hole at least 30 m away from streams and make sure everything is properly buried.

The most exciting Drakensberg hikes are the ones up to the summit plateau. Clothing should protect you from sub-zero temperatures you are likely to encounter over 3000 m, and you should carry good waterproofs, thermal underwear, a fleece, woolly hat and gloves. Even on a short day hike in the Little Berg in summer a waterproof jacket and a sweater are essential.

Maps A map, a compass and a good knowledge of map reading are essential for hiking in the Drakensberg. Ezemvelo KZN Wildlife produces a series of six comprehensive 1:50,000 maps, which usefully also cover the Lesotho side of the mountains. Contact Ezemvelo KZN Wildlife in advance.

Staying in the park

There is a huge choice in the area, including within Ezemvelo KZN Wildlife accommodation and in private establishments on the fringes of the park. Ezemvelo KZN Wildlife offers a wide range of facilities, from luxury lodges and chalets through to campsites, mountain huts and caves. All of the camps are basically self-catering and, although there are some camp shops which sell food, the choice is limited. It is far better to come prepared and buy your food beforehand in the nearest large town. An entry fee, which includes a community levy and an emergency rescue levy, is payable each time you enter a protected area administered by Ezemvelo KZN Wildlife. This is included in the cost of accommodation; it is only day visitors who pay an entry fee at the gate.

The areas bordering the national park have a number of privately run self-contained holiday resorts. These tend to offer numerous facilities and activities such as horse riding, golf and swimming pools, and while they are sometimes rather distant from the mountains themselves, most offer outstanding views of the Drakensberg.

Reservations for **Ezemvelo KZN Wildlife** ① *T033-845 1000, www.kznwildlife. com*. Bookings can be made by telephone or online; camping reservations must be made directly with the officer in charge of the campsite, see individual areas for details.

Northern Drakensberg → *For listings, see pages 161-172.*

The scenery of the Northern Berg is exceptional in its grandeur, and is perhaps the most photographed section of the range. The Royal Natal National Park is the most popular of all the resorts in the Drakensberg, and although there are some good hikes outside the park, they don't really compare with the sheer majesty of those within its boundaries.

Arriving in Northern Drakensberg
The usual approach from the north and Gauteng to the resorts and the reserves in the Northern Drakensberg is from Harrismith and the N3. The R74 heads 37 km south from Harrismith past the Sterkfontein Dam to the top of Oliviershoek Pass. Once over the pass, the road continues east to Bergville and Winterton, which also provide access from the N3 from the Durban direction.

Oliviershoek Pass
The 1730-m Oliviershoek Pass was named after Adriaan Olivier who was one of the first Voortrekkers to descend from the Orange Free State in the 1830s. He claimed a farm for himself at the foot of the pass. As the R74 ascends to the top of the pass from the north it begins to climb through pine forests. Although the mountains here aren't as spectacular as Mont-aux-Sources (see below), they do have their own quiet charm and it is worth stopping off at one of the few restaurants on this road. The R74 in this area also provides access to numerous private resorts bordering the Royal Natal National Park.

Royal Natal National Park

ⓘ The park can be reached from the R74 from both Harrismith (60 km) or Bergville (45 km), the turn-off is 8 km south of the Oliviershoek Pass from where it is a further 14 km to the park gate, T036-438 6411, gates Oct-Mar 0600-1900, Apr-Sep 0600-1800, office and shop (selling curios and limited supplies) 0800-1630, R40, children (under 12) R20, car R40.

The highlight of a visit to the park is the first view of the massive rock walls that form the **Amphitheatre**. The **Eastern Buttress** (3009 m) is the southernmost

① Northern & central Drakensberg

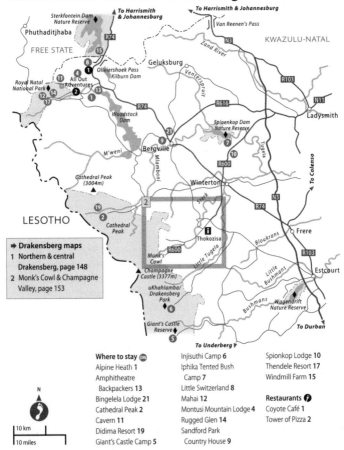

Where to stay 🛏
Alpine Heath **1**
Amphitheatre
 Backpackers **13**
Bingelela Lodge **21**
Cathedral Peak **2**
Cavern **11**
Didima Resort **19**
Giant's Castle Camp **5**

Injisuthi Camp **6**
Iphika Tented Bush
 Camp **7**
Little Switzerland **8**
Mahai **12**
Montusi Mountain Lodge **4**
Rugged Glen **14**
Sandford Park
 Country House **9**

Spionkop Lodge **10**
Thendele Resort **17**
Windmill Farm **15**

Restaurants 🍴
Coyote Café **1**
Tower of Pizza **2**

→ **Drakensberg maps**
1 Northern & central
  Drakensberg, page 148
2 Monk's Cowl & Champagne
  Valley, page 153

peak of the 4-km of cliff face, which arcs northwards towards the **Sentinel** (3165 m) forming an impressive barrier. On the plateau directly behind the Amphitheatre is **Mont-aux-Sources** (3299 m) named by French missionaries in 1836. This mountain is the source of five rivers: the **Elands** which flows into the Vaal; the **Khudeda** and the **Singu** leading into the Orange/ Gariep River in the Free State; and the **Tugela** and the **Bilanjil** which lead into Natal.

The most impressive of these is the Tugela which plunges over the edge of the Amphitheatre wall, dropping around 800 m through a series of five falls. The gorge created by the waters of the Tugela is a steep-sided tangle of boulders and trees which at a point near the Devil's Tooth Gully has bored straight through the sandstone to form what appears to be a tunnel around 40 m long.

The national park was established in 1916 when farms around the Amphitheatre were bought by the government to protect the land. Tourism started around this time and the park has been popular since then. Queen Elizabeth II visited the park in 1947, five years before she became queen; since then, the national park and the (now closed) hotel are prefixed by the word 'Royal' in memory of this visit.

Hiking There are over 130 km of walking trails around the Royal Natal National Park, many of which are easy half-day strolls. Even the hikes that don't climb up to the top of the escarpment wind through beautiful countryside of grassland dotted with patches of yellowwood forest and proteas set against the stunning backdrop of the Amphitheatre. The office sells hiking maps and a leaflet describing the many possible walks around the park.

The 20-km hike up to **Mont-aux-Sources** (3299 m) can be completed in a strenuous day's walk. The path starts at **Mahai Campsite** and heads steadily uphill following the course of the Mahai River. The path climbs steeply around the eastern flank of the Sentinel (3165 m). Just after the Sentinel Caves is the notorious chain ladder, built in 1930, which takes you up a 30-m cliff face. Once on top, Mont-aux-Sources is only 3 km away and involves no more serious climbing. The views from the top of the escarpment are splendid as they stretch out over KwaZulu-Natal.

The walk up the **Tugela Gorge** is a 14-km round trip which begins at the car park below Tendele Camp. The path heads up the gorge and follows the Tugela River passing through shady patches of yellowwood forest. Higher up along the valley there are rock pools which are ideal for swimming in. After around 6 km at the entrance to the gorge there is a chain ladder; from here you can either wade through the gorge or climb up the ladder and walk along the top. There are magnificent views here of the Devil's Tooth, the Eastern Buttress and Tugela Falls.

The 8-km trail to **Cannibal Cave** heads north from the road leading to **Mahai Campsite**. The route follows the Goldie River for 1 km before crossing over and following the ridge north again until it passes close to Sunday Falls. The path then rises over Surprise Ridge and on to the Cannibal Cave. The walks from the **Rugged Glen campsite** are over rolling hills and although there are some good views of the Amphitheatre, they don't compare with the hikes from the Thendele Resort and Mahai campsite.

Bergville

This quiet country town is in the centre of a maize and dairy farming area. It was established and named after a retired sea captain in 1897, and two years later at the onset of the Anglo-Boer War a blockhouse was built by the British, which today stands in the grounds of the local courthouse. Most visitors will either be passing through en route to the resorts in the Northern Drakensberg or be heading northeast towards Ladysmith and the Battlefields. The main reason for stopping is to visit the helpful **Drakensberg Tourism Association** ① *Municipal Building, Thatham Rd, Bergville, T036-448 1557, www.drakensberg. org.za, Mon-Fri 0900-1700*, which provides information on the whole region.

Central Drakensberg → *For listings, see pages 161-172. See map, page 148.*

From Winterton the road to Monk's Cowl, with its string of resorts, curio villages and golf courses, is one of the most heavily developed areas of the Drakensberg. While you may see more tourists in this region, the scenery is no less spectacular and access is easier than in other areas of the park. This is also home to the internationally famous Drakensberg Boys' Choir. Further south, the Giant's Castle Reserve is the most spectacular of the Central Berg resorts. It has two camps: Injisuthi and Giant's Castle Resort. Here, the basalt cliff faces rise up to 3000 m and stretch out to the north and south for over 30 km. Kamberg Nature Reserve is situated centrally in the foothills of the mountains, and is one of the best places to see San rock paintings.

Arriving in Central Drakensberg From the N3 you can get to Winterton via the R600 if coming from the north, or R74 if coming from the south. Two kilometres south of Winterton on the R600 there is a signposted turning west to Cathedral Peak, 43 km. The R600 continues on south to Monk's Cowl (Champagne Valley), 33 km. Injisuthi is 53 km from Winterton. Take the turning to Loskop off the R600 on the way to Monk's Cowl, 13 km south of Winterton at the junction next to the Thokosiza Centre (see below), and before reaching Loskop there is a dirt road on the right; follow the signposts to Injisuthi from there. To get to Giant's Castle the access points off the N3 are from Estcourt and Mooi River in the KwaZulu-Natal Midlands (page 123). Kamberg can be reached from Mooi River or Nottingham Road.

Winterton

Winterton is 23 km south of Bergville on the R74, and this small village with tree-lined streets is an important centre for the surrounding maize, beef and wheat farms. It was founded in 1905, three years after the Anglo-Boer War, when settler farmers constructed a weir across the Little Thukela River for irrigation. Winterton is also the last place to stock up on supplies for visitors to Cathedral Peak or Monk's Cowl. There are a couple of petrol stations and small supermarkets on Springfield Road (R74) in the village, though the better choice is in the chain supermarkets in the larger towns before you get here.

Cathedral Peak

① *Signposted from Bergville (48 km) and Winterton (41 km), T036-488 8000, www. kznwildlife.com, gate 24-hrs, office 0700-1900, shop (selling curios and limited supplies) 0800-1900, R30, children (under 12) R15, or R50/25 with a visit to the Rock Art Centre, trips to Mike's Pass R60 per person, minimum 4, 0900, 1200 and 1600.*
Cathedral Peak is the main point of access to some of the wildest areas of the central Drakensberg, and provides some of the most spectacular scenery for hikers. Driving into the area, the road dips through leafy valleys, with the views gradually opening up as you get closer to the park. The park itself is ringed by dramatic peaks with views of the Cathedral Spur and Cathedral Peak (3004 m), the Inner and Outer Horns (3005 m) and the Bell (2930 m). An alternative to hiking round the peaks is to go on a ride up Mike's Pass in one of the parks' vehicles, which go three times a day (book at the office).This is a steep 4WD 35-km mountain road to a viewpoint from where there are spectacular views of the Little Berg. The Mike in Mike's Pass was a Mike de Villiers, who played a crucial role in its commissioning to access part of the Little Berg for ecological research.

Hiking There is a good network of paths heading up the Mlambonja Valley to the escarpment from where there are trails heading south to Monk's Cowl and Injisuthi or heading north to Royal Natal National Park. There are designated caves and mountain huts on the longer trails. Didima Resort or the **Cathedral Peak Hotel** are good bases from which to set out exploring the area on a series of day walks and maps are available. The 10-km hike to the top of **Cathedral Peak** (3004 m) is one of the most exciting and strenuous hikes in this part of the Drakensberg, and the views from the top are unforgettable.

Cave paintings The sheltered valleys in this area are thought to have been one of the last refuges of the San, and this is one of the best places to see San cave paintings in the Drakensberg. An excellent introduction is just past the entrance to the park, at the **Rock Art Centre** ① *Didima Resort, T036-488 8025, daily 0800-1600, coffee shop and craft centre.* The stylish thatched building holds a series of displays interpreting the art found in the surrounding mountains.

A key thread in the museum is the eland, a vital aspect in San mythology and culture, with some life-size replicas in the entrance. The museum begins with an introduction to the culture and lifestyle of the San, with a look at archaeological finds, quotes from some of the last San descendants, and descriptions of the symbolic meaning of some of the most famous paintings. At the back of the museum is a replica of an open-topped cave, complete with starry sky and fake camp fire, where recordings of San folklore stories are played.

Monk's Cowl and Champagne Valley

The R600 road to Monk's Cowl passes through one of the most developed areas of the Drakensberg. Looking down from Monk's Cowl the view of KwaZulu-Natal is dotted with hotels, golf courses and timeshare developments and the area is locally dubbed 'Champagne Valley'. However, **Champagne Castle**, **Monk's Cowl** and **Cathkin Peak** are still impressive features in this landscape. The entrance to Monk's Cowl is 33 km west of Winterton where there is a Ezemvelo KZN Wildlife campsite and several interesting hikes. On the way there are numerous resorts and attractions in the valley off the R600.

The first stop should be the **Thokosiza Centre**, 13 km from Winterton on the R600; a tourist complex that is home to a number of arts and crafts shops, the **Thokosiza Restaurant** (see page 168), and the **Central Drakensberg Information Centre** ① *T036-488 1207, www.cdic.co.za, daily 0900-1700*, which stocks useful maps and brochures and can help arrange accommodation. The turn-off to Injisuthi is also at Thokosiza (see below).

About a 20-minute drive from the Thokosiza Centre, the **Drakensberg Canopy Tour** ① *on the right of the R600 just after the turn-off to the Champagne Sports Resort, T083-661 5691, www.drakensbergcanopytour.co.za, departures daily 0800, 1000, 1200, 1300 and, R495 per person, no children under 7, includes refreshments*, is set in a patch of indigenous forest in the shadow of Cathkin Peak. It is one of many canopy tours now around South Africa (see www.canopytour.co.za for the other locations). It's a great way to see the forest canopy from platforms in the trees and on rock faces some 40 m above the ground. The platforms are connected by steel cables that you swing across on a harness. The experience lasts about three hours.

Drakensberg Boys' Choir School ① *on the right of the R600, 4 km after the Champagne Sports Resort, T036-468 1012, www.dbchoir.co.za*, has one of the most beautiful locations for a school in the whole of South Africa and was established in 1967. The school is highly accredited in its own right, but is most famous for the choir that has performed all over the world. Boys aged between nine and 15 have performed in front of the Pope and 25,000 people at the Vatican City, sung with the Vienna Boys' Choir in Austria, and have been proclaimed top choir at the World Festival of Choirs. The choir has even received a special award at Disney's Magic Kingdom. During term time the choir performs (anything from Beethoven to Freddy Mercury) on Wednesday at 1530 in the school's impressive auditorium (check the website for dates; booking essential).

About 2 km beyond the school, turn off the R600 to reach **Falcon Ridge** ① *T082-774 6398, 1030-1230 except Mon and Fri, 1-hr bird shows 1030, R40, children (under 12) R15*, a rehabilitation centre for rescued birds of prey, mostly injured from flying into power lines. The daily falconry show is a big attraction, and you can don a glove and have your photo taken with a large raptor.

Monk's Cowl ① *at the end of the R600, 33 km west of Winterton, T036-468 1103, www.kznwildlife.com, gates 0600-1800, office and shop 0800-1530, tea garden 0800-1630, R35, children (under 12) R18*, taking its name from the peak between the Champagne Castle and Cathkin peaks, is a popular part of the uKhahlamba-Drakensberg Park for camping, day hikes or a stop at the tea

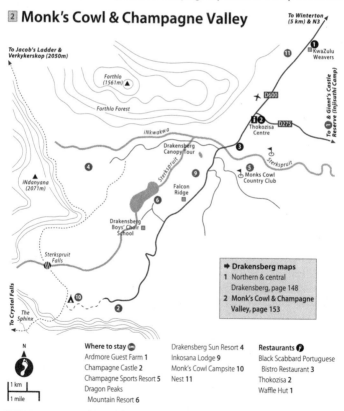

② Monk's Cowl & Champagne Valley

To Winterton (5 km) & N3

To Jacob's Ladder & Verkykerskop (2050m)

Forthlo (1561m) ▲

Forthlo Forest

iNkwakwa

KwaZulu Weavers ❶

⓫

D600 ✈

D275

Thokozisa Centre ❶❷

❸

To Giant's Castle Reserve (Injisuthi Camp)

Drakensberg Canopy Tour

Sterkspruit

iNdanyana (2071m)

❹

❾

Sterkspruit

Falcon Ridge

❻

❺ Monks Cowl Country Club

Drakensberg Boys' Choir School

Sterkspruit Falls

To Crystal Falls

The Sphinx

▲❿

❷

➡ **Drakensberg maps**
1 Northern & central Drakensberg, page 148
2 Monk's Cowl & Champagne Valley, page 153

N

1 km
1 mile

Where to stay 🛏
Ardmore Guest Farm **1**
Champagne Castle **2**
Champagne Sports Resort **5**
Dragon Peaks Mountain Resort **6**

Drakensberg Sun Resort **4**
Inkosana Lodge **9**
Monk's Cowl Campsite **10**
Nest **11**

Restaurants 🍴
Black Scabbard Portuguese Bistro Restaurant **3**
Thokozisa **2**
Waffle Hut **1**

room at the reserve's entrance, and is usually visited on a day excursion from the resorts in Champagne Valley.

Hiking Maps are available from the office for the short hikes around Monk's Cowl and the paths are clear and well signposted. They vary from one hour to a round trip of six hours, and are graded from easy to difficult. Places to visit include **Nandi's Falls** (5 km), **Sterkspruit Falls** (2 km) and **The Sphinx** (3 km). The paths cross areas of proteas and some woodland and some go past gloriously refreshing rock pools.

The route up to **Champagne Castle** (3377 m) is a 20-km, two-day hike which involves a steady slog uphill, but no climbing skills are needed.

Injisuthi ① *38 km from the Thokosiza Centre on the R600 or 65 km from the N3 near Estcourt, both routes go via Loskop, T036-431 7848, www.kznwildlife. com, gates Oct-Mar 0500-1900, Apr-Sep 0600-1800, office and shop (selling curios and limited supplies) 0800-1230, 1400-1630, R30, children (under 12) R15.* Injisuthi is an isolated camp high up in the Giant's Castle Reserve (Giants Castle Resort is accessed further south – see below). The valley is covered with large areas of yellowwood forest and grassland, and looming over the camp are the awe-inspiring mountain peaks of **Champagne Castle** (3248 m), **Monk's Cowl** (3234 m) and **Cathkin Peak** (3149 m). **Mafadi** (3446 m), **Injisuthi Dome** (3410 m), and the **Injisuthi Triplets** – Eastern Triplet (3134 m), Western Triplet (3187 m) and Injisuthi Buttress (3202 m) – are some of the highest peaks in South Africa and have become magnets to South Africa's climbers. The game in Injisuthi Valley used to be abundant and the Zulu word *Injisuthi* actually means 'well-fed dog' as hunting parties here were often so successful. San also thrived here and left many cave paintings.

Hiking There is a selection of trails for day hikes beginning at the campsite and following the Injisuthi Stream to the southwest. Poacher's Stream is a tributary of the Injisuthi and this path leads off Boundary Pool (3 km) where it is possible to swim. Following the Injisuthi further up the valley are Battle Cave (5 km), Junction Cave (8 km) and Lower Injisuthi Cave (8 km). Giant's Castle Resort is a three-day hike from Injisuthi following the contour path south. The trail can be exhausting but it does pass through spectacular mountain scenery including Popple Peak. Reservations for sleeping at Lower Injisuthi Cave and Bannerman Hut have to be made in advance.

Cave paintings There is a daily **guided walk** ① *minimum charge R235 for up to 3 people, each additional person R60, book at the office the day before,* 7 km, to **Battle Cave** and other San sites. Battle Cave is named after one its cave paintings, which shows two groups of San attacking each other. Figures are shown running into the fight with arrows flying between them. There are hundreds of other paintings on the cave walls of animals that used to live here, including lions, eland, rhebok, an elephant and an antbear.

Giant's Castle
ⓘ *62 km from the N3 near Estcourt, or 66 km from the N3 at Mooi River, T036-353 3718, www.kznwildlife.com, gates Oct-Mar 0500-2200, Apr-Sep 0600-2200, day visitors must leave before sunset, office and shop (selling curios and limited supplies) 0800-1630, R30, children (under 12) R15, Izimbali Restaurant 0730-2100.*
This reserve was established in 1903 when there were only 200 eland left in the whole of what was then Natal. Over the years, the reserve has successfully helped the eland population to recover and at present they number around 2000 in the Drakensberg. Blesbok, mountain reedbuck and oribi are some of the other mammals you are likely to see here. A wall of basalt cliffs rises up to over 3000 m and the peaks of **Giant's Castle** (3314 m), **Champagne Castle** (3248 m) and **Cathkin Peak** (3149 m) can be seen on the skyline. The grasslands below the cliffs roll out in a series of massive hills, which give rise to the Bushman's River and the Little Tugela River. The Izimbali Restaurant here has a deck with a lovely view over the valley.

Hiking The shorter walks explore the forests and river valleys within a few kilometres of the camp, whilst the longer ones take up to three days and can reach areas as far afield as Injisuthi. A comprehensive leaflet detailing the hiking choices is available from the camp office.

The 7-km hike up to **World's View** (1842 m) follows a path north along a ridge overlooking the Bushman's River. The climb up to the top is not too strenuous and the views looking over Wildebeest Plateau to Giant's Castle and Cathkin Peak are well worth the effort. The best time to see the peaks of the mountains is early in the morning as clouds tend to descend in the afternoon.

The more challenging walks to **Langalibalele Pass**, 12 km, **Bannerman Pass**, 20 km, and **Giant's Castle** involve a long uphill struggle to reach the top of the escarpment. The hike up to Giant's Castle at 3314 m takes three days and means using Giant's Hut as a base camp for two nights. The second day's hike from the hut to Giant's Castle Pass, 12 km, rises up through scree slopes and loose rubble. From the top of the pass it is a further 1 km to the peak. Giant's Hut is 10 km from the main camp and there are several well-marked paths which lead to it.

Cave paintings The **Main Cave Museum** ⓘ *R30, children (under 12) R15, booked and paid for at the camp office, tours go on the hour 0900-1500 from the museum gate,* is half an hour's walk from the camp and must be visited with a guide and has a large wall covered in paintings and a simple display on the archaeology of the cave and the San who lived there.

Lammergeyers

Lammergeyers (or bearded vultures) are one of the world's rarest and shyest vultures. They live a mostly solitary existence in isolated high mountain areas in the Pyrenees, the Atlas Mountains of Morocco and in the Drakensberg and Lesotho.

They live on a diet of dried bones, waiting for a carcass to be cleaned by other vultures before they will start to feed. The lammergeyer flies off with bones from the carcass and drops them onto rocks below. The bones crack open enabling the bird to feed on the nutritious bone marrow inside.

The **lammergeyer hide** at Giant's Castle (1 May to 31 September, T036-353 3718, www.kznwildlife. com, R645 for a minimum of three and up to six people) is a popular attraction and advance booking is necessary. Visitors are taken up to the hide by vehicle and walk back. In addition to the lammergeyer you can expect to see the lanner falcon, jackal buzzard, Cape vulture and the black eagle.

Kamberg Nature Reserve

ⓘ *55 km from Mooi River on the N3, 52 km from Nottingham Rd on the R103, both routes go via Rosetta; the last 19 km are on dirt roads, T033-263 7312, www.kznwildlife.com, gates Oct-Mar 0500-1900, Apr-Sep 0600-1800, office and shop (selling curios and limited supplies) 0800-1300, 1400-1600, R30, children (under 12) R15.*

This reserve is at relatively low altitude, the highest point being **Gladstone's Nose** at 2265 m, and is therefore known for its birdlife, with over 200 species recorded here. However, the scenery is not as spectacular as at some of the other reserves, although the Clarens Sandstone around Kamberg does have its own special appeal, and there is some good San rock art within the reserve.

Kamberg is probably best known for its trout fishing; there is a hatchery open to the public and the Eland and Erskine dams stocked with brown and rainbow trout which can be fished all year round. Rods are available for hire from the office and a bag limit is set at three fish per day.

Hiking The trails around Kamberg are quite leisurely and involve no steep climbs. The **Mooi River Trail**, 4 km, has been designed with wheelchair access in mind, and is a relaxing stroll past willows and eucalyptus trees along the banks of the Mooi River. Longer trails, such as the hike up to **Emeweni Falls**, are detailed in a booklet available in the camp office.

Cave paintings There are several rock art sites in the reserve, but the main site worth visiting for the sheer number and quality of the paintings is Game Pass Shelter, which can be visited on a three-hour round trip **guided walk** ⓘ *0900,*

1100 and 1230, book the day before or phone ahead T033-263 7251, R50 per person, and is preceded by a DVD presentation at the state-of-the-art **San Rock Art Interpretation Centre**. The experience is a great way to get a handle on the Drakensberg's San rock art given that Kamberg was one of the first sites ever to be seen by Europeans around 1915. It was the detailed paintings in the Game Pass Shelter that revealed the meaning of San rock art to archaeologists; in a sense, 'cracked the code'. Among the many scenes on the rock wall here is one of a human with hooves instead of feet holding the tail of a dying eland. This is thought to have shamanic meaning and to be connected to a trance-like state. Just outside the shelter there are some fossilized dinosaur footprints.

Southern Drakensberg → *For listings, see pages 161-172.*

The southern section of the Drakensberg stretches along the Lesotho border from the Giant's Castle area and along the Eastern Cape border. Although it is the least visited part of the mountain range, simply because it lies a bit off the beaten track in terms of being on the way to somewhere else, the scenery here is no less spectacular, and it's only roughly just over two hours' drive from Durban. The area is best known for the Sani Pass, a spectacular track crossing over to the mountains to Lesotho, reaching 3000 m at its highest point.

Arriving in Southern Drakensberg Underberg is the main access point to the Southern Drakensberg resorts. You can get there either from Mooi River and Nottingham Road in the KwaZulu-Natal Midlands, if approaching on the N3 from the north, or via Bulwer and the R617 from Howick on the N3 if coming up from the south. Both Underberg and nearby Himeville are sleepy farming villages but have shops, and are convenient stop-offs for provisions en route to the Ezemvelo KZN Wildlife camps or the Sani Pass. Despite its relative isolation, the **Underberg Express** offers bus transport to/from Underberg and Pietermaritzburg and Durban, which helps make this beautiful area of the Drakensberg accessible for budget travellers.

   Southern Drakensberg Tourism ① *Clock Tower Centre, Main Rd, Underberg, T033-701 1471, Mon-Fri 0800-1600*, is another helpful office and can book local accommodation.

Underberg
Underberg was established in 1917 when the railway from Pietermaritzburg reached the area, and is still very much the main service centre for this part of the Drakensberg; its name refers to the town's location beneath the mountains. It is a typical old-style South African farming town, with a mix of basic shops, pubs, dust roads and visiting farmers bustling about. The junction

with the road to Himeville is where the petrol station, banks, supermarkets and the tourist information office can all be found.

Himeville
Just 5 km north of Underberg and founded in 1893 and named after Sir Alfred Hime, a road engineer elected Prime Minister of Natal in 1889, Himeville is a small prosperous village reminiscent of England. Arbuckle Street runs through the village centre where there is a supermarket, post office, museum, hotel and petrol station. **Himeville Arms** is the main hotel; its distinctive Tudor architecture wouldn't be out of place in an English village. Opposite, there is the small **Himeville Museum** ① *T033-702 1184, Tue-Sun 0930-1230, free but donations accepted*, in the old fort and prison built in 1900. It is an early sandstone building with exhibits on settler and agricultural history and one of the better displays on the San.

   Himeville Nature Reserve ① *Oct-Mar 0500-1900, Apr-Sep 0600-1800, free*, is set on the outskirts of Himeville, where there are two dams surrounded by grassland, and it takes about 30 minutes to stroll around. The 105-ha protected area is a home for waterbirds and the occasional blesbok and black wildebeest.

Cobham
① *On the road between Underberg and Himeville, a signposted turning leads down a dirt road (D7) to Cobham (13 km), T033-702 0831, www.kznwildlife.com, gates Oct-Mar 0500-1900, Apr-Sep 0600-1800, office and shop (selling curios and limited supplies) 08000-1300, 1400-1530, R30, children (under 12) R15.*
This is a fascinating wilderness area and is an ideal base for many exciting hikes. The land rising up towards the escarpment has been gouged with steep-sided gorges filled with thick yellowwood forest. The view above the cliffs of the escarpment is of the Giant's Cup, lying between Hodgson's Peaks, and the Drakensberg stretching out to the north and south. The Mzimkulu River rises here and flows to Port Shepstone. This area is relatively undisturbed by human activity and the clean waters of the high Drakensberg streams are a sanctuary for Cape clawless otters and spotted-necked otters. People rarely see them, as they are very shy animals, but they tend to be active at dusk and dawn. White droppings on riverbanks are a sign of their presence; the distinctive colour comes from the calcium of the crab shells that make up a large proportion of their diet.

Hiking There are five day hikes of various lengths from 4-18 km, most of which leave from the campsite. The most notable longer hiking trail in the Southern Drakensberg is the **Giant's Cup Hiking Trail**, a 60-km five-day trail through the foothills of the mountains from Cobham (officially the start is at the foot of Sani Pass) to Bushmen's Nek and the trail lies almost entirely in the Cobham and Garden Castle reserves. Some sections are steep, but manageable even for younger children, and accommodation is in mountain huts. A variety of animals may be spotted along the trail, including eland, dassies (rock hyrax) and porcupines. Birds are less common at these higher altitudes but birds of prey such as the black eagle and the jackal buzzard may be seen. The trail must be booked in advance through **Ezemvelo KZN Wildlife** ① *T033-845 1000, www.kznwildlife.com.*

Sani Pass

The road from Himeville to Sani Pass (15 km) rises steadily through rolling hills covered in grassland and patches of pine plantation until it passes the **Sani Mountain Lodge** and the 3000 m peaks on the escarpment come into view. **Hodgson's Peaks**, at 3256 m and 3229 m, the **Twelve Apostles** and **Sani Pass**, at 2874 m, are at their most beautiful after snow. The road is one of the most dramatic in Africa and is the only route leading into Lesotho on its eastern border with South Africa.

Sani Pass was originally used by traders transporting goods by mule into Basutoland. A trading post was opened in the 1920s at Good Hope Farm at the bottom of the pass, which was the closest store to Mokhotlong in Lesotho. Then the Sani Pass was little more than a bridle path, but it was upgraded to a road in 1955 after the first 4WD Land Rover managed to complete the ascent. Maize and trade goods, including a fair number of guns, were taken up, while wool and hides were brought down. Trade still continues on this route, although these days most traders supplying shops in Lesotho have their own 4WDs and prefer to drive to the larger warehouses in Pietermaritzburg to stock up on goods. The Good Hope trading post closed in 1990 but the remains of the buildings can still be seen at the bottom of the pass. The provincial government of KwaZulu-Natal has recently decided to have the Sani Pass road tarred, and the project should be completed in the next few years. Some of the flat part of the road from Himeville and up towards the South African border post has already been tarred. It might be a loss for adventure tourism as it's a thrilling ride up by 4WD, but for the poor rural people of Lesotho, economically completely dependent on South Africa, it would definitely mean progress.

Tours and hikes The pass is a popular attraction with tourists, and organized trips to the top of the pass and over the border to Lesotho are available from Underberg, the **Sani Pass Hotel** and **Sani Lodge**. Travellers are taken up by 4WD; the road is terrifyingly steep and winding but the views are outstanding. The tours are a good way to discover local history and wildlife and include a visit to a Basotho village to see sheep shearing, maize cultivation or beer making. A picnic lunch in the Black Mountains or lunch at the **Sani Mountain Lodge** is included; don't miss a glass of warming mulled wine at the pub at the Sani Mountain Lodge– at 2874 m it is the highest pub in Africa.

The most rewarding hike in this area is the day hike up to the top of Sani Pass at 2874 m. There is a car park at the South African border post from where it is a further 14-km hike to the top. The trail is quite straightforward and just involves following the road. A number of shorter walks visit **Gxalingwena**, **Kaula** and **Ikanti Shelter**. These cave-like dwellings are home to a number of San rock paintings. Regulations stipulate that for the protection of the paintings, they must only be visited with a registered guide. These can be arranged from the **Sani Pass Hotel** or **Sani Lodge**.

Vergelegen
ⓘ *35 km north of Himeville on a signposted dirt road, T033-702 0712, www.kzn wildlife.com, there are no gates and all visitors must report to the office during office hours, Mon-Sat 0700-1200, 1300-1630, Sun 0800-1200, R30, children (under 12) R15.*
The 21,000 ha Vergelegen is one of the most remote and rugged reserves in the uKhahlamba-Drakensberg Park and as such receives fewer visitors than most other reserves. The majority of it is made up of the high Mkhomazi Wilderness area, where the prominent feature is the towering peak of **Thaba Ntlenyana** (3482 m); the name means 'pretty little mountain', hardly a fitting name for the second tallest mountain in Africa after Kilimanjaro. The summit actually lies on the Lesotho side of the border, but there are hikes on the South African side from the top of the escarpment in the reserve. Some of the most inaccessible and demanding hiking trails in the Drakensberg are here, and permits are available at the camp office. There's no formal accommodation but you can camp and stay in caves on the hikes.

Lotheni
ⓘ *45 km north of Himeville on a signposted dirt road (after Vergelegen), or 62 km from Nottingham Rd about half of which is gravel, T033-702 0540, www. kznwildlife.com, gates 0600-1800, office and shop (selling curios and limited supplies) 0800-1230, 1400-1630, R30, children (under 12) R15.*
The landscape at 3984 ha Lotheni is mainly rolling grassland rising up towards the High Berg and Redi Peak at 3298 m. The grassland is interspersed with patches of protea woodland, tree ferns and the rare Berg bamboo. Streams cutting down through the rock have formed narrow wooded gorges, which have been stocked with brown trout. The trout season lasts from September to April and during these months accommodation at weekends can be fully booked. Spring is also a popular time for visitors who come to see the magnificent wild flowers. There's a little museum at the camp in an old homestead with an interesting collection of early settler farming implements.

Hiking There are three leisurely day hikes and two overnight trails in the reserve, for which maps can be bought in the camp shop. All three day walks go to the Lotheni River; during hot weather it is safe to swim when it is not in flood although the water flowing straight off the mountains can be icy. Of these, the **Jacobs Ladder Trail** starts at the office and is only about 2 km long so is suitable for younger children.

Garden Castle and Bushman's Nek

ⓘ *38 km west of Underberg at Drakensberg Gardens Golf & Spa Resort (see page 167), the gate is on a gravel road that goes beyond the resort, T033-701 1823, www.kznwildlife.com, gates Oct-Mar 0500-1900, Apr-Sep 0600-1800, office and shop (selling curios and limited supplies) 0800-1300, 1400-1600, R30, children (under 12) R15.*

Garden Castle is the southernmost reserve in the uKhahlamba-Drakensberg Park and incorporates the beautiful Bushman's Nek Valley. The area is characterized by many unusual sandstone buttresses and other formations and is home to eland, grey rhebok and reedbuck. The landscape consists mostly of grassland with patches of proteas and tree ferns. There are many tarns in this part of the Drakensberg where waterbirds and wildlife can be seen. There are magnificent views up into the mountains on a clear day, with the mountain peaks of **Walker** (3322 m), **Wilson** (3342 m) and the **Rhino** (3051 m), towering over the reserve.

Hiking There are five day walks here, for which maps can be bought in the camp shop. The most strenuous is the 18-km trail up to **Rhino Peak** (3051 m), which juts out like the head after which it is named, and there is a knife-edge ridge to the 'horn'. **Engagement Cave** and **Sleeping Beauty Cave** are 8 km from the park office and are easily visited in a morning. There are also plenty of huts and caves to spend the night in on longer hikes.

⏱ uKhahlamba-Drakensberg Park listings

For hotel and restaurant price codes and other relevant information, see pages 12-16.

● Where to stay

While the prices for some of the private mountain resorts in the Drakensberg may seem high, remember many consist of family units sleeping at least 4, and some,

even if they are standard doubles, include all meals.

Oliviershoek Pass *p147, map p148*
$$$$ Montusi Mountain Lodge, follow signs along the R74 towards Royal Natal National Park, T036-438 6243, www.montusi.co.za. 14 smart thatched chalets surrounded by lawns, with private terrace and staggering

views towards the amphitheatre, plus 6 self-catering cottages (**$$**) dotted around the estate. Good restaurant and small bar, guided walks into the park including to San rock art and the top of the amphitheatre, trout-fishing, horse riding, pool, and Zulu village visits.

$$$ Alpine Heath, below Oliviershoek Pass, follow signs along the R74 (Cavern Berg Rd), T036-438 6484, www.alpineheath.co.za. A well-established resort with 100 self-catering chalets with 3 bedrooms, 2 bathrooms, lounge with fireplace and DSTV, and patio with mountain views. Facilities include 2 pools, gym, spa, tennis, shops, restaurant and pub, and horse riding and mountain biking can be arranged.

$$$ The Cavern, 10 km, follow the signs heading off the R74 towards the Royal Natal National Park, T036-438 6270, www.cavern.co.za. Large complex set among gardens and woodland offering accommodation in 55 comfortable thatched cottages. Wide range of activities including horse riding, bowls, pool, spa, and evening entertainment. As well as meals, rates include guided hikes. A superb location and good choice for families.

$$$-$$ Little Switzerland, signposted off the R74 next to the petrol station, just below Oliviershoek Pass, T036-438 6220, www.littleswitzerlandaccomodation.co.za. Another large family resort with 66 thatched cottages and self-catering chalets set in a 2000-ha reserve, with indoor heated pool, spa and gym, activities include horse riding, hiking, fishing, canoeing and tennis, and there's a kids' club and babysitters.

$ Amphitheatre Backpackers, 21 km northwest of Bergville on the R74, T036-438 6675, www.amphibackpackers.co.za. Excellent backpackers, the main building is a converted sandstone house with log fires, dorms, doubles and camping, hearty home-cooked meals, packed lunches to take with you on over 30 hikes in the area, guided hikes to the top of the amphitheatre and to the Cathedral Peak summit and day trips into Lesotho. If you don't have your own transport, this is a perfect introduction to the mountains; the Baz Bus makes a detour to here on its route between Durban and Johannesburg, or you can get a regular bus to Harrismith and they'll pick you up for a small fee.

$ Windmill Farm, on the R74 at the top of Oliviershoek Pass, 23 km northwest of Bergville, T0716-570811, www.windmillfarm.co.za. Tucked among giant pine trees and perched along the edge of the plateau at the top of the pass, 9 simple and cheap brick and thatched bungalows, fully equipped for self-catering but bring your own towels. Terrific views but it can get chilly up here.

Royal Natal National Park
p148, map p148

$$$-$ Thendele Resort, Ezemvelo KZN Wildlife, T033-845 1000, www.kznwildlife.com. Stunning location with unrivalled views of the amphitheatre from 26 chalets with fireplace, terrace and *braai* sleeping 2-4, 2 cottages sleeping 6, and a deluxe lodge with 3 en suite bedrooms. The cottages and lodge have cooks who prepare food supplied by the guests, while the chalets are self-catering. The camp's setting makes it one of the most popular in the entire Drakensberg, so must be booked months in advance. The shop sells maps, books, souvenirs and a few basic groceries.

Camping

Mahai, T036-438 6310. Spacious campsite spread along the Mahai River with pleasant lawns bordered by large pine trees and 120 sites, most with power points, modern ablution blocks, washing machines, good views and footpaths lead straight up into the hills, very popular (it can be crowded and noisy at weekends).

Rugged Glen, T036-438 6303. Small site to the north of the park, with 20 sites, some with power points, shaded by pine trees and a central ablution block. Horse riding is available here (see What to do, page 171).

Bergville p150, map p148

$$ Sandford Park Country Hotel, 4 km northeast of town on the R616, T036-448 1001, www.sandford.co.za. Country hotel dating back to 1852, with 50 rooms, some in separate rondavels, slightly dated furnishings, but neat gardens, large pool, hiking and canoeing, and restaurant and characterful pub. Affordable base from which to explore both the Drakensberg and the battlefields.

$$-$ Bingelela Lodge, 3 km northwest of town off the R74, T036-448 1336, www.bingelela.co.za. A working farm with 12 comfortable, rustic, thatched cottages set under blue gum trees, 2 are self-catering, pool, large à la carte restaurant and friendly pub with several fireplaces serving good South African cuisine and wood-fired pizzas.

Cathedral Peak p151, map p148

$$$ Cathedral Peak Hotel, at the end of the road past the entry gate to the reserve, T036-488 1888, www.cathedralpeak.co.za. All-round resort established in 1939 in a stunning location close to the high peaks of the Drakensberg, popular as a base for hikers and for weddings in its own stone chapel, with 90 luxurious rooms, several restaurants and bars, 3 pools, 9-hole golf course, horse riding, mountain biking, squash and tennis, gym and spa. Rates include meals.

$$$-$$ Didima Resort, in the reserve, just before **Cathedral Peak Hotel**, **Ezemvelo KZN Wildlife**, T033-845 1000, www.kznwildlife.com. Large resort themed around the San rock art and the thatched chalets have been designed to look like caves, 63 2-bed chalets built back to back so can be converted into 4-bed units, 1 6-bed chalet and a honeymoon suite. All have DSTV and fireplace, and there's a restaurant, bar, small shop and pool. The conference centre/wedding chapel has a full-height glass wall framing a view of Cathedral Peak. Also here is the **Rock Art Centre** (see page 151).

Camping

Cathedral Peak Community Campsite, reservations, T036-488 8000. 30 sites with power points with a quiet, tranquil feel and mountain views, good ablutions and communal kitchens, and campers can eat at the restaurant. There are also 12 caves in which overnight hikers can camp.

Monk's Cowl and Champagne Valley *p152, map p153*

All the accommodation listed below is signposted off the R600. The distances shown are from each hotel to the entrance to Monk's Cowl.

$$$$-$$$ Drakensberg Sun Resort, 13 km, turn off opposite the **Champagene Sports Resort** for 5 km, T036-468 1000, www.tsogosunhotels.com. Located in the scenic Cathkin Peak area and centred around an attractive lake, 78 good standard rooms, the **Lakeview Restaurant**, **Grotto Bar**, spa, 2 swimming pools, trout fishing dams, sundowner cruises on the lake, pitch and putt golf, and horse riding.

$$$ Champagne Castle, 2 km, T036-468 1063, www.champagnecastle.co.za. Traditional Drakensberg family resort in a spectacular mountain setting, with 72 smart rooms, set in the main lodge and annexes with thatched roofs, surrounded by attractive leafy grounds. Restaurant, bar, horse riding, trout fishing, tennis, pool, spa. Rates include all meals.

$$$ Champagne Sports Resort, 9 km, T036-468 8000, www.champagnesportsresort.com. Pleasant, typically South African family large resort with beautiful views, but avoid if there's a large conference on. 152 rooms and 92 chalets with bright furnishings, stylish bathrooms and balconies. impressive 18-hole golf course, large buffet restaurant, sports bar, 4 pools,

tennis, squash, horse riding, gym and spa. Rates include breakfast and dinner.

$$$-$$ The Nest, 13 km, T036-468 1068, www.thenest.co.za. A 3-star resort with 55 rooms in thatched rondavels with verandas and mountain or garden views, bright furnishings and wooden furniture. Restaurant, bar, guest lounges, pool, bowls, horse riding, croquet and guided hikes. Rates include all meals and afternoon tea.

$$ Dragon Peaks Mountain Resort, 4 km, T036-468 1031, www.dragonpeaks.com. Mix of B&B and self-catering chalets and cottages sleeping 2-12, plus a **camping** and **caravan site** (**$**) with power points. Restaurant with outdoor lapa area, 2 pools, tennis and horse riding, plus a small supermarket, and a rather unusual thatched wedding venue on an island in the middle of a dam. The **Drakensberg Boys Choir School** is within walking distance.

$$-$ Ardmore Guest Farm, 18 km, turn off opposite **The Nest** and it's 5 km on on the D275, T036-468 1314, www.ardmore.co.za. An alternative to the large resorts with superb views and lovely gardens overlooking a dam. 8 good-value rooms, B&B or full board, excellent farm-style meals, 4-course dinners are taken at a long table with hosts and other guests, also known for its ceramic and weaving art studios on the farm.

$$-$ Inkosana Lodge, 7 km, T036-468 1202, www.inkosana.co.za. Established backpackers with fine views of the mountains, set in a large garden with pool. 4 small dorms, doubles, some en suite, rondavels and camping. Large dining area with hearty home-made meals on request or kitchen for self-catering. Can give lots of advice on hiking and can arrange other activities in the valley such as horse riding.

Camping
Monks' Cowl Campsite, literally at the end of the road, T036-468 1103, www.kznwildlife.com. Delightful campsite in a stunning spot with views back across the valley, with 38 pitches, some with power points, bordered with indigenous trees and shrubs. The office has a tea garden (open 0800-1600) for light meals and also provides hikers' picnics in backpacks with cutlery and a slot for a bottle of wine. Order these the day before.

Giant's Castle Reserve
p155, map p148
$$$-$$ Giant's Castle Camp, Ezemvelo KZN Wildlife, T033-845 1000, www.kznwildlife.com. 44 chalets sleeping 2-6, with lounge, TV and fully equipped kitchen. Shop sells a wide range of books and curios but only a limited selection of dried and frozen food and has a petrol pump. **Izimbali** restaurant and pub (0730-2100) if you don't want to self-cater. Swimming in summer is permitted in the Bushmen's River below the camp. There are also 2 hikers' caves about 4-5 hrs' walk from the camp.
$$ Injisuthi Camp, Ezemvelo KZN Wildlife, T033-845 1000, www.kznwildlife.com. Remote camp with 15 simple self-catering chalets sleeping 2-6 with fireplace and *braai*, no plug points but gas fridge and stove and lighting from 1730-2200.

The shop here only sells basic groceries and firewood so visitors need to bring all other supplies with them.

Camping
Injisuthi Campsite, reservations, T036-431 9000, www.kznwildlife.com. There are 20 sites at Injisuthi that can accommodate 120 people, plus 3 2-bed pre-erected tents, and shared ablution blocks. There are also a number of hikers' caves in the vicinity.

Kamberg Nature Reserve *p156*
$$-$ Main Camp, Ezemvelo KZN Wildlife, T033-845 1000, www.kznwildlife.com. 5 self-catering chalets, 1 5-bed and 1 6-bed rustic thatched cottages, communal lounge area with DSTV and freezer facilities. The shop here only sells basic groceries and firewood so visitors need to bring all other supplies with them. **Stillerus Cottage**, is 8 km from the main camp and sleeps 10 (minimum 6) and has gas lights, stove and fridge.

Underberg *p157*
The best choice of accommodation is either on Drakensberg Gardens Rd towards **Garden Castle & Bushman's Nek** (see page 161), or on Sani Pass Rd towards **Sani Pass** (page 159).
$$ Umzimkulu River Lodge, Coleford Rd, 22 km from Underberg off the R617 towards Bulwer, T0762-379112, www.umzimkuluriverlodge.com. Tranquil retreat set on a bend in the Umzimkulu River with 8 lovely self-catering farm cottages sleeping 2-10 set well apart from each other, restaurant and pub, trout fishing and

canoeing on 2.5 km of river frontage, picnics on an island in the river.

Himeville *p158*

$$$ Moorcroft Manor, 2 km from Himeville on the Sani Pass Rd, T033-702 1967, www.moorcroft.co.za. Smart rural retreat with 8 spacious rooms, some with Victorian baths, decorated with antiques, good restaurant with bar and outside terrace, mountain views, provides picnic lunches for hikers, and can organize trout-fishing and the day trip up Sani Pass.

$$ Himeville Arms, Arbuckle St, T033-702 1305, www.himevillehotel. co.za. Historic hotel dating to 1904, the 15 comfortable rooms with period furniture can be rather gloomy in summer, but are cosy in winter with well-stocked log fires, plus 9 cheaper backpacker rooms in shared rooms with 4 beds (**$**). The excellent **Arms Pub**, restaurant (see Restaurants, page 169), small pool, and can organize the tour up the Sani Pass.

Cobham *p158*

Cobham campsite, T033-702 0831, www.kznwildlife.com. The campsite here is very basic with an open area for setting up tents and you need to be totally self-sufficient, though there are *braais*, basic toilets and hot showers and campers may swim in the river below the campsite if it's not too cold. There are a number of hikers' caves within a 4-5 hr hike from the camp.

Sani Pass *p159*

$$$ Sani Pass Hotel, 22 km from Underberg on the Sani Pass road, T033-702 1320, www.sanipasshotel.co.za. A large resort hotel built in 1958 in a beautiful location with over 70 rooms either in the hotel building or in luxury cottages in the gardens, and rates include breakfast and dinner. Facilities and activities include fly-fishing, tennis, bowls, horse riding, quad-biking, there's a 9-hole golf course, spa and swimming pool, and 4WD tours are on offer up the Sani Pass.

$$-$ Sani Lodge, 19 km from Underberg on the Sani Pass road, T033-702 0330, www.sanilodge. co.za. The **Underberg Express** will drop here if you are coming from Pietermaritzburg and Durban, see page 128. There is a mixture of dorms, double rooms, en suite rondavels, and family cottages, and plenty of space to pitch a tent. Large kitchen, comfortable lounge with open fire, veranda with a superb uninterrupted mountain views, restaurant, tea garden, farm stall and packed lunches are available for hikers. It's close to the start of the **Giant's Cup Hiking Trail** (see page 158), and owners Russell and Simone Suchet started the Lodge in 1992 and are experts on hiking in Lesotho and organize several tours and guided hikes (see page 172), including an excellent Sani Pass tour by 4WD.

$$-$ Sani Mountain Lodge (formerly Sani Top Chalet), top of the pass, next to the Lesotho border post, T078-634 7496, www.sanimountain. co.za. In the most wonderful location overlooking the dramatic road below, this historic inn offers 9 en suite rooms in cosy stone rondavels out back, plus 3 backpacker rooms and 2 6-bed dorms with shared bathrooms, and you can camp in summer. While the accommodation (and bedding) is warm, be prepared for below-freezing temperatures in winter when it can snow. Activities include fantastic hikes to some awe-inspiring viewpoints along the escarpment, including to Thabana Ntlenyana (Africa's 2nd tallest mountain; see page 172), plus pony-trekking on Basotho ponies and possibly snow-boarding and sledging in winter. The lodge has a pub (the highest in Africa) that offers *gluhwein* and a restaurant warmed by roaring wood fires. If you're driving, the option here is to drive and park overnight at the South African border post (0800-1600) and the lodge will pick you up in their 4WD at 1130 or 1530 for R250 per person each way; pre-book. By doing this you get the ride up the pass too.

Lotheni *p160*

$$$-$$ Lotheni Hutted Camp, Ezemvelo KZN Wildlife, T033-845 1000, www.kznwildlife.com. 12 self-catering chalets and 1 6-bed cottage with gas fridges and stoves and there are communal freezer facilities. The shop here only sells basic groceries and firewood so visitors need to bring all other supplies with them. Electricity 1700-2200 only. Simes Cottage is an old farmhouse with exclusive use of a dam for trout fishing, sleeps 10 and has gas-powered kitchen but need to bring own bedding.

Camping

Lotheni campsite, reservations, T033-702 0540, www.kznwildlife.com.

The 14 campsites at Lotheni, are a secluded 2 km from the hutted camp and it's a beautiful spot. The only facility is an ablution block with hot and cold water.

Garden Castle and Bushman's Nek *p161*

$$$ Castleburn Resort, 25 km west of Underberg and 10 km before Garden Castle on Drakensberg Gardens Rd, T033-701 1405, www.castleburnresort.co.za. A beautiful location overlooking Lake Madingofani which attracts eland and mountain reedbuck, with 58 thatched self-catering chalets sleeping up to 4, some have extra beds in loft space for large groups, great mountain views, popular for hiking and trout fishing, restaurant, pub, pool, mini-golf.

$$$-$$ Drakensberg Gardens Golf & Spa Resort, 34 km west of Underberg on Drakensberg Gardens Rd, just before the gate to **Garden Castle & Bushman's Nek,** T033-701 1355, www.goodersonleisure.co.za. A large 3-star resort with 82 rooms in cottages, some self-catering, full range of facilities and activities including swimming pools, spa, hiking, horse-riding, canoeing, trout fishing, the southern Drakensberg's only 18-hole golf course, and a 12-km mountain-bike trail up into the mountains.

Camping

Hermits Wood Campsite, at Garden Castle, T033-701 1823, www.kzn wildlife.com. There are 10 camping sites and an ablution block with hot and cold water but no electricity and campers need to bring their own lights, though a gas freezer is available. The shop here sells curios and basic groceries. Eland have been known to wander through the camp. There are also 12 hikers' caves and 3 rustic huts sleeping up to 30 on the **Giant's Cup Hiking Trail** (see page 158).

⑦ Restaurants

All the large mountain resorts have restaurants and bars on site. Much of the other accommodation is self catering; as a result there is little need for restaurants in the region.

Oliviershoek Pass *p147, map p148*
$$-$ Tower of Pizza, 6 km from the R74 turn-off, below Oliviershoek Pass, T036-438 6480, www.towerofpizza. co.za. Tue-Sat 1200-2030, Sun 1000-2100, open on Mon in season. Pleasant farm restaurant with tables on the stoep and a menu of pizza, pasta, tramezzini, salads and desserts; does takeaways if heading to nearby self-catering accommodation. The Tower refers to a grain silo that is now the wood burning pizza oven. Also offers B&B accommodation in 6 comfortable rondavels (**$$**)
$ Coyote Café, on the R74 on the south side of the pass at the entrance of **Little Switzerland** (page 162), T036-438 2515. Daily 0730-2030. Friendly café with a broad wooden deck overlooking the Woodstock Dam, serving breakfasts, lunches, afternoon teas, and also good for early dinners on the way to self-catering accommodation.

Winterton *p151, map p148*
Cafés
Pig & Plough, Springfield Rd (R74), T036-488 1542, www.amblesidefarm. co.za. Mon-Fri 0730-1700, Sat-Sun 0830-1700. Farm shop, deli and coffee shop, great English breakfasts and light lunches including wood-fired pizzas, and there's a children's playground, animal petting farm as well as a dam with ducks to feed. Also rents out a quaint 3-bedroomed farm cottage (**$$**) next to the Little Tugela River.

Monk's Cowl and Champagne Valley *p152, map p153*
$$-$ Black Scabbard Portuguese Bistro Restaurant, on the R600, 3 km before the **Champagne Sports Resort**, T0786-23 9126. Daily except Tue 1200-2030. Basic place with rickety tables and bench tables, but well-loved by locals for the authentic Portuguese chicken and espetada da Madeira, decent prawns, and steak egg and chips. Good value for money and wonderful views.
$$-$ Thokosiza Restaurant, Thokosiza Centre, on the R600, 13 km southwest of Winterton, T036-488 1827. Mon-Fri 0900-2100, Sat-Sun 0900-2200. Popular coffee shop and restaurant in this cultural/craft/tourist centre, and within less than 30 mins' drive of most of the resorts on the R600. Pleasant wooden tables on a shady deck and cosy interior, long menu of burgers, wraps, salads, and some Italian and Thai dishes, and reasonable wine list. There's also a deli and wine shop in the centre.
$ The Waffle Hut, at KwaZulu Weavers, on the R600, 10 km west

of Winterton, T036-488 1500, www.
kwazuluweavers.com. Daily 0800-
1630. Tables on the stoep decorated
with Zulu murals, serving waffles –
try the chocolate chip and ice-cream
one – plus breakfasts, light meals
and legendary milkshakes, plus a
kids' menu and takeaways.

Underberg *p157*
$ Lemon Tree Bistro, Clock Tower
Centre, Main Rd, T033-701 1589.
Daily 0830-2200 except Mon when it
closes at 1700. Hearty breakfasts, light
lunches, coffee and cakes and a bistro-
style menu in the evening, plus good
produce in the deli and winery and
small selection of interesting books.

Cafés
Pucketty Farm Stall, Main Rd, on the
way out of the village on the R617
towards Bulwer, T033-701 1035, www.
puckettyfarm.co.za. Daily 0800-1800. A
good stop for self-caterers for its fresh
home-baked goodies like pies and
quiches, plus pâtés, cheeses, jams and
marmalades, pickles and chutneys and
home-made ginger beer. There's also a
tea garden with outside tables under
a weeping willow and an art gallery.

Himeville *p158*
$$$-$$ Moorcroft Manor, see Where
to stay, page 166. Daily 0730-2130.
Restaurant in the lodge of the same
name, stylish dining room with
beautiful terrace, breakfasts, light
lunches like ploughman's platter or
gourmet steak sandwiches, upmarket
menu with a French feel for dinner.
Bookings are essential.

$$-$ Himeville Arms, see Where to
stay, page 166. The **Arms** (1100-late)
is the local pub with lots of character
(and characters) with cosy wooden
interior and crackling fire selling pub
grub. The **Torridon Restaurant** (0730-
0900, 1230-1500, 1830-2100) serves
country cuisine including good steaks,
fresh local trout and some traditional
sticky desserts and again there's a fire
to sit next to with a nightcap.

⊛ Festivals

Underberg *p157*
**Easter weekend Splashy Fen
Festival**, www.splashyfen.co.za.
South Africa's most popular outdoor
music festival held over 4 days on
Splashy Fen Farm. Similar to the
summer festivals held in Europe,
with camping and fringe activities,
arts and crafts market, food stalls
and children's entertainment.

O Shopping

Bergville *p150, map p148*
There are a couple of supermarkets
to stock up in before heading into
the reserves, though the better choice
is in the chain supermarkets in the
larger towns before you get here. The
shops at the campsites stock
only the most basic supplies. On the
roads to the mountains, look out for
farm stalls selling fresh produce.

Monk's Cowl and Champagne
Valley *p152, map p153*
KwaZulu Weavers, 10 km west of
Winterton on the R600, T036-488

1098, www.kwazuluweavers.com,
0800-1630. Colourful handwoven
rugs made from wool and mohair.
Attached is a popular handmade
candle shop and **The Waffle Hut**,
is here (see Restaurants, page 168).
Thokozisa Centre, on the R600, 13 km
west of Winterton, T036-488 1207.
Daily 0900-1630. A one-stop tourist
centre (the **Central Drakensberg
Information Centre** is here) with
attractive thatched shops and galleries
surrounded by indigenous gardens
selling arts and crafts, home decor
items and wines, and an excellent
restaurant (see Restaurants, page 168).

Underberg *p157*
The **Underberg Village Mall**, on the
Himeville road has banks and ATMs, a
small supermarket, pub and coffee shop.

☉ What to do

uKhahlamba-Drakensberg Park
p142, maps p148 and p153
Adventure activities
All Out Adventures, near the turn-offs
to the Cavern and Montusi Mountain
Lodge, off the R74, below Oliviershoek
Pass, T036-438 6242, www.allout
adventures.co.za. 0900-1630, closed
Tue out of season, no need to pre-book
but phone ahead in quieter seasons.
Fun activities for young and old; a flying
trapeze (R110 for 2 flights), a bungee
bounce (R70), where you're put in a
bungee harness and then bounce very
high from a trampoline, a big swing
(R110) from the top of a pine tree, a zip-
liner slide (R110), and a canopy cable
tour (R440) to various platforms in the

trees. Children (under 12) get discounts
and combo tickets are available. Also
organize paintballing and quad-biking.
Coffee shop serving snacks.

Climbing
The website of the KwaZulu-Natal
section of the **Mountain Club of
South Africa**, www.kzn.mcsa.org.za,
is a useful source of information for
experienced rock climbers.
Peak High, T033-343 3168, www.peak
high.co.za. Contact for details of guided
climbs in the Drakensberg, and about
the possibility of ice climbing the
Lotheni Falls, which are usually frozen
from mid-Jun to mid-Aug. Strictly for
experienced mountaineers only, with
full equipment, including an ice pick.

Fishing
Trout were introduced into the rivers
of the Drakensberg around 1900 and
over the years fly-fishing has become
popular. Fishing licences are available
from some of the offices at the camps,
and some rent out rods and tackle.
Enquire with **Ezemvelo KZN Wildlife**,
T033-845 1000, www.kznwildlife.com.
Many of the private resorts also arrange
trout fishing.

Golf
In good weather, the Drakensberg are
a spectacular backdrop for a round of
golf. There are several courses including
at the **Cathedral Peak Hotel**, see
Where to stay, page 163, T036-488
1888, www.cathedralpeak.co.za,
9 holes; **Monk's Cowl Country Club**, on
the R600, Champagne Valley, T036-468
1300, www.monkscowlgolfclub.co.za,

9 holes; **Champagne Sports Resort**, see Where to stay, page 164, T036-468 8000, www.champagnesportsresort. com, 18 holes; and in the southern Drakensberg, the **Drakensberg Gardens Golf & Spa Resort**, see Where to stay, page 167, T033-701 1355, www.goodersonleisure.co.za, 18 holes; and **Sani Pass Hotel**, see Where to stay, page 166, T033-702 1320, www.sanipasshotel.co.za, 9 holes.

Helicopter flights

Westline Aviation, has 3 bases: at **Tower of Pizza** (see Restaurants, page 168), T073 6-25 1655, www. towerofpizza.co.za; **Dragon Peaks Mountain Resort** (see Where to stay, page 164), T083-652 7493; and **Cathedral Peak Hotel** (see Where to stay, page 163), T036-488 2055, www. berghelicopter.co.za. Offers helicopter scenic flights over the mountains from R790 for 15 mins; check the website for options which include landings halfway up Cathedral Peak to take in the sweeping views with a glass of champagne. This company also assists **Ezemvelo KZN Wildlife** in mountain rescue operations.

Horse riding

The full length of the Berg is negotiable on horseback and most of the larger resorts offer horse riding. **Rugged Glen**, in the Royal Natal National Park (see page 148), has stables at the **Ezemvelo KZN Wildlife** campsite, enquire at the park office or phone ahead for times, T036-438 6422, www.kznwildlife.com. Guided horse trails are from R75 for half an

hour to R220 for 3 hours; very popular during the holiday period when it's best to book in advance.

Khotso Horse Trails, Bergvlei Farm, 10 km from Underberg on Drakensberg Gardens Rd, T033-701 1502, www. khotsotrails. co.za. Mountain rides for beginners and advanced riders from 1 hr (R150) to a full day (R500 including lunch), plus specialist adventure 2-3 day rides to Lesotho. Also has simple farm accommodation (**$**) in dorms in a log cabin with shared kitchen and bathroom or in self-catering thatched rondavels.

Mountain biking

Mountain biking in the Drakensberg is hugely popular, and the routes are by no means extreme and pass through some spectacular scenery. Many of the resorts rent out bikes and have short trails on their properties. You can also rent bikes from **All Out Adventures**, see page 170, for R350 per day to ride on the Drakensberg MTB Trail; this is 100 km of trails marked out that link many of the resorts in the northern Drakensberg, as well as **All Out Adventures**. A trail pass costs R100 per day, or R180 for up to 5 days, and includes a map, and can be bought from **All Out Adventures** or **Montusi Mountain Lodge**, **Alpine Heath**, or the **Cavern** among other resorts.

Tour operators

Based in Underberg, **Major Adventures**, Underberg Hotel, Main St, T033-701 1628, www.major adventures.com; **Sani Pass Tours**, Trout Walk Centre, Sani Rd, T033-701 1064, www.sanipasstours.com; and **Thaba Tours**, Clocktower Centre, Main Rd, T033-701 2888, www.thabatours.co.za, all offer daily 4WD day trips to the top of Sani Pass for about R550-650 per person with a stop for (optional) lunch at the Sani Mountain Lodge.

Drakensberg Adventures, Sani Lodge (page 166), 19 km from Underberg on the Sani Pass road, T033-702 0330, www.sanilodge.co.za. Great selection of tours in the area, and Russell is a formidable guide for the Sani Pass excursion (R580 per person) and local hikes. Also offers hikes to San rock art, visits to local Zulu families where you can spend the night, overnight or 2- to 3-day trips into Lesotho, and guided climbs of Thabana Ntlenyana (Africa's 2nd tallest mountain).

⊖ Transport

Northern Drakensberg
p147, map p148
Baz Bus, reservations Cape Town T021-422 5202, www.bazbus.com, runs from **Ampitheatre Backpackers**, Oliviershoek Pass to **Johannesburg** and **Durban**.

Central Drakensberg
p150, map p148
Baz Bus, reservations Cape Town T021-422 5202, www.bazbus.com, runs in both directions between **Johannesburg** and **Durban**, drops-off and picks-up outside of the **First National Bank**, Winterton.

Southern Drakensberg *p157*
Underberg Express, bookings T033-701 2750, www.underbergexpress. co.za, runs between **Underberg**, **Howick**, **Pietermaritzburg**, **Hillcrest**, **Kloof**, the **Pavilion Mall**, **Durban**, **Umhlanga** and **King Shaka International Airport**. It departs Underberg Tue-Sun at 0800 and arrives in central Durban at 1100 and at King Shaka International Airport at 1130, from where it leaves again at about 1300 and arrives back again in Underberg at around 1730. There is a service on Mon that departs Underberg at 0500, so adjust times of arrival accordingly. The full one-way fare between Underberg and the airport is R600. Fares and timetables can be found on the website. There is also the option to get on or off in Pietermaritzburg to connect with the **Baz Bus** and other buses heading towards Johannesburg.

⊕ Directory

Winterton *p151, map p148*
Medical services Emmaus Hospital, Springfield Rd (R74), T036-488 1570. This is a public hospital so anyone with decent medical travel insurance would be advised to go to the private **Medi-Clinic** or **Netcare** hospitals in Pietermaritzburg (page 128).

Contents

174 Index

Footnotes

Index → *Entries in* **bold** *refer to maps*

A
accommodation 12
  price codes 13
air travel 6
alcohol 15
Aliwal Shoal 63
Amanzimtoti Bird Sanctuary 61
Amatikulu Nature Reserve 78

B
backpacker hostels 13
Ballito 76
  listings 93
banking hours 20
Battlefields Route 129
Battle of Spion Kop 133
Baz Bus 9, 13, 59, 74, 162
beer 15
Bergville 150
  listings 163
biltong 15
Blood River 136
border crossings 9
bunny chow 34
business hours 20
bus travel 8, 10

C
camping 13
Cape Vidal 92
  listings 99
caravan parks 13
car hire 10
car travel 9
Cathedral Peak 151
  listings 163
cave paintings 144, 151
coaches 8, 10
Cobham 158
  listings 166
consulates 18
crime 21
cuisine 14
currency exchange 20

D
Department of Home Affairs 22
diarrhoea 18
diving 108
Dlinza Forest 80
Dolphin Coast 75, **76**
Drakensberg Boys' Choir School 152
drink 15
driving 9, 10
Dundee 135
  listings 139
Durban 24, **25**, **32**
  beachfront 37
  Berea 39
  city centre 30
  Golden Mile 37
  listings 45
  Indian district 35
  Victoria Embankment 36
Dutch East India Company 28
duty free 17

E
Elephant Coast 78
embassies 18
Empangeni 83
  listings 95
Eshowe 80
  listings 94
Estcourt 123
  listings 126
exchange rates 20

F
food 14
Fynn, Henry Francis 29

G
game lodges 14
Garden Castle 161, 167
  listings 167
Giant's Castle 155
Giant's Castle Nature Reserve 150
  listings 165

Gingindlovu 78, 99
  listings 94
Greyhound buses 10
guesthouses 12

H
Harold Johnson Nature Reserve 77
  listings 94
Hawaan Nature Reserve 42
heatstroke 19
Hibberdene 64
Hibiscus Coast 64
hiking 146, 149, 151, 154, 155, 158
Himeville 158
  listings 166
HIV/AIDS 18
Hluhluwe 87
  listings 97
Hluhluwe-Imfolozi Game Reserve 84, **85**
  listings 96
holidays 19
hostels 13
hotels 12
  price codes 13
Howick 121
  listings 124, 126

I
Illovo 62
immigration 22
indentured labourers 29
Injisuthi camp 154
Intercape buses 10
international airports 6
iSimangaliso Wetland Park 88
Ithala Game Reserve 81
  listings 95

K
Kamberg Nature Reserve 156
  listings 165
Karridene 62
Kingsburgh 61

Kosi Bay Nature Reserve 111
listings 114
Kruger National Park 86
Krugerrands 53
KwaZulu-Natal coast 61
KZN Wildlife 120

L
Ladysmith 129, **131**
listings 138
seige of 132
Ladysmith Black Mambazo
129, 134
Lake Eland Game Reserve 65
Lake Sibaya 108
lammergeyers 156
licensing laws 15
Lotheni 160

M
malaria 19
Maputaland **79**, 104
Margate 66
listings 70, 74
Midlands Meander 121
Midmar Dam Nature Reserve
122
listings 125, 127
minibus taxis 11
Mission Rocks 92
Mkhuze Game Reserve 106
money 20
Monk's Cowl 152, **153**
listings 164
Mpenjati Nature Reserve 67

N
Napoleon, Louis 124
Natal Midlands 116
Ndumo Game Reserve 109
listings 114
Northern Drakensberg
147, **148**

O
Oliviershoek Pass 147
listings 161, 168
Oribi Gorge Nature Reserve 65
listings 70

P
Pietermaritzburg 116, **118**
listings 124
Port Edward 67
listings 71
Port Shepstone 64
listings 69

R
rail travel 8, 9
Ramsgate 66
rand 20
restaurants 14, 15
price codes 13
Richards Bay 83
listings 95
Riverbend Crocodile Farm 67
road travel 8, 9
rock art 151, 156
Rorke's Drift 137
Royal Natal National Park 148
listings 162

S
safety 21
Salt Rock 76
Sani Pass 159
listings 166
Scottburgh 62
self-catering apartments 14
Shaka 29, 77
Shelly Beach 66
Siege of Ladysmith 132
Sodwana Bay 107
listings 112
South African Tourism 22
Southbroom 67
listings 71
Spioenkop Dam Nature
Reserve 133
listings 139
St Lucia 90, **91**
listings 98
supermarkets 15

T
taxis 11
tax refund 17
telephone 21

Tembe Elephant Park 110
listings 114
time 21
tipping 22
Tongaat 77
train travel 8, 9
Translux buses 10
transport 6-12
turtles 89

U
uKhahlamba-Drakensberg Park
133, 142
Umhlanga 41
uMkhomazi Wilderness Area
160
listings 167
Umkomaas 62
Umtamvuna Nature Reserve 67
Underberg 157
listings 165
Uvongo 66

V
Valley of 1000 Hills 43
VAT refund 17
Vergelegen 167
Vernon Crookes Nature
Reserve 64
Verulam 77
visas 22
Voortrekker Museum 117
vultures 156

W
water 15
Weenen Game Reserve 133
listings 138
weights and measures 22
wine 15
Winkelspruit 62
Winterton 151

Z
Zululand 75, **79**
Zululand Historical Museum 80

Join us online...

Follow **@FootprintBooks** on Twitter, like **Footprint Books** on **Facebook** and talk travel with us! Ask us questions, speak to our authors, swap stories and be kept up-to-date with travel news, exclusive discounts and fantastic competitions.

Upload your travel pics to our **Flickr** site and inspire others on where to go next.

And don't forget to visit us at footprinttravelguides.com